K

09-BTJ-862

Judy & Liza & Robert
& Freddie & David
& Sue & Me . . .

Judy & Liza & Robert & Freddie & David & Sue & Me . . .

A Memoir

Stevie Phillips

ST. MARTIN'S PRESS · NEW YORK

www.stmartins.com

The Library of Congress Cataloging-in-Publication Data is available upon request.

ISBN 978-1-250-06577-3 (hardcover)
ISBN 978-1-4668-7277-6 (e-book)

St. Martin's Press books may be purchased for educational, business, or promotional use. For information on bulk purchases, please contact the Macmillan Corporate and Premium Sales Department at 1-800-221-7945, extension 5442, or write to specialmarkets@macmillan.com.

First Edition: June 2015

10 9 8 7 6 5 4 3 2 1

For Nico and Dylan.
Swing for the fences.

CONTENTS

ACKNOWLEDGMENTS

Inclement weather almost kept me from a party where I enjoyed a serendipitous meeting with Sally Richardson, who bought this book shortly thereafter. Thank you, Sally. I now think of that cold, wet winter night as a sunny day. And thank you, Michael Flamini, my editor at St. Martin's, who framed every suggestion with such kind consideration. I want to include in my thanks the entire team at St. Martin's for their wonderful support. I'm grateful to my amazing agent, Al Zuckerman, for his caring and expertise, and I also owe a great deal of my good fortune to Richard Marek, without whose early attention this book would not exist. Finally, there is my close friend Albert Poland, organizer of the first Judy Garland fan club, which is no more than a coincidence in our friendship . . . or perhaps a sign of the universe at work. His understanding and appreciation for the gift Judy Garland gave the world gave me the encouragement I needed to keep the important things in focus.

Introduction

I'm in the bedroom of Judy Garland's suite at New York's Plaza Hotel. It's just past four thirty in the afternoon on a cold November day and Judy is still in bed, late for the four o'clock meeting in my office with her business manager, Charlie Renthal. That's why my boss has sent me over: "Get her here," David Begelman ordered.

"What do you want to wear?" I ask Judy sweetly. She doesn't answer me. I stand there—like the dummy I was at twenty-five—staring at her. She takes the Salems off the nightstand, removes a cigarette, and puts it in her mouth. She takes a pack of matches, strikes one, and sets her nightgown on fire. What?! A small flame appears. Oh no! Lightning explodes in my head. Please God—not now! But I have no time for this thought. For thinking at all. Time collapses. An instantaneous chill overtakes me. What if—? She could die. Every possible terror collides in me at once as I grab the blankets and smother the flame about to consume the pale-blue nylon gown. Judy offers no resistance—and no help. Done. It is over. Another catastrophe averted. Why am I still so cold and frightened? Her leg is slightly burned. She puts her hand on it, examines it, and gets out of bed. The bedding is only scorched. I shiver and stare.

My hands are icicles. I am in a state of complete shock. I don't know what I feel besides icy cold. Not a word from her about it. She heads to the bathroom. "I better wear tights," she tells me.

This ugly incident wasn't the first, and it wasn't the worst. That came when she attempted to kill me instead of herself. Drugs were responsible, and I'll get to that. I will show you a woman whose mind was destroyed by prescription drugs and alcohol. But let me stay with the Plaza for a moment so that I can explain that while self-immolation was hardly a daily event, it did occur sometimes when she reached the depths of her despair on the emotional roller coaster she was riding, a trip that was picking up more speed all the time during the four years we spent together in the early sixties.

When she was "up" she was totally manic, her fast-paced conversation larded with brittle laughter; when she was depressed, it was nothing like a normal depression, for she could not hear the sound of a human voice. She was in a foreign country. Deeply felt pain, however, was a constant in the daily existence of this troubled and immensely talented woman whose life was spiraling down and, at the same time, gaining momentum in helping to shape my own.

I had recently turned twenty-five when she set her nightgown on fire at the Plaza; Judy was thirty-nine, and we had known each other slightly less than a year. Although there was only a 14-year difference between us, it might as well have been 114. I was still an innocent; she had lost her innocence before I was born.

If timing is critical—and it has always been for me—Judy and I connected at a moment when she needed company and I needed an opportunity. That moment would forever change my life. Judy had virtually retired. She had fled the United States, where in Hollywood she'd been labeled unreliable, and she was quietly living a healthier lifestyle abroad when my first real employer pitched a comeback to her. She was bored enough doing nothing in London to jump at the chance. But while she was mentally ready for another shot at stardom on the silver screen, she still was not emotionally stable enough. The outcome was at once triumphant and tragic. The triumph was her immediate success when she reappeared on the American scene; the tragedy was the reemergence of the rampaging insecurities that fostered her reliance on drugs and alcohol. As her anxieties took over again, prescription drugs once more dominated her daily life and finally killed her.

For a lonely, latchkey, star-struck kid from a Conservative Jewish household, being sent on the road with Judy was like being shot out of a cannon into the fast-and-furious lane. Once there, I had no choice but to grow up quickly or go away and forget about the life in show business I had dreamed about. It was with her that I discovered my staying power and the determination necessary to accept a harrowing existence. Along the way she became my greatest teacher.

As I turned from twenty-five into thirty and from thirty into forty, Judy was by then long gone from my life, but I discovered that in fact she had never left me. I came to realize that many of the decisions I made were filtered through a brain stem overloaded with things I had learned from being with her, from my exploring and finally understanding who she was personally as well as professionally. She taught me both how to and how *not* to live. She was the major ingredient in the special lens through which I have seen, lived, and dealt with my life. Even today, what comes out on the other side of my filtration system is heavily influenced by that education. Given what I've gone through, I realize I'm still standing because of the greatest lesson Judy Garland taught me: how not to fold.

Judy Garland was hardly the only celebrity in my life whose insecurities led to the kind of abuse that destroys all happiness. My day-to-day was filled with the addictions of others, most notably Liza Minnelli, whom I represented for fifteen years at the peak of her career. Their desperate lives were not what I had grown up expecting, not what I stood in line for, but once my ticket was stamped, I entered into the theater of abuse for most of my professional career.

I could have opted out—at great cost to myself. Instead I chose to stay in—also at great cost to myself. Eventually I discovered that there were many different kinds of addicts in the world of entertainment, no different from the universe outside its cloister. I saw the dysfunction this kind of behavior causes. I saw firsthand how alcoholism damages the families of stars and their associates, how it ends friendships and relationships. However, in spite of my disapproval and my disgust with addiction, I nonetheless managed to fall into the same dumps the addicts were in without ever taking any drugs or enjoying more than the occasional glass of wine.

Most addicts I dealt with at arm's length, but a few I wrapped my arms around and married. Those missteps tested the limits of my endurance. I allowed myself to be sucked into personal relationships that I failed to examine.

I might not have finally succumbed to a breakdown had I only listened to the men who courted when they spoke, but it took me a while to learn how to listen. Addicts can be most charming and seductive. Certainly Judy was when she was in her best of all possible worlds. When it came to my personal life, I threw caution to the winds.

So to an extent this book is also about what can happen to an enabler on the sidelines. I am that person, and only one of millions like me. I never saw myself as a victim. I was righteous, self-confident, judgmental, and imperious—until the day I wasn't anymore.

Judy may have been my greatest teacher, but she was not the only one. I was extremely fortunate to find a wonderful mentor, Freddie Fields, one of the all-time best agents on the planet, who—along with his partner, David Begelman, a sick puppy—played an enormous role in my career. Their arrival in my life was a matter of good timing, the result of shifting professional circumstances that opened a door for me at the right moment. Ultimately Freddie, a sportcoated, charming smart aleck, gave me the skills I required to become effective in the motion picture industry at a time when the only women in the agency business were locked in rooms reading screenplays, manuscripts, and books. He taught me what the agency business was mostly about: representing stars. He made me understand that it didn't matter where you sat in New York, Hollywood, or anywhere else if you had the right clients. I became a client signer, and the stars I represented were the real deal, big-money talent who could make the Hollywood cameras roll.

The remarkable lesson I learned from these egocentric stars is that they are always right. The reason I know this is that nobody in showbiz ever disagrees with them. Nor did I. Handling superstars gave me clout, and I used it to fight for the things I wanted in my career: money and position. But I was selfish. I fought entirely for myself until the time came—and for me it was late in coming—when I finally saw the light of a new day dawning, and I recognized that I might have the capacity to make a small difference in my corner of the world. And I did that too.

Part 1

Beginnings

CHAPTER ONE

Who the Hell Is Stevie Phillips?

Okay, here's the obligatory where-I-was-born segment. It might give you an idea about how a person could ever grow up to become a talent agent who deals with megalomaniacs and addicts.

Was my showbiz career preordained? Here are some freaky facts. I was born on August 9, 1936, in a hospital in the middle of the Broadway theater district. Even though my parents lived in Hoboken, New Jersey, where there were plenty of hospitals. But they picked this inconvenient place on West Fiftieth Street because it was cheap and they could afford having me if I made my debut there. Alas, the broken-down Polyclinic outlived its usefulness, and the eyesore met the wrecking ball decades ago. But while it existed it was the go-to place for ailing show folk. My birthing doctor, whose name was Phillips—same as mine—was simultaneously in the room next door, giving life support to a comedian named Joe Howard who'd had a heart attack. It's a comedy sketch: Dr. Phillips running between rooms yelling "Push!" in one room and "Don't push!" in the other. All he needed was a red fright wig. Joe Howard must have been one helluva guy. I discovered he was not only a comedian but also a Broadway producer—which I now know (having been one) is ridiculously hard—and yet Howard additionally managed to be a director, writer, composer, and lyricist. He wrote a famous song, "Goodbye, My Lady Love." The title of Howard's famous song also strikes me as a little scary. I think it all means something—maybe.

My very first childhood memory comes from the summer of 1939 when I was taken to the World's Fair in Flushing Meadows, New York. I am sitting on Edgar Bergen's knee talking to Charlie McCarthy. I can see myself there; I remember what I was wearing and what Charlie wore.

A year later we moved into an apartment on the top floor of a small building in Washington Heights a few blocks from the George Washington Bridge. Our apartment had bare wood floors that announced my father, whose footfalls I came to dread. He was a vain, vile-tempered man who once, in a rage, threw all my clothes out our sixth-floor window onto the street below because I hadn't hung them up. Somehow that translated into not respecting him or the money he made selling children's wear. What my father called "a good spanking" would now be called something else entirely. He is also the reason there are no pictures from my childhood, no picture of Charlie and me.

Selling children's wear was hardly comparable to designing strategies for world peace, but it took all my parents' time and energy. They were never home. I was alone and lonely except when I was in my friends' happier homes. I saw their parents much more than I did my own.

At seven thirty every weekday morning a housekeeper named Evelyn arrived. Do not think "warm family retainer." Evelyn never came close. She was black in mood as well as in color, and always gave the impression that she was not happy being there. She put the same cream-cheese-and-jelly sandwich with a banana into my lunch box every day for years. In all the time she was with us, I don't recall so much as a hug from her. Evelyn didn't know or care what I did or where I went as long as I showed up on time for dinner. She was discharging her obligation. That's all I ever was to her, an obligation. Salvation for me lay in escape from home.

The most wonderful escape was going to the movies. On Saturdays twenty-five cents gave me a wonderland to live in for an entire day. Loew's 175th Street with its starlit Casbah etched in bas-relief on the walls and ceilings was where I looked up, closed my eyes, and entered a different future. I yearned for a Technicolor world replete with riches, song, dance, and excitement of all kinds. I would be at the box office, my quarter in hand, as soon as the doors opened, and there I would remain until dinnertime. I loved the serials and the newsreels, but most of all I loved the musicals. Judy Garland in *Meet Me in St. Louis* was the girl I longed to be, with long straight hair and soft curls and a house next door to the handsomest boy on the block.

Nothing at home was anything like Judy's house in St. Louis. Apartment 6H was filled with drama and dysfunction and lots of the ugly behavior that characterized my parents' marriage. Nowadays I assume my parents' screaming matches were part of a dynamic they depended upon because they both participated so enthusiastically. The screaming was about money, about the retail business, about family—my mother's, mostly—but it really wasn't about any of those things.

Finally I understand that arguing is never what the anger is about. My father was carrying baggage that came from another place: the loveless home of his own childhood. My grandfather, I discovered, was a world-class philanderer, a stage-door Johnny who lusted after Ziegfeld chorines and bedded more than a few. When I was the tender age of ten, my father took me to a memorabilia-packed walk-up in Hell's Kitchen to visit my grandfather for the very first time as he lay dying in the arms of a former Follies star whose faded beauty was a reminder of the knockout she must have been when she was young. I thought it strange, even at ten, that my father had brought me along to witness his father's death, but it turned out to be the most intimate moment I ever shared with my dad. My grandfather had been the role model for my father, an excellent student.

There you have it. I'm part of a family in which not one single member had any interest or practical involvement in showbiz, and yet my early life was coincidentally touched by it time and again. As I grew older, the coincidences became a mainstream of events, until it was clear to me that showbiz was indeed where I belonged. A cliché I know, but here goes: It was all in the stars.

CHAPTER TWO

What Do You Do with a Jewish Princess?

I knew that after college I'd try making a career in entertainment, so I replaced education studies (my mother thought I should be prepared to teach in case I "had to" go to work) with comparative literature: "From all your great literature will come nothing but starvation!" There were plenty of women who worked—my mother was one of them, and a role model for me—but most of them held jobs out of their need for a paycheck, and many of them were looking for husbands so that they could stop working. They were not, in the main, remotely interested in career building. They wanted out. I wanted in. My enormous ambition has been one of the few personality disorders I haven't wanted to change. My mother was aware of this, and she decided she'd better find me a husband and put all my nonsense to rest.

She and her best friend, her older sister, Julie, convened to figure out my future in a very organized fashion, and husband hunting morphed from merely an idea into an intense pursuit. The starting point of this organized search was the synagogue. Who in the congregation did they know had a son the right age, preferably a doctor or a lawyer? My mother remembered a German family living in the Fourth Reich, so called because of the many German-Jewish refugees who settled there. They had a son who would be just about the right age and she phoned them. Chutzpah? (Leo Rosten in *The Joys of Yiddish* defines the word as "gall, brazen nerve, effrontery, incredible 'guts'; presumption plus arrogance such as no other word, and no other language, can do justice to.")

I told my mother what she was doing was embarrassing, but she was determined to find out the son's marital status, and there was no other way but head-on. In the conversation with this family of German refugees, she hit pay dirt. "He's an attorney from a good family. Now I remember the parents," she said. "We used to say hello in the shul." (At that point she had not attended services for more than a dozen years.) "You'll be a mother with a baby in a carriage. You won't need to work hard all your life like me."

So off we went to observe the Sabbath (which I never did, nor did she really) in a temple where we were no longer part of the congregation. I sat on a bench five rows ahead of my mother's pick, turning every now and then in order to steal a glance without being seen. Caught in the act. He smiled at me.

I agreed to go out with him. He was considerate and attentive, and best of all he owned an old Pontiac convertible. We drove to City Island for lobsters, to Brooklyn for dinner with his friends, to the beach for the day. We shared our love of movies and theater. No bells rang, but being with him felt good. I never for a moment thought I was in love, and *no*—just in case you're wondering—we never slept together before we married. In 1957 "nice" Jewish girls didn't do *that*. I expected him to ask me to marry him, and he did it charmingly on bended knee while putting a perfect two-carat diamond ring on my finger.

Finally, one sunny April afternoon, on the day Greeks celebrate their independence, we got married at the Plaza Hotel in the "Gold and White Suite" on the second floor, overlooking the very corner where the Greek marching bands turned from Fifth Avenue into Central Park South. Given that I was also celebrating my independence, marching bands seemed entirely appropriate, even though the martial music of the parade drowned out the entire ceremony. I couldn't hear a word the rabbi said.

The irony in all this is that my mother pushed me into marriage with a man who was even more starstruck than I. It was an accident to be sure, but then again, maybe no accident at all. Had it not been written somewhere in the stars that I should be in show business, my new husband might have discouraged me from a theatrical pursuit; but this kind and honest man adored every aspect of entertainment. All he ever wanted in life was to be an actor, but instead he passed the bar to satisfy his parents—just as I was trying to satisfy mine by marrying.

He quickly decided he was going to live his dream vicariously through me. I had his full support to delve into the world of showbiz, and that was all I needed. I felt capable of finding my own way, starting at the bottom of the ladder. The rest was determination, something I owned in abundance. I would make it. I just had to. I would finally realize the dream I had dreamed all those Saturdays in the uptown movie palace.

CHAPTER THREE

Girl on the Bottom

In 1958 the only start-up jobs available, besides retail, were for women with decent secretarial skills. It was a time when, after you got your college degree, graduate work generally meant that you took a course in either the Pitman or Gregg method of stenography, and only then did you have a skill worth selling, one that put you on a collision course with a low glass ceiling. Of course if you graduated from Vassar, Smith, Holyoke, or any of the other Seven Sister schools, and you had good social connections, you might acquire an entry-level position as an editorial assistant at a top publishing house or classy magazine like *Harper's Bazaar*—that is, until you married and moved to a start-up mansion in Greenwich. Inasmuch as I wasn't one of those Muffy, Buffy, Duffy, or Libby socialites about to enjoy my coming-out, I went straight to the Kelly Girl secretarial school for my continuing education, recognizing that my bachelor of arts degree in literature might occasionally help me in cocktail conversation.

From the moment I started working, I knew it was the right choice for me. Not all the shit jobs were, but then I was 100 percent prepared to pay my dues. My mom was wrong about working. I didn't find it hard at all; of course, unlike her, I was not standing on a retail sales floor twelve hours a day. I was sitting in bright airy spaces, reading most of the time, and best of all, at the end of the week I had a paycheck in my hand that gave me the first real power I thought I'd ever had: buying power. But it wasn't *only* about the money. Working reinforced my thinking that I could have it all: fame, money, and power. And there was at least a tiny bit of genuine altruism. I also wanted to make a contribution to society. I thought from the beginning that entertaining people was a great way to do that.

With my skill set in place, such as it was (no hundred-words-a-minute me), I launched my attack on "the industry" by going to a temp employment agency, where I asked to be sent out for entertainment work. There were lots of jobs available, and I was regularly employed at a network (both CBS and NBC) or at advertising desks (McCann Erickson stands out because some jerk hit on me until I finally quit), where I read through whatever files were available to me, an eager participant in my own little master plan to figure out how people functioned in the industry. I thought I could learn by reading contracts and memos.

I was placed in some jobs for a few days, some for more. Sometimes I would just up and quit after I'd sucked out of a particular office as much worthwhile background as I could. And I had plenty of time to do it. My boss of the moment, always a man, made up his mind before I got there that there was no point in my doing anything other than answering the phone until his regular girl got back. When asked why I was reading a file (and that wasn't often) I simply said I needed something to read. The boss smiled. I was a girl, after all. How could I know what I was reading? But I thought I had a good plan because I was actually interested in everything I read. I might have forgotten my Shakespeare, but I could indeed remember contractual terms and conditions. I could remember who got paid what for every show on the air. I counted on the fact that this was not useless information, that one day I could get to a place where I could actually use the info I was stockpiling.

Not all the early jobs were terrible. I stayed at ABC Television for a few months and had a wonderful time, though certainly not at the start in the typing pool, which was a drag and hard, boring work, typing columns of numbers that, without context, made no sense.

Luckily I was rescued from the pool after only a week and a half, told I would now be a "production assistant," and sent to the stage floor of a little game show called *Who Do You Trust?*, starring Johnny Carson. Though happy to be plucked out of the pool, I'm sorry to say I believe the only reason I was chosen over the other more efficient women who had longer tenure was my appearance. I was tall and slim; I had a good figure, and, although no great beauty, I was nice looking. I knew I attracted men's attention, and I liked it. I was a flirt. So sue me.

My new job definition was "Help anyone who needs help." Typing was the least of it. What I remember most is running off copies on the mimeograph machine and chatting a lot. You couldn't just deliver a copy without having a little chat. For five minutes I thought this was the beginning of the rest of my life. Not so. But it's worth two minutes of recollection.

I was awkward as a young woman (not so terribly different now): a tangle of long arms and legs that found their way into a space slightly ahead of the rest of me, mixing it up with whatever was in their path. There were always offending inanimate objects, taking on lives of their own against my daily progress. One day in my second week as production assistant I was running across the stage on some momentous mission when the camera cable reached out and brought me down.

Now I am lying spread-eagle in front of the entire TV audience while Johnny Carson is doing the warm-up. "There she is, ladies and gentlemen—I give you the Jewish Elizabeth Taylor!" Oh no,

Johnny's not talking about *me*?! "Smile, Stevie, you're on camera." On big monitors no less, placed strategically around the audience of 499 giddy spectators laughing at my expense. Elizabeth Taylor had nothing to worry about, but then the audience could see that for themselves. I was still a natural brunette, and my green eyes—all that remains of that naive, young woman of twenty-three—were then, and still are, my best feature. Johnny could see they were not violet like *her* beautiful eyes. In fact he could see they weren't violet even after he'd had a number of strong belts. I was always generously invited along for pre-warm-up drinks at Sardi's bar next door.

The way that guy knocked back two double shots showed me he'd had a lot of practice. Still, Johnny had no trouble standing up or doing stand-up, whereas I, on one simple, well-nursed glass of wine, would fall down. Sadly, when the show was canceled at the end of the season, so was I.

This experience reinforced something I already knew, something that has been true since the beginning of time: Being attractive helps. I wasn't totally dim. I always knew I could count on my appearance to some extent. But I also understood from the get-go that competence and intelligence matter more.

CHAPTER FOUR

Can I Tell You About "Menial"?

How I wish my mom had hung around long enough to see how things worked out. She was, however, only there at the start, and it was a slow start. I didn't actually get my foot on the first rung of the success ladder until I got a job at the hugely successful agency called MCA (Music Corporation of America). I wanted a permanent job there, and I had no idea if they were hiring when I popped in to Personnel to fill out an application. The reason I found MCA so appealing is that it was across the street from my husband's first private office.

As a young lawyer with his own practice, he couldn't afford a secretary. I could type up his few letters on my lunch break and then again at night after work. As well, an agency represented another area of show business that I was curious about, one that I thought might lead to something. MCA hired me on the spot because I was a college graduate. Most of the other secretaries were not.

I had no difficulty doing whatever jobs MCA gave me while also doing my husband's work. And he was totally grateful. Our marriage projected the appearance of picture-book perfection, but it was a lie. All of it. I liked him, but when we had sex I lay in bed feeling nothing even though he was such a considerate lover, always eager to please me. Our lovemaking was not unpleasant but far from exciting, and I faked my responses. In that as in everything else, creating a great impression was always easy, and it saved me from embarrassing honesty. I was totally disingenuous, clearly not the doting helpmate and sweet little wife. My ambition far exceeded the feelings I had for him. I was selfish and self-involved, thinking exclusively of number one. I felt guilty even thinking about home and hearth because he was so kind and generous, so anxious to make it work.

As my career progressed and he saw less of me, he never raised an objection. He wanted to have children; I did not. I knew from day one that one day I would leave him, and children would complicate it. I hung in far longer than I should have. I knew it was over for me the first year. Guilt kept me there for five. But the bottom line is that he was the keeper, and I blew it. There were so many wonderful things about him to love—his thoughtfulness, kindheartedness, honesty, and loyalty, just to name a few—and I was too young and stupid to realize it.

Given the marriages that followed, I can now say he was the only decent man I married, and he was much more than simply decent. It no longer embarrasses me to talk about it because as I matured I developed enough grace to apologize to him, and we became good friends.

MCA was a class operation, and its overall appearance reflected that. The halls were paneled in mahogany throughout, and, hanging everywhere one looked, were antique equestrian prints matted exquisitely in matching black-and-gold frames. There was a lot of French country furniture, much of it the real deal. The heavy doors with their beautiful brass hardware matched the paneling, and I mention the doors specifically because many, many years later, when I'd become the occupant of one of those grand offices, the little Boston terrier I took to the office daily missed me so much during my lunch dates that he eventually gnawed his way through my door. One morning when I came to work, I found a sweet note on my secretary's typewriter from Lew Wasserman, the great gray eminence himself, asking me to replace the door. And I did—at no small expense.

"Uncle Lew" to some, "Mr. Wasserman" to me, he was the mastermind who built MCA into *the* studio conglomerate that dominated Hollywood. What started out as a company that booked musicians and bands grew, under his management, into a mega-monster agency that represented singers, dancers, producers and directors, writers of screenplays and books, and famous actors and actresses of the day, including such legendary stars as Bette Davis, Cary Grant, Tony Curtis and Janet Leigh, and, of course, Ronald Reagan, whom this kingmaker would later help become president of the Screen Actors Guild. A dealer of unmatched stature, Wasserman alone was responsible for installing his candidate as the head of the Motion Picture Association of America.

His influence extended well beyond the Sunset Strip into governors' mansions, Senate chambers, international boardrooms, and the White House. He held sway over dozens of labor unions, and he became the cultural statesman for the entire entertainment industry. He and his wife, Edie, whom I met only once, brought glamour to Las Vegas by lending the city their stature and bringing along their friends. Maneuvering together, they helped shape the television industry into the business we know today.

Additionally Wasserman found time to pioneer the blockbuster film, and with his golden touch was responsible in large part for the successes of *Psycho, Jaws,* and *E.T.* And, as noted, he also found time to charge me for the door my dog ate. I am grateful to be able to boast that many years down the road we became buddies of a sort when he inadvertently discovered, through an offhand remark

I made, that I was interested in current affairs. After that I looked forward to his New York visits because I would be invited into his palatial office suite to discuss party politics. The Iran hostage crisis was in the headlines, and it amused me that Uncle Lew asked me what I thought President Carter should do. I knew he was toying with me, and I loved it. On a more serious level he encouraged me to become more involved in the Democratic Party, in which I was a card-carrying member and he an important fund-raiser. At that point I was a Broadway producer working under one of Uncle Lew's corporate banners. But—back to beginnings!

I didn't mind the awful low-man-on-the-totem-pole job that MCA gave me: something called "floating secretary," which paid $69.50 a week, even less than the starvation wages I'd received at temp jobs. At first it was not at all different from the temp jobs; Personnel had me replacing secretaries who were ill or on vacation.

The upside was that I got to work for all the important agents in the organization: vice presidents like Sonny Werblin, who a few years later went on to buy the Titans, the team he renamed the Jets. I was now on my best behavior, for I was a permanent employee who I felt would soon be placed in an office that suited me. Part of that choice, I was encouraged to believe, would be mine, pending availabilities, of course. I read everything I was allowed to see, and at Mr. Werblin's desk (though there only briefly). I started to learn what "tough" meant. Old Sonny didn't mince words. "Shut the door, you idiot. I don't want anyone to hear me," he told one of the younger guys. I wanted to hear him.

Some of the agents I temporarily worked for seemed overwhelmed, and some dazed and confused as they wandered around the halls seeking information, but not Sonny Werblin. I admired his take-no-prisoners approach: Deal with what you're supposed to know, and take responsibility for it. After working for him, I looked for the tough guys. I asked for the difficult jobs on the music side, where the agents were frantic. I stayed late. I worked insanely hard, which attracted attention. I attracted attention. I knew how to subtly size up the powerful men. And they knew the look. Suddenly Sonny Werblin and Larry Rosenthal—the two top guys in New York—started to notice me, and the next thing I knew, Personnel was asking me what I wanted to do. When they ask you what you want to do at an agency, you say: "I want to be an agent"—unless you're a complete dummy. And so I did. I became an agent-in-training.

What that means is four things: You get a raise (totally modest), you get to sit inside your boss's office and listen in on his calls on an extension (except when the calls are personal), you get to be the gatekeeper and custodian of the calendar (which starts to put you on the shit lists of people who can't get in the door), and you get watched by those who make decisions—which is the only part that really matters. As far as I know, I was the only young woman accorded this privilege.

My "takeaway" from my early days at MCA has also been true since the dark ages: Hard work matters. When I looked at a ton of papers that had been piling up, I didn't wait to be asked, I made the pile go away. I didn't ask if I could finish the long memo in the morning. I made sure it was on "his" desk by the time he came in even if it meant staying late. I was efficient, organized, and as mistake-proof as possible. I knew that if I did a good job, I would be rewarded, and I was, for when I was called in to my first closed-door meeting, it was to discuss what I wanted to do with the rest of my life.

CHAPTER FIVE

The New Kids on the Block

I had been an agent-in-training only a few months when something unexpected happened. MCA was brought up on antitrust charges in Washington, DC. The government accused the agency of taking commissions from performers more than once for the same job, and Lew Wasserman was forced to choose between staying in the agency business or holding on to his new acquisition, Universal Pictures. Mr. Wasserman, whom I remember back then only as the man in the midnight-blue suit whose forbidding presence silenced all elevator chatter, decided in his infinite wisdom to keep the more profitable Universal. The agency doors were closing immediately. In one day all the lovely accessories that graced the offices and corridors of MCA vanished. It happened so fast it was as if a magician came through the halls and waved a wand that made things disappear. Neither a magician nor thieves in the night were responsible: It was the agents who ran through the halls grabbing everything that wasn't nailed down. Expensive lamps, blotters, trash baskets, leather pencil boxes and desk sets, some of the horsey prints, and the extant office supplies all left through the front door. Just about everything, short of the wall paneling and the largest pieces of furniture, was carried off.

A few days before MCA's doors closed for good, Personnel sent me as a floater into a double-office suite shared by Freddie Fields and David Begelman. Of all the guys I'd worked for, these two were the hippest, the coolest, and the most exciting. Freddie was the nattily sport-coated wisecracker; David, the very model of sartorial elegance—turned out every day in one of the dozen or more that he owned of the same exact suit; blue shirt by day, white by night— was the brilliant raconteur. Both were in their late thirties; both were sharp-witted, smart, flamboyant hotshots. They could call Rock Hudson, Doris Day, Ronnie Reagan, and Marilyn Monroe and get their calls picked up, but they had not signed these West Coast clients. Freddie had brought Dean Martin and Jerry Lewis with him from his prior job, and they were his ticket of admission to MCA. He was the agent responsible for Phil Silvers, who was a big Broadway, Hollywood, and TV star at the time, and he was married to the singer-actress Polly Bergen, who was also in great demand.

Freddie got his pal Begelman into the company, and together they were trying to hustle comedians popular in the Borscht belt. They always brought me into their inner offices for dictation when calling someone impressive so that I could be impressed. Seemed to me they spoke to the A-list only when I was around. They were show-offs in the most charming way, full of themselves and aware of it, keeping things light all the time. When we left the building together they did their "crowded-elevator shtick," which never failed to delight me. David might say something like: "She was so sick: sneezing, coughing, running a high fever. I tried desperately to keep away from her, but she was crawling all over me." And then he would let out a huge fake sneeze, and I would watch as everyone in the elevator shrank into the corners, backing into one another to gain as much distance as possible from him. Or Freddie would do the one about the rash and then just happen to notice it on his hand. "Omigod, David!" he'd say, feigning abject horror. "What's this? Do you think I caught it?" Nobody in the elevator had the slightest idea what "it" was, but from the horror etched on all the faces, you knew they thought "it" was at least as awful as the bubonic plague and clearly not worth catching. I would be giddy with laughter, trying my hardest not to give it up. They were both the most amusing men I'd ever met, and they liked that I liked them.

Actually, at the start I had a crush on them both, but it wasn't a physical thing; it was about their style. I loved their act, their two-man vaudeville show. They may have borrowed their shtick from the Borscht belt comedians they hung with, but I didn't know that then. I simply thought they were hilarious. Sadly, I found myself comparing my husband with these two characters. He was so much kinder and sweeter, but he couldn't make me laugh like they did. He didn't have this pizzazz. On the other hand, he was real, while all the pizzazz was phony baloney. That I understood this didn't matter.

So when these two colorful characters told me they were going to open their own office, asking if I wanted to come along with them, I jumped all over it. Both their secretaries opted to stay with Universal because each, having been with the parent company more than ten years, was fully vested in the rich MCA pension plan. I heard the universe speaking loud and clear, telling me that Freddie and David would get to the top, telling me to bet on them, and if I was clever I could ride their coattails to success. Of all the agents that were flushed out into the larger world the day MCA's doors closed, these were the two that would make it big-time.

A woman entering show business in the sixties was nothing more than a scribe—not even. I was only a tad more noticeable because I was attractive and had a sense of my own style, even on a limited budget. I inherited vanity from my father and cared deeply about my appearance. I was also a flirt and always anxious to be thought of as pretty by men. Flirting was, sadly, one of the few ways to be noticed in an office back in the day. A nice smile and a clever remark went a long way toward helping a woman realize even the smallest of ambitions.

One didn't—I certainly didn't—get an opportunity right away to demonstrate that my trendy hairdo framed a head with a brain in it, and although my two bosses were ready to acknowledge that I might have a brain, they weren't ready to acknowledge it financially. Men got cash for Christmas; I got a handbag. It was a beautiful handbag, bought for me at Bendel's by Freddie's beautiful wife, Polly. I peeked inside with trepidation, hoping to find a check for even a hundred dollars, but there was none. Worse, I was still called on to fill in as a babysitter as a favor. You know what "favor" means.

The women's movement didn't fully get under way until Betty Friedan published *The Feminine Mystique* in 1963. Prior to that women were invisible or, if noticed at all, seen mainly as sex objects— certainly not as people with leadership potential. For most, work was only a means to an end. I, however, yearned for a meaningful career, a way of life, and I was beginning to understand just how impossible that was. I heard a little voice saying, Hey, wait a minute here. I'm just as smart as some of these palookas. I want the same chance they got. This had nothing whatever to do with sisterhood. I was thinking exclusively of myself.

Fortunately for me, the bet that I made paid off. Freddie Fields and David Begelman started a company that grew to be one of the two or three largest agencies in the world. Although at the start they took advantage of my office skills, often leaving me at the end of a long day with enough typing to keep me working until midnight, I never once complained. (Sometimes one of them would come back at about ten with a thank-you and a buttered roll from Danny's Hideaway.) I sucked up and soaked in everything. I had my eye on the summit from the start, and, by making the compromises to my marriage that I found necessary, I did in fact ride their coattails to success. A good part of the reason it happened had everything to do with Judy Garland.

CHAPTER SIX

How Good Is Real?

Suddenly Judy Garland is standing in front of me. She has walked into the reception area of Freddie Fields Associates all bundled up. This very cold December afternoon at the end of 1960 is one that I will never forget. Thirteen-and-a-half-year-old Liza is with her. Judy's hair is short. Not as I remembered her. Liza's hair is halfway down her back. Not as most of you have ever thought of her. Judy, who has met Freddie only once at that point, has come to the office in order to meet his partner, David, to see exactly whom she has gotten back into business with. It is a red-letter day for me. The girl whose life I fell in love with, my idol, is standing three feet from me, and I am about to be introduced. I may be nothing more than part of the wallpaper to her, but I am giddy with anticipation, delight bubbling up inside me. I imagine I am one big step closer to my childhood dream of walking through the screen and making Judy's life mine. In that moment on that fateful day, I forget I have heard she can be trouble. I forget she is no longer welcome in Hollywood. I forget that what I loved was Judy's screen life. My mind wipes out everything but the feel of her hand in mine. There is no way in that electric moment that I can imagine anything but the rainbow. And of course there is no way I can imagine putting out a fire she will set to herself at the Plaza ten months down the road.

"I found Judy in a tiny second-floor walk-up in an uninteresting neighborhood in London," Freddie has told us. "I confronted a small Buddha unable to earn more than five hundred bucks for any appearance. It looked like she spent most of her time eating." Judy then tells him she wants to get back into films, and Freddie makes her a promise tied to her weight: The more she loses, the bigger the movie roles will get. Judy takes up the challenge; her diet will start completely on Freddie's dime. Using plane tickets he has happily paid for, she gets on the plane to New York with her three children, Liza, Lorna, and Joey. Freddie has a limo bring her from Idlewild Airport directly to the office. She takes my hand and flashes her million-dollar smile.

She has become Freddie's third client. His wife, Polly, and his best friend, Phil Silvers, have loyally followed him into his new company. These two have given him not only a launching pad, but also a head start in earnings. His dream, however, has been to do something spectacular, something that will attract major attention from the entire industry and kick-start the company on the road to success. Freddie has divined that the answer is Judy Garland. He is determined to arrange a comeback that will restore Judy to her former stardom and glory. This is the miracle he needs to put his new management company, Freddie Fields Associates, on the map.

My becoming Judy's shadow (I don't know what else to call myself here) was totally unplanned. David sent me to her hotel with some papers for her signature. After she signed them, she asked me to sit and talk for a while. She needed company—not wanted, *needed*. It was clear from the first that she hated being alone. The children could be parked in a room next door (and in fact they were), but they were company only when she wanted to be with them. I was adult company, and I was immensely flattered. *Beyond!* I had been

with the company all of four months at the time and didn't expect
to actually talk to a star other than on the phone when I said, "I'll
put you through now." I want to remind you that I was nothing
more than the office's all-purpose schlepper, file clerk, typist, steno-
grapher, babysitter, coffeemaker/-getter, and the occasional mes-
senger, which is what brought me to Judy's door at the Drake.

And when I walked through that door, I opened a whole new
chapter in my life. Only what I thought was going to be a thrilling
chapter became instead a whole book, and not the kind of book
I would ever have imagined. Entering that room changed my life
from ordinary into something else entirely. I walked in a total innocent, perhaps a bit lonely and worn down by family dysfunction,
but still just a girl.

Judy did her impressions of Freddie, and she was not only funny
but also a good mimic. I would discover that her imitations were
always slightly skewed to the ridiculous and coupled with a soupçon
of nastiness that comes from anger. But all I knew on that particular day was that we laughed and generally had a pleasant time. She
was on her best behavior then and maybe for a few days more. She
had some old friends in New York to go out with whom she hadn't
seen in a long time.

Short of a week, however, her good behavior was finished. And
then the calls started to come—calls to Freddie and David in which
she demanded their undivided attention. If she couldn't reach them,
she got pissed. And then she settled for me, and I became no longer
available to them. She was plummeting back into what the guys
would quickly learn was her normal behavior, and while the elevator was going down she would keep one of us on the telephone
endlessly, making it impossible for that person to do anything else
but talk to her all day.

Freddie and David understood immediately that being with her
24/7 was not going to work for them. They couldn't do business.
They decided in the very first week that they could not endure fol-

lowing her around on the concert tour they were planning. Judy was needy to the point of desperation, and they had to find a way to handle it. They'd taken notice that when I was around she was always happier—or if not happier, at least satisfied. This presented them with a unique opportunity to use me, and being the good users they were, they were totally willing to sacrifice me to appease the entertainment gods who were allowing them to build a company.

Would Judy ever be salable again? Could she be counted on to show up on time? Would she show up at all? The game plan was to book her into large venues and prove to the Hollywood community that she still had a huge following. F&D (kindly allow me to abbreviate them) wanted to establish a reliability factor, to show the world that she could perform night after night and deal with a difficult schedule.

Although he didn't talk about it much, Freddie had started his career as a kid in the Borscht belt, where being a waiter gave anyone who wanted it an education in personal appearances. He learned a lot about nightclub acts, about production, about lighting and stage design. He decided to take me with him on Judy's first few concerts in Texas to show me the light cues; he taught me how to call the show (which meant giving the light cues to the electrician backstage) and watched me do it a couple of times.

Given that I could, I became her stage manager. Then, having discovered that I was a fast learner who could handle other road chores such as the load-in, the stage setup, and the sound check, he cut back his handholding. F&D could stay in New York while I went to such cities as Buffalo and Birmingham, Pittsburgh and Cleveland, places they had no interest in (and not exactly places I had dreamed about traveling to either).

F&D thought they were home free, and to a large extent they were right, for they now had a wage-slave assistant for Judy who could double as a constant companion. It was my husband who suddenly, after only a year and a half of marriage, had no one. But he didn't see it that way. Although I would sometimes be gone for a good part of every week, during which he had to fend for himself, he thought this was a groundbreaking career opportunity, and with the generosity that was so characteristic of his good nature, he was happy for me.

I, on the other hand, was grateful for the chance to get away from the marriage. Being on the road with Judy persuaded me that I didn't have a clue about marriage, or my role in it. More to the point, I was now swelling with hope that I was well on my way to the success I lusted after, and marriage was damn inconvenient. I was running Judy Garland's shows. I was traveling in limousines, and talking with authority to members of the press. I was full of myself.

When you worked with Judy, you took good care to take good care of her. It was expected that anyone in that job would want to do that, and I did. Judy Garland was, after all, a public treasure, beloved by millions for her brilliant body of work and cherished by children all over the world who had grown up watching *The Wizard of Oz* year after year. She was an object of universal adoration, and deservedly so. And now, my having acknowledged that, my having made the all-important disclaimer, I have to tell you that "time-intensive" doesn't begin to describe what it was like to work with her. She was demanding beyond any dictionary definition. As jaded as it may sound, the thrill of being with her night and day faded fast.

Road manager was only just the start of it. I grew quickly into much larger boots—with nasty cleats and steel-tipped toes. I had no choice in the matter (except quitting, not an option). In addition to handling the load-in, the stage setup, and the sound check, I now also handled the press. For me there were precious few hours between the end of one concert and the start of another. A day with

Judy ended around four in the morning, and the new day began with the load-in for the next concert at 10:00 a.m. Time was not my friend. There was never enough of it. And, of course, traveling with Judy was necessarily all about her all the time. The things I might do for myself like occasionally go to a hairdresser or take my clothes to the cleaner didn't happen because I had no free time. I saw to it, however, that every radio interview started on time, that her hair was always perfect, that her designer clothes were meticulously pressed. I made sure that a bottle of her liebfraumilch was no farther than her grasp and that she would never have to ask for it lest that make her the slightest bit uncomfortable. A lovely glass and the bottle magically appeared wherever and whenever. She preferred to do her own makeup but wanted me in the room when she did it in case she couldn't find something right in front of her. This had everything to do with her compulsive need to have someone there, and nothing to do with lost lipsticks. She simply could not stand to be alone.

Freddie and David started to believe that I could fend for myself, and if I couldn't—well, that was my tough luck. I was expendable. Once I'd left to go on tour with Judy, I was out of their hair and beyond their care. What happened to me in the boonies was not important. If I became roadkill, someone else would pick up the body. For as long as I lasted, I was giving them breathing room.

However, having discovered that my serving Judy solved a huge problem for my two bosses, I wanted to make sure that no other person ever replaced me. I wanted to impress them; I wanted to become indispensable to them. For this I needed to appear supremely confident, and, in truth, I wasn't confident at all. I was a twenty-four-year-old innocent who knew almost nothing about the workings of show business, and in terms of worldly experiences, I hadn't amassed any. I was hardly more than a clumsy grown-up child in trendy clothing, only a small step ahead of the demure secretaries who still wore straw hats and white gloves in the summer.

The eighteen-wheel semi that rolled all night with the risers, the lights, the music stands, the scores, and the costumes pulled into the new venue in each city sometime after nine. It was then that I would have to start functioning on about three hours' sleep if I was lucky. I went to each load-in already dressed for that night's concert, because I knew there wouldn't be any chance to change. By two in the afternoon my makeup usually looked as if it had been applied with a trowel. I wasn't exactly a natural beauty, and without eyeliner and eyebrow pencil, my green eyes disappeared into my olive complexion and I became featureless. But the road was intense and permitted no time for personal touch-ups. I ran up and down the aisles all day long like a perfect Miss Know-It-All, with authority I granted myself to talk for one of the world's greatest entertainers.

Although she was starting to make money again, we hadn't enough extra to pay for a roadie (those guys we see before a concert dragging cables around the stage, checking the amplifiers and the setup) and so I was the one dragging the cables and I was still getting my secretarial wages of $150 a week. It was just the two of us together, traveling on the cheap. She did the only important thing. She sang. I did everything else, beginning with calling the show from the light booth.

After a while every city looked the same to me—that is, what I got to see of it, which was precious little. Occasionally Judy sent me out into the city to look for a pair of new tights or one of the smocks she loved wearing. Her liver was distended, and maternity smocks hid a figure problem that would endure until she dropped more weight. Often we were on the road for four days and back in New York for three, and on those days when I was home, I role-played the little wife, trying to make all the road anecdotes entertaining to my husband and our friends. Judy would go home to the children, who were now settled in an apartment I'd rented for her at the legendary Dakota.

After I caught up on my sleep I always went to the office to catch up on the filing and to be debriefed, my menial mind-set still firmly locked in. And then one day when I went to FFA, I discovered that Freddie had hired someone new, someone permanent. No more temps replacing me. I was no longer their secretary. Freddie had found an elegant man named Jeff Hand who was part valet, part social secretary, and part confidant. Whatever he was, he was above filing. But I had no time to worry about that, for all too quickly concert time would roll around again, and it was back to planes and limos, hotels and halls.

But there was something else going on here besides simply getting Judy out onstage and getting the job done. Sure, it was a fast-track education in working a show, but way more important, it was a high-speed education in addiction, in the human behavior of a very troubled soul. I couldn't put Judy in the same category with anyone I'd ever met in my life up to that point. And yet, peculiarly enough, it wasn't my first exposure to people who have to drink.

My mother's older sister, her best friend, my aunt Julie, was known as "Julie, Queen of the Bowery." This was in the days when the Bowery on the East Side of lower Manhattan was a haven for every alcoholic in New York City. The street lined with polite commerce on what is now called Third Avenue was then lined with no-frills bars cheek by jowl along ten dirty blocks, where drunks wallowed in the gutter. My aunt, who never touched liquor, owned the largest of these establishments.

This came about because when her husband came home from World War II an alcoholic, he bought this huge beer hall where he could feed his need while serving the public—serving them much more than beer, but nothing quite as good. He died young—not unexpectedly—of cirrhosis and left Aunt Julie the business. My mother's clan, the Weiss family, were all rather tall and stately, but not Julie. She was the runt of the litter. Yet this little lady would stand behind the bar and serve former judges and inmates alike the swill that constituted their total diet. My aunt told me she could be fined if she was caught by the ABC (Alcoholic Beverage Control) board serving a drunk. But drunk was all there was. So when someone fell asleep at one of the tables, Julie would go over and get him up, sometimes throw him out. She could manhandle those guys, some twice her size. In the end this led to two unfortunate incidents in which the drunks fought back.

The first ugly episode caused Julie a broken wrist. The second and last little contretemps ended in several broken ribs. She was seventy-three at the time. Around the holidays business swelled to a point where customers could be three-deep at the bar and unpaid assistance was required. My uncles and my mother would help serve behind the bar, and I would stay in the back avoiding, detection while drying glasses. Other than that I was nothing more than an amused witness. Her only competition downtown was from "Tomato Mary," another woman right next door. I never found out why she was called that, but I imagined it was from a red face caused by too much drink.

Men of the Bowery inhabited a different world from Judy. She belonged to a world that I very much wanted to be a part of, and now she was drinking as much as they, and her world also no longer felt normal to me. Was it typical for so many to drink so much? As I moved around the country with Judy, I was learning that in show-biz alcoholism was a part of many people's "normal"—people who were high-functioning professionals, well regarded and highly respected, and preferred to orbit in a refined stupor.

CHAPTER SEVEN

Have You Heard of Haddonfield?

Every concert was thrilling. I never saw Judy phone it in, no matter how exhausted she was. Her performances were always joyous, and in some cases so intense I worried that she would spin off into some emotional hell. That never happened. Instead each appearance collided happily with the highest of audience expectations. I watched fans in very different cities react exactly the same way—streaming down the aisles in order to mob the apron of the stage, hoping to get close enough to shake her hand or to throw a rose she might pick up.

Love of her was the common denominator everywhere, and that never got old. It made me really happy, sometimes teary-eyed happy, to see her win big. But I also felt a sadness that always floated just on top of the happiness like a storm cloud, and if I drew my eyes up and away from the ecstatic audience for a moment, I saw it lying in wait. Noël Coward wrote an exquisite song that Judy usually included in her performance: "If Love Were All." It contains the lyric phrase "a talent to amuse." Judy understood what that meant as surely and as deeply as anyone ever did, and she owned that talent. There were times when she understood that her talent to amuse was her undoing because it made everyone want to take advantage of her. Sadly, she was right.

By the time I started traveling with her, she had allowed her life experience to make her unhappy, suspicious, and often mean, and therefore her talent to amuse was the only thing she had left that anyone cared about. So there were also moments when I stood backstage at the end of the performance thinking, Would these ecstatic fans feel the same way about her if they knew what I know? It was a sinister feeling. It was ironic that all anyone loved her for was her talent, because all she ever really wanted was to be loved— not just for her talent but for herself. And that was what she herself made impossible. Midway through the tour, she had turned my open heart into a dry little seed.

Although the concerts were always wonderful, what came before and after was not. Sometimes it was plain awful, and a few times almost tragic. The before and after could not have withstood a spotlight. Often getting her onstage could involve a contest of wills, a test of my endurance, a hard sell, chicanery, or all of them. It could sometimes precipitate events that I couldn't handle well. But there was one I wished I had filmed. My mind flies to the before at the arena in Haddonfield, New Jersey. Preparations for that night's concert were unique.

The arena was a shit hole. No other way to describe it. It was old and dirty, and when I walked into the dressing room I knew instantly we were in trouble. The large room was a cement bunker. Broken lockers, their doors falling off, lined one wall. Old jockstraps hung from rusty hooks, a few littering the floor. The windowpanes on the short wall contained twenty-five years of grime, grime that was growing mold. Two wooden chairs and a table with a broken leg completed the decor. The stench was so strong it was like a wall trying to stop me from entering the room. It had been collected from the accumulated perspiration of all the basketball and hockey teams that had ever played in the premises. It threatened to straighten my curly hair were I to remain there more than five minutes. The bathroom was unusable, and one had to hope the rats and mice would be annoyed enough by our presence to stay hidden from view. Sadly, the only mirror was in the john. The concert promoter that night was the nicest old man, Felix Gerstman, who had been presenting concerts all his adult life. What was he thinking?

I had to do something fast because the arena's maintenance department assured me this was the best dressing room in the whole place. There wasn't even an unused, unlocked office we could use. I knew it would be advisable for Judy to dress at the hotel; however, that was turning out to be a nightmare, the main problem being that I had all her clothes with me. She accepted no calls before five, and that was when the critical sound check took place. I had to be in the hall for that. If I went back to the hotel to dress her after that, we would never make curtain time.

I spent my lunch at a five-and-ten loading up on all the cleaning products I could carry (the backstage crew laughed when I suggested mopping to them); I also bought the biggest mirror I could find, lots of white towels, a bedpan, and a large screen. I mopped and I fumigated, I wiped and I repaired, and I have to say that it looked no better when I finished than when I'd started. But the makeup was laid out the way Madam liked, on clean white towels in front of a mirror, and if push came to shove, she could pee in a pan behind the ersatz shoji screen I'd purchased. Talk about beyond the call of duty! I was wrecked and held my breath with terror at what was coming. And when it came, I was still not prepared.

While waiting for the limo to pull up to the stage door, I figured that warning Judy about what to expect might be a good idea. Wrong! It was a mistake that stemmed from my inexperience. Here's an agency road rule: Never share your bad news in advance because it's pointless to suffer before you have to. When Judy saw the hall, her face dropped; when she saw the dressing room, she wanted to drop *me*. Her features froze into an angry mask, and the silence that followed was more intimidating than any of the words she might have chosen. If it's true that anger turned inward becomes depression, it was proved again that night. An old arena wasn't something Judy could accept, even knowing that in two hours she'd be gone from it forever, and a lot richer to boot. It was instead a reflection of her awful life, an opportunity to make others suffer for her present unhappiness.

By 8:00 p.m. she still hadn't talked to me, but she had started crying nonstop and occasionally sob-speaking through the tears to no one in particular. "All the years of hard work, and this is where I end up—in a fucking rat hole. I'll kill Freddie fucking Fields—and that cocksucker Begelman. How dare they. . . ." It was a sorrowful outpouring, causing the mascara she was applying to stream down her face in greasy black rivulets. Every so often she would stop the prep altogether and cry flat out for five minutes. And all the while we heard footfalls on the iron steps just above the dressing room, made by the eager concertgoers getting to their seats in the upper deck. The din was beyond awful, more icing on this layer cake of despair.

"Judy, it will all be over soon," I said.

"What will be over soon? This concert or my fucking life?"

"This concert." I tried to sound repentant. That sometimes worked.

"Shut up; you're no better than the rest of them." "The rest of them" meant virtually everyone in her life up to that moment. She held everyone she'd ever met responsible for her feeling like a victim. Clearly I wasn't to blame, but I was the only one there to absorb her anger. I, too, felt like a victim. Even though I could still rationalize that I was merely a victim of circumstance, a circumstance that would end, it didn't help. It was a feeling I'd gotten used to, but don't confuse "being used to" with "being comfortable with." I felt as if my body temperature was dropping. At times I would actually start to shiver as if seized by a cold dread that I would soon be facing a much larger problem—that she would not perform. What then? Never once was I able to reassure myself that Judy would finally do what she had committed to. There was always a chance that she would not, or worse, that she would do something awful, and I would be left to explain. And I would be blamed.

Great entertainers like Jack Benny, George Burns, Nat King Cole, Frank Sinatra, Dean Martin, and Sammy Davis, Jr., were now making huge sums of money in Las Vegas. Could Judy do that? Could she get there again? And if she could get as far as Las Vegas, could she get all the way to Hollywood? So much depended on these concerts. My job depended on these concerts! It had been explained to me early on that getting her out on the stage on time each night was my job—all 150 percent of it. (The extra 50 percent was about getting through the show without a glitch so that I wouldn't get scorched at the end of it.) Never gonna happen tonight, never gonna happen tonight. . . . The loop ran around in my brain, repeating nonstop. Eight thirty, and she was redoing the mascara for the third time. How long would it be before ten thousand people began clapping in unison, or worse, stamping their feet over our heads?

After the mascara came the instant face-lift. Those of you unfamiliar with this procedure probably never hung out in Gray's Theatrical Drugstore while it still occupied the corner of Forty-third and Broadway. The facelift came in two pieces that looked like ordinary flesh-colored Band-Aids. Each had adhesive on one side that went against your skin just like any other Band-Aid, but at other end of the material there was an elastic string with a hook on the end of it; the corresponding piece had the same elastic with an eye. One could put the two pieces on either side of the face by the ears, connect the two elastics under the hair, and voila—everything that gravity had dragged down got drawn up tight again. The trick was to get them on straight. If they went on askew—as was totally possible under these volatile circumstances—you might end up with a crooked smile or, worse, singing out of the side of your mouth.

Judy took out her lifts and began taping them on. Application normally took five minutes. Judy's hair was done last. On this frightful night her hair hadn't even been started. Nine o'clock was looking like a possibility if she would just stop crying. I was chattering on a lot about Freddie and David; defending them, telling her how much they really cared about her. It was exactly the wrong conversation. Crying, cursing, crying, cursing. She couldn't get the lifts on straight, and there was a possibility she would give up trying and storm out. But just then came a knock on the door. I prayed for a miracle, and it was standing in front of me in the figure of "Freddie fucking Fields." Thank God, I thought.

With his sensitive antennae and completely intuitive understanding of divas, Freddie sized up the situation in seconds. "Judy, Judy, Judy," he started, doing his Cary Grant bit. I could see her lip curl. Undaunted, he pressed on.

"You know Roz Russell didn't use just two lifts when she went into makeup." He had her attention, although she feigned indifference. Freddie went into full action-figure mode: He was using lots of exaggerated hand and arm gestures as he identified all the places Roz Russell put her lifts.

"She would put two low on her forehead, and where you're using two, she glued on four." A smile was starting to crack Judy's gloom look.

"She used six on either side of her neck." Judy had now turned around to face Freddie, her amusement impossible to conceal.

"And the master string came out her ass. When you pulled it, she smiled!" Hysterical laughter followed. No one enjoyed a good laugh more than Judy. And since put-down humor was Judy's favorite kind, Freddie had found a receptive audience. All was forgiven.

"Freddie, we will not be doing shit holes like this ever again."

"I didn't know there were any places this old."

"Well, you should have known. You're as old as this place is." She was laughing when she said it, and flying into her clothes while the hairdresser of the moment tried to work around the flurry of sudden activity. She did a great show that night. Better than great! The audience may have had to wait an extra hour, but they got their money's worth.

We drove back from Haddonfield that night in Freddie's limo. I was relegated to sitting in front with the driver, and since the glass privacy partition separating the driver from those seated in back had been employed, I, too, could hear nothing until the glass came down and Freddie ordered the driver to get off at the next exit. We then drove into a less-than-lively town somewhere in lusterless New Jersey and went into a bar so that Judy could "relax."

It was a cold night, and Freddie took pity on the driver and me, allowing us to come inside, where we sat at a small cocktail table while Freddie and Judy stood at the bar. From where we were sitting I could see a woman who was overwhelmed by Judy's sudden appearance. She could not contain her excitement, and because of it—and not for any other reason—her hands were all over Judy. This happened all the time, and Judy just hated people touching her. Freddie to the rescue. He engaged the woman in conversation, and as he did so, he started undressing her, making her more comfortable. Judy immediately picked up on it, and she also kept talking to the woman who was almost too excited to notice what was happening. By the time the woman finally pushed Freddie away she was down to her bra. Everyone in the bar, except herself, was hysterical. Judy was almost on the floor. In the end the woman was a good sport. She got the autograph she wanted, and we laughed all the way home.

Freddie taught me that humor works wonders. Well—not exactly a newsflash, and easier said than done; however, I embraced the idea. I simply knew that I would have to learn to see things cock-eyed as well as straight on. And I do.

CHAPTER EIGHT

Boston

The "before" the show in Boston was another thing entirely. It is still one of my most painful memories these fifty-two years later. We were staying at the Ritz-Carlton, at that time arguably the best hotel in the city. Judy had an elegant gold-and-white suite overlooking Boston Common gardens and pond. She'd decided to dress in the suite that night, which was unusual because she disliked dressing at the hotel prior to any concert, and she gave me no reason why she was changing her routine. It meant, however, that I would have to return from the setup to the Ritz to collect her.

At seven I left the Boston Garden, went back to the hotel, went up to the suite to put together the Act 2 costume change, and as I stood asking her about taking additional eyelashes to the hall, she slit her left wrist with a razor, cutting deeply into an artery. The moment was made even grislier by the fact that when she made the cut she was looking at me and smiling.

I learned many things that night that I could have gone on through life never needing to know. One was that blood doesn't leak out; it spurts, it arcs. I can see it still on the gold-and-white bedspread, on the flocked wall covering and matching drapes, and on me. I was wearing my new favorite outfit, my first-ever ensemble, a three-piece outfit manufactured by my husband's uncle, from whom I bought the most wonderful designer rip-offs wholesale. The fabric of my wool challis blouse matched the lining of my coat. I definitely loved it too much. That night when I walked into her room I thought I looked so snazzy. But all I see now is her blood all over my once-beautiful ensemble, on my skirt and coat. My hands. My hair. I stood there horrified. This was her normal! This is what she did. This is who she was. This is the kind of a teacher she was.

I was beginning to understand that these events were all about manipulation and control. Judy's suicidal episodes gave her power. With every horror she became the center of "his" attention. "'His' attention" was owned by the man of the moment. She craved his love much more than the adoration of her fans. They were strangers. It would soon be over for her—this episode—and she would go on to the next, but not so for me. I would never forget it. It would be seared into my memory, and I would replay it forever. You know what else? I still feel sorrier for me.

So why slit her wrist on that particular night? Let me repeat it: It's a love story. On that particular night she did it for David, for the love of this man who was, at this moment in time, the single most important consideration in her life. (I often wondered—still do today, and will for as long as I live—if I could have sat her down in a totally sober moment—of which there were none—and asked her: Judy, what's more important to you? Being in love? Or singing? What would her answer have been? Some may think they know that answer, and they may be right. But I do not know it. I never have, and I don't think I ever will.) But let me get back to her heart, and her affair with David Begelman.

After an absence of a few weeks, Begelman was back in New York. Judy was in thrall to him. Obsessively. They'd been having an affair for some months, and the affair was forever tripping down a rocky road; for the last many weeks it had been caught on some insurmountable boulders due to David's disappearance. Judy did not, like other women, tell everything to her hairdresser, because her hairdresser sometimes changed as often as her wardrobe. I was her confidante; she told me everything, and I knew about the affair from the beginning. I often wished I did not, because David was my boss. It put me in the very uncomfortable position of being in the middle when Judy sought insider information. She would ask me questions about his wife, Lee, and where he'd been on certain nights, questions I couldn't answer—sometimes because I didn't know, and sometimes because I didn't want to.

Recently he'd gone on a trip abroad, and had dared to take his wife along with him. And how did Judy know that? Not from me. She'd checked with his housemaid, whose confirmation had sent her into a tailspin. She could not be jollied out of it. I faced daily questions like: "Do you think he's sleeping with Lee?" What was I supposed to answer? My best shot at a response was: "How could he be sleeping with her if he's in love with you?"

Answering her question with a question wasn't really answering her question at all, and I preferred doing that to lying. Judy was sure that David was in love with her. And I was happy to leave it right there. I knew the truth, and it was ugly. David was ugly. I had now been in his employ a year and a half, and I was learning what a liar he was. The truth would have hurt. The truth might have cured some other person, but not Judy, who lived in a make-believe world.

She would sometimes tell me the romantic things David told her, and I knew they were all lies. She giggled like a schoolgirl when she confided: "We're making wonderful plans to travel." Travel with David? He was a different kind of addict: a gambler and a workaholic who went on vacation only when forced to by his wife, and this is exactly what had happened. Lee Begelman had her social set, a finite group of wealthy couples, the wives of which performed good works mostly for themselves, and who spent hours on the phone each day discussing how to spend their husbands' money. One day Lee announced that they were all going yachting in the Greek Islands, and off David went with a small library to forfend against the boredom he suffered around Lee's entitled entourage. He told Judy he was going to London on business. "What plans are you and David making?" I asked Judy. "We'll rent a marvelous big yacht just for the two of us, and we'll cruise the Greek Islands." There's no other word for it. David was a cruel man.

It hurt me to see Judy taken in by David's outrageousness, but I could not or would not attempt to convince her that David loved no one but himself. She believed what she wanted to believe, and in spite of their fights about his prolonged absences, regardless of his limp ad-libbing about his failure to get a divorce, Judy remained a believer. And now David had come to Boston to attend her concert and was dressing in a room almost next door when she slit her wrist. Judy Garland would show him. Judy Garland would die for him. Who was Judy Garland really punishing? It wasn't David Begelman.

I made a tourniquet out of a towel and a hairbrush. Then I picked up the phone to call David while Judy sat docilely by. She didn't cry or scream or have any reaction at all, for that matter. She was standing when she did it; now she sat down on the bed and, staring straight ahead, calmly waited for David to arrive. David immediately called for a doctor, and one arrived in record time; in fact he got there so fast it made my mind spin a fiction that Judy had stationed him downstairs in the bar in advance for her own nefarious purpose. That, of course, is ridiculous, but I do have a sense that she knew what she was doing, that in fact she had planned it. Could she have known that what she had done or the way she had done it was not serious enough to cause a major problem? It sounds awful to even think such a thing because the slice she made looked ghastly, but that may be the truth of this horror. Maybe this was not so much a suicide attempt as it was a scream: I hurt! Come take care of me. Come love me!

It was a gash in a life careening out of control, a huge, ugly gash that would hopefully make David see her, and see the pain that was tearing her apart. If she did it for effect, the effect on me was shattering. I was angry that she would do such a terrible thing to herself, and, at the same time, do it to me. My anger filled a space in my being like air filling a balloon. And I didn't know how to show it. I even felt guilty for having it. How could I be angry at someone who was so sick? Well, it is possible. The anger stayed with me for a long time, for years, until the balloon inside me got so old and weak that all the anger seeped out. Only the picture remains.

Put her in an institution. Get her the help she needs! That's the scream that was raging in me. It never came out of my mouth. Could anyone have institutionalized Judy without her permission? Maybe not, but it didn't matter because there were no candidates. Everyone was too busy exploiting her. To this day I think I should have tried harder to get her the help she so obviously needed. I should have appealed to David to get her serious attention. I should at least have tried. I didn't. I knew then as I know now that any plea for saving Judy would have been gratuitous, made for wanting to hear the sound of my own voice—for all the attention such a plea would have received. But maybe had I at least given lip service to this tragedy I might have felt less guilty. Here's my cop-out: I was only a foot soldier doing my duty. And my duty was to obey orders. There was only Do the job and shut up, or quit. I'll say it again. Quitting wasn't ever an option.

When I describe what followed, you may find it despicable. I do. I was repulsed by my own behavior, but I knew I was doing what Judy wanted me to do. "Here's a hundred," David said, peeling a bill off a large roll and putting it into my hand. "Buy enough bracelets to cover the bandages." Judy sat by, admiring David's take-charge capability. There wasn't an iota of protest from her. Under the circumstances one might think she would want to go to the hospital, or at least pull the covers up over her head. Wasn't anyone going to cancel the concert and give her tender, loving care? Heavens no! Judy was now ready to go out onstage, and if Judy intended to perform that night knowing full well that she had slit her wrist on the way to the theater, so be it. If buying bracelets to cover her wrist was the only thing I had to do to hold on to my job this night, I would do it. "Hurry," Judy told me. I ran out into the streets of Boston to find a store where I could buy enough cheap bangles to cover the bandages the doctor had put on her wrist. It wasn't so easy at seven o'clock on a Saturday night, but I was on a mission and I would do whatever I had to—beg, borrow, or steal—to get her onstage. And get there she did. She did such a wonderful show no one could have suspected she wasn't at the top of her form. On second thought, maybe she was.

That Judy desperately needed help was clear even to a naive dummy like me. I was brought up to believe that when someone was ill, you took him or her to the doctor. But the point here is that "doctor" (as opposed to pill pusher) was not the help she wanted. It wasn't the kind of help she felt she needed, and it wasn't the kind of help she would have accepted. It was a hard lesson for me.

CHAPTER NINE

Reality Checks

I was wearing chicken soup stains the day Judy called me out on-stage to sing "Just in Time" with her. No, I'm not making this up. I didn't think it would ever happen, although she had threatened to do it at the last concert, and that day was now here. It was the culmination of a tour to establish her reliability that had taken us on the road for months in 1961, against the hope that Hollywood would take another chance on her. Freddie's strategy had proved successful. Alas, that afternoon I spilled soup down the front of my beautiful, almost-new, brown wool A-line dress when a lumpy electrician backed into me with a ladder in a place where I should never have been standing. This is what happens when you drink your lunch standing up.

The lovely Lanz dress, soft and warm when I'd zipped it up early that morning, was now ruined and still wet around the chest area from repeated soakings in several of the Armory's bathrooms. I hadn't brushed my hair all day, and one heel was barely hanging on to its shoe. Judy couldn't've cared less about what I looked like as I stood in the wings as usual for the encores, a towel hung over my right arm like a Victorian maitre d', and the earphones I'd used in the light booth to call the show still hanging around my neck. She did take away the liebfraumilch in my right hand and passed it off to a stagehand paging the curtain, lest I walk out holding booze the audience might think was hers. Then she grabbed my arm and pulled, and suddenly I was out onstage, framed in the spotlight, and totally terrified that I was really going to have to sing. My throat was closing with the fear of it, and I was positive no sound would come out.

Thousands of miles traveled had brought me to that moment. Many of them traversed over well-paved roads. Boring rides in limousines. Overheated or freezing limos. On the way to airports, from airports to hotels, from hotels to gigs, from gigs to restaurants—or wher-ever else we went at two in the morning—from "wherevers" back to hotels, and finally back to airports. Those rides became too te-dious to endure—except for the day in which her hand began a trip from my knee, where she had placed it when the car lurched, to my crotch. As it slowly crept no more than an inch every two or three minutes, I started to panic. Her move wasn't inadvertent. Judy did nothing inadvertently. Like Alice, I grew smaller and smaller as I shrank into the upholstered corner on my side of the car. Her arm, however, grew longer and longer as it stretched across the length of the backseat.

Omigod! What am I going to do? It was, for me, a close encoun-ter of the unwanted kind. In an instant my body turned rigid, and I stopped breathing while every possible weak-kneed simpering re-sponse like, I don't think so. Please! Not my thing. I wish you wouldn't collided in my head. I rejected them all. Breathe, Ste-vie. Dare I look at her? I mustered all the courage I had and turned in her direction. I hesitate to recall the pained expression I must have worn. Take another breath and say something, I commanded my-self. Nothing would come out. Her hand was now fully in my crotch, and she was staring straight ahead. Then she turned and smiled. What did it mean? Why was I even thinking about that? What should I do? The idea of being intimate with Judy revolted me. I wanted to reject her. And it wasn't just because she was a woman, although a relationship with another woman did not interest me. It was because I didn't like her. That was the biggest Oh no!

In that minute I knew, as surely as I knew my name, that I no longer liked her and I could admit it to myself. I loved her talent, but I didn't like her. The pass might not have been as distasteful if it had come from someone else. Beyond that, there was that other big Oh no! She was the great Judy Garland, and I was her assistant cum roadie cum wet nurse cum all other things menial. I was scared. Will I lose my job if I take her hand away? Will I offend her? These insipid questions were exploding in my head. Breathe, Stevie.

And then suddenly it didn't matter. If I lost my job, so be it. It all happened in that moment. I took another deep breath, and then I took her hand and put it back in her lap. I looked at her and smiled. And when I did, I understood that I had the courage of my conviction. After that I would never doubt it again. She smiled back, and we both moved on. It was another step forward in my real education, but I'm grateful that I was not tested again. She kept her hands to herself after that.

Having car sex with Judy Garland was in no way the right answer to alleviating boredom, but after a while one simply had to do something. I was drowning in my own miserable small talk. "Tell me what it was like working with Gene Kelly in *The Pirate*," and then there would be little snatches of fun when she talked about working with Mickey, Fred, and Gene. But I was not knowledgeable enough, or insider enough, to discuss the great professionals like the producer Arthur Freed and the other creative geniuses that she had worked with, like the composer Roger Edens and the choreographer Busby Berkeley.

In these countless car rides I went with her through every movie she'd ever done, patting myself on the back each time I remembered some silly casting detail, while unintentionally boring her to death. And when she was bored she was nasty. I was predictable in my style, formulaic in my conversation, and, with Judy, limited mostly to praise of her voice, her clothes, her wit, and her last performance. Thank God she never tired of praise.

Away from her I tried recapturing the feelings I had had for her before we met. She was, after all, the living incarnation of my childhood dream. But it became more and more difficult even to pretend I was in awe when we were together. The dream disappeared when the real Judy Garland entered the room. Clearly I had nothing in common with her, or she with me. She was sophisticated; I only thought I was. I was totally naive. Going on her concert tour was the first time I'd been out of New York. She was worldly; I was inexperienced. My husband was the first man I'd slept with.

When she was in her best of all possible worlds, Judy had a great imagination, and one day while on our way to somewhere, she told me she'd come up with a suggestion to relieve our limo despair. "I'm going to teach you the Mort Lindsey arrangement of "Just in Time" (a superb song written by the Broadway king Jule Styne for the show *Bells Are Ringing*). Judy didn't bother to ask if I could sing. If I couldn't I might then become the victim of some of her outrageous nasty humor for a couple of rides. Truth is I sang in tune and played the piano a bit.

Let's talk for a minute about what Judy thought was funny. She had a fine, funny, and fertile creative mind. She loved hearing a good joke; she would howl with laughter, and she was a good joke teller herself. But her best indoor sport was put-down humor, the Don

Rickles variety that identified a human target and then eviscerated it with a sharp blade. It was mean humor and often dealt with one's physical attributes. For instance, Billy Barty, the wonderful elfin actor who was featured in movies and countless TV shows once the little box became so popular in the fifties, did not fare well with her. All things small in stature got "Barterized." She loved to toss a good "bart." Of Debbie Reynolds's husband, Harry Karl—whose manners she deplored—she quipped: "He eats two-minute eggs with his fingers." Then there was also more subtly nasty humor.

One of my favorite Judy moments happened in an elevator at the Beverly Hilton. Judy and I stepped in on the twelfth floor. Richard Nixon and another gentleman stepped in on the tenth. Nixon looked at Judy and then turned toward the front, showing her only his back. On the fourth he turned around and said, "And you must be Judy Garland." She smiled politely and, without missing a beat, replied, "And you're Richard Nixon." Back to the car and "Just in Time"!

Mort Lindsey's arrangement was brilliant, and difficult. It contained eleven halftone key changes: one modulation every eight bars. A whole-tone key change is hard enough to sing, but a halftone is impossible—unless, of course, you're Judy Garland with a voice of liquid magic. When she performed the song onstage, it was nothing less than amazing. You could only listen in total awe of where that voice could go and admire the versatility of her enormous talent. She could take a melody anywhere, put it through the wringer, and squeeze tears out of the audience. On the other hand, when I attempted to make the halftone changes that came so effortlessly to her, I was lucky that Jule Styne was nowhere within earshot. But repetition, herein the substitute for talent, finally put me on the road to nine, ten, and, yes—at last—eleven key changes. I thought I was home free. Not so fast.

Once I had mastered the key changes in the melody, she started singing the harmony along with me. The new fun was seeing how far I could now go before I crashed. The answer: not very far. "You better get it right," she warned, "because in the last concert I'm going to call you out onstage to sing it with me." It was a teasing moment she was relishing, and so was I. It was always good to see her in a good mood.

"I dare you." I told her. "Daring me is treading on very dangerous ground," she warned. I had no doubt that was true. The Judy Garland I'd come to know was willing to try anything—twice—to avoid a rush to judgment. She made it easy to believe that trying kinky things was fun for her. There were always sly sexual intimations about relationships with women that were titillating and bore further investigation, but that was *really* treading on dangerous ground, and after the touching incident in the limo, I didn't want to go there. But the stage was not dangerous ground, it was sacred ground, and that was different. Performance was something she didn't share except with superstars. Judy was the single and complete owner of whatever concert stage she walked out onto. I could count on her not wanting to share her moment with me—not even as a joke.

"You better be prepared," she warned. "I'm gonna do it." Not bloody likely, I continued to think. The only nonsuperstar she ever got out on the concert stage with her was Liza, which fell into another category entirely. Occasionally she would call Liza up from the audience to spell her for five minutes. It gave Judy an opportunity to catch her breath, mop her wet head, and gulp down some water. She would sit with her legs hanging over the apron—mugging and stealing the scene—while an earnest thirteen-year-old Liza kicked up her heels to her own choreographed rendition of "Swanee," and I, up in the booth, intoned a prayer that Li's unwashed underwear—

peeking out from under her short skirt—couldn't be seen by the audience.

So there I was, wearing the chicken soup and standing next to her on center stage while she's prattling on about how she couldn't have done a thing on the tour without me, and I'm staring out into the audience without any grace of word or movement. I am this big soup-stained, exhausted-looking creature frozen in the glare of the spotlights, nothing delicately deerlike about me. To complete this "deer-in-the-headlights" cliché, the car she's driving is about to roll on over me and kill me. I see it coming, and I can do nothing to stop it. I will die there in front of thousands about to enjoy this joke at my expense. Judy turned to Mort Lindsey, her conductor, nodded, and I heard, or thought I heard, the intro for "Just in Time." Then came the downbeat along with a poke in my ribs, and there I stood, stupidly singing.

As it turned out, I got through the first key change without falling apart and moved right on to the second. I know I was smiling—and not because my childhood tap-dance teacher, Charles Lowe, taught me always to smile at recitals—because I'd managed not to mess up the song for her—yet. I can remember that I was even starting to enjoy myself just a little. Can you be scared to death and enjoy yourself at the same time? I know the answer. Yes!

But wait a minute. What happened to the music? I'm suddenly aware that I'm standing there singing alone. No Judy. No accompaniment. And now I'm being pushed off the stage. I see the wings coming up in front of me like big, flat, black maws about to swallow me, and I hear her mimicking the vaudevillian who coined the phrase "Give the little lady a big hand." Hey, hold on there! What did I do wrong? I got it right. That's what. I had held on and sung, made three correct key changes. The joke didn't work.

She saw I wasn't going to become an object of derision. She wouldn't be able to make fun at my expense. She didn't need a straight man, she needed a foil, and I was going to be flat-out square, dull, and boring. The usual. Of *course* she wasn't going to sing with me. Of *course* I wasn't going to sing with her. Judy never shared a stage with anyone. Until she had to. Gee, Judy, thanks for the memories!

CHAPTER TEN

Love—or Something Like It

Judy wanted romance around the clock. She was starving for it. The love she got from her audience was never enough. Not even close. The minute she was not in front of the footlights, she craved male attention. She could not feel attractive or beautiful without being told so by a man. When *he* was present, Judy sublimated so it could be all about *him*. He was everything as long as he adored her. Without a man, 50 percent of her was missing. And this was David Begelman's moment.

I'd watched, and listened in on phone calls in which David promised his wife and his clients that he would take care of business for them in ways that were never fulfilled. For instance, it was no more than routine for David to assure the fine comedian Shelley Berman that he would call Warner Bros. on his behalf, a call that would never happen and for which there was probably never any intent. But substitute the name of anyone else in Shelley's place, and the deal with David was always the same. He was a slime. However, going well beyond the ugly episode in Boston, David—the scoundrel, the liar, the thief—could do no wrong as far as Judy was concerned.

David wasn't beautiful by any means. He had a large nose, flaccid cheeks (always by 5:00 p.m.), and beady eyes. Somehow all this ugliness came together in its own interesting and gruesome way, distinguishing him from the rest of the ugly powerful men he ran with. He was tall, and his height, coupled with immaculate tailoring, helped to hide his protruding belly. His shoes were hand sewn in Italy, his shirts made to order in London and shipped in boxes from Bond Street every six months, and his suits custom tailored at one of the most expensive Park Avenue ateliers. He loved only the best, most expensive things for himself, and he lived like a sheikh on what he earned, borrowed, and stole.

What did we all see in David? I include myself along with Freddie Fields, Judy, Lee Begelman, and a legion of showbiz friends. We were all so blinded by a little charm that we couldn't see the truth: He was no good. In fact he was worse than that. He was toxic, fatal for all his wives, but most of all for Judy. He took aim and leveled a shot across her bow that filled her with his poison and overwhelmed her. His was the charm of a psychopathic personality: totally flamboyant, witty, intelligent, and intellectual on the one side; a liar, a cheat, a complete fraud, irresponsible, and self-destructive on the other.

He was a world-class womanizer who loved the seduction. Women were enchanted with him because he was a wonderful raconteur, extremely alert, quick witted, and totally attentive. Judy responded to him instantly because he kept her endlessly amused. Her enchantment began on the first day they met, when she walked into Freddie Fields Associates to meet the partner she'd heard so much about. I watched from my desk outside Freddie's glass-enclosed private office until Freddie closed the mechanically operated draperies, cutting off my view. Nor could I hear anyone, but I could imagine David greasing on about how wonderful Judy looked, how lucky he was to be sitting there with her, and how lucky she was to be sitting there with him. She would have laughed politely and perhaps raised a question about the latter, whereupon David would have assured her that she would now become richer and more famous than ever before. It would be the starting point from which, over the next few months, David's professed adoration would grow to unbelievable heights.

It would be easy for Judy, so wanting to believe she was adored, to cross the Rubicon and imagine that this man held her in something more than simple professional esteem. And he was willing to prove that in bed. It didn't take long, however, for Judy to decide she wanted him exclusively to herself.

And so, with David's encouragement, Judy managed to persuade herself that they would soon be husband and wife. The affair had started a few months after she became a client. And perhaps, by bedding her, David was determined to ensure that she, and her income, would remain tied to FFA. The wonderful success that was coming for Freddie and David hadn't yet arrived.

Meanwhile, David's wife, Lee, was a woman who would not be denied. She also wanted her charming husband around all the time, and she demanded all the baubles and perks he could afford—and many that he couldn't. Divorce wasn't anywhere on her radar, and she resented not only the time David spent with Judy but even the mere mention of Judy's name. David let Lee buy the expensive clothes she wanted, allowed her to keep refurnishing their apartment, put up with her need to be seen at every opening, gala, and charity event—all in the interest of placating her so that she would remain silent when he needed to buy some time with Judy. Then he would go on the occasional after-concert honeymoon with Judy in order to placate and silence *her* for as long as he could. It didn't work with either woman. They each wanted it all, and it was all so apparent to me. David seemed to enjoy the enmity he saw growing between the two women. That was his kind of gruesome pleasure.

The Newport concert offered Judy just such a weekend opportunity, and the two "lovebirds" planned a little idyll among the idle rich. (Judy had a long list of society friends.) When the concert was finished she took off with David into the starry night, while I stayed behind to pick up the pieces, literally. I packed a rental car with all the extra clothes, the costumes, the makeup, and the meds, and I left for Cape Cod. By the time I left Newport on the way to Hyannis, it was well past midnight.

As my office's real-estate agent par excellence, I had struck pay dirt. I'd found Judy a house on the water near the Kennedy compound. It was a big old clapboard home with a wraparound porch right across the road from the president of the United States. Judy had been enjoying spending time at the old house when she was not working. My marching orders were to take the car with everything to the Hyannis house. Judy had no concerts immediately following Newport, so after the "David honeymoon," she would relax with the children and party with the vacationing Kennedy clan until she went back to work.

It was not part of anyone's plan for me to get lost en route. I was traveling on the outskirts of small towns where there was minimum lighting, and on narrow country roads where there was none. It's not a long trip from Newport to Hyannis, but I managed to turn it into one.

Sometime after three I finally found myself in the right neighborhood. The street where Judy rented was pitch black and deserted, and I was anxious and dead tired as I tooled along at about three miles an hour. Suddenly from out of the bushes sprang a half-dozen men with their guns drawn and pointed at me. I was hustled from the car, frisked, and asked to sit on the pavement while they searched the car's contents.

Initially I was too frightened to realize what had happened, but as I sat on the stone-cold road in my thin pink-and-white-checked cotton pants with a gun pointed at me, I realized that my welcoming committee was the Secret Service. I relaxed because I thought I could explain myself, but they didn't know that Judy was renting across the street. How could that happen? I found it hard to believe how deficient their intelligence gathering had been, amazed they didn't know the name and complete background of every neighbor, but there it is. Indeed they were curious about such a large carton of drugs in the backseat of a rented car, all bearing Judy's name. You couldn't find this many drugs anywhere but a pharmacy. And there I was trying to explain what the various drugs were for when I didn't even know myself, but it was a way of trying to make them understand that I was who I said I was. Anyway, my explanation fell on deaf ears. At some point the situation started to strike me as even a little funny, but my armed guard was not amused. Nor at four in the morning was anyone willing to knock on any door, for which I didn't have a key. While the Secret Service kept the rented Chevy in tow, I was taken into custody, where I remained (on the road) until around dawn, when one of the men accompanied me to Judy's house. It was a long cold night.

Only one thought warmed me, and that was my knowing it was David Begelman who was now sitting in some fancy hotel suite holding the gin rummy cards instead of me. Okay, so maybe it wasn't gin rummy; it was whatever game he was playing with her.

The good news was that they didn't confiscate the drugs. And I got terrific mileage out of the story, first with Judy, who thought it was a riot, and then with many lesser lights. But I also realized that life with Judy took me down many dark roads where real danger lurked.

David continued to press his luck to the limit, constantly lying to both Judy and Lee. On occasion he seemed to have fun making me witness his little game. While I sat in his office ready to take dictation that he said had to go out immediately, I would listen to him lying to Lee on the phone about the work he had to do, and then he would put on his jacket and leave to go dine with Judy, and he did so in restaurants for which I made the reservations, most of them Lee's favorites.

Sometimes I managed to rationalize this, persuading myself that both women were unbearably demanding, and to keep his head above water David would of course need to tap-dance around the truth a little bit. But I really knew better. He was a snake. He didn't know how to tell the truth, and it amused him to show me how outrageous a liar he could get away with being. Like Judy, he loved an audience. It's almost as if he needed me to know just who he was.

He didn't seem to care one iota about his wife, and he told everyone that Judy also meant nothing to him. Given the treatment they both received at his hands, this had to be true. I remember the dinner when I was invited to join him and some friends at Danny's Hideway, the famous steak house, where David held court and made his ugly declarations. In fact, on the night I was there he made one of the most disgusting statements about Judy that I've ever heard made about anyone, saying to the group, "A ragpicker wouldn't throw a hook into her!" And this was the man Judy Garland adored. He was a pig.

After working with him for two years, however, it was apparent to me that David was more than just a pig: He was a sick pig. It's easy to say of someone who makes ugly remarks, "That guy is sick." It's a cheap expression that gets tossed around a lot. But even as naive as I was at twenty-five, I thought David needed psychiatric help. He was always setting himself up to be punished. And no matter how bad the punishment, David raised the ante so that the next punishment would be worse. Las Vegas and London were prime examples.

The stakes for him were always high. In Las Vegas people get punished every minute, but very few plummet into the David class. I couldn't believe what I saw. There for Judy's opening night in 1962, what her on-again, off-again lover set himself up for confirmed my sense that he was sick and in great need of help. But the only help he sought was more punishment.

Watching David at the craps table meant waiting to see just how far he would go, how far he would push the envelope. It was always to a place way beyond his means. Wanting to win but setting himself up to lose, he was a fascinating paradox to observe. One simple example of how this "prospective punishment" worked was when I was with him in the casino at the Sahara Hotel one night during Judy's engagement. He signed an IOU for fifty-thousand dollars. I watched as he successfully gambled and parlayed his winnings into more than one hundred thousand dollars; then he stood there losing until not only were his winnings gone but also the borrowed fifty, as well as the next seventy-five. He did that more than once on that trip alone.

As I think about it now, I can't imagine the casino management lending this person, relatively new to them, those sums unless they made Judy Garland a guarantor. More likely he took the money in her name. The outcome: Strange men in shiny black suits then came to the New York office unannounced, carrying their shiny little black suitcases. I called them "the bent-nose brigade," and it clearly was more than coincidence that they showed up right after Judy was in Las Vegas. I could imagine, after David closed the drapes and locked his office door, that guns came out of those attachés. What he had to give in return for his life was undoubtedly more Judy engagements. But that was not yet punishment enough. Much more was still to come.

By the time the "London incident" occurred, Judy was employable in Hollywood if not exactly back on top. Freddie and David had gotten her several movie deals, including *Judgment at Nuremberg,* for which she was nominated for an Academy Award, and *A Child Is Waiting*. *I Could Go On Singing* was the third starring film under the FFA management. During all this time—from the end of the concerts in 1961 through the making of the films—I was the go-to person for Judy whenever she was in New York, and always on call no matter where she was. David and I accompanied Judy to England on the press junket for the world premiere of *I Could Go On Singing*. The plane, filled with American press, took off for London, where we had approved a schedule that would require total efficiency. All of the English entertainment press was at the airport awaiting her arrival. Meanwhile, the universe had a different plan. Fog, of the densest kind, socked in Heathrow, making it impossible to land. Although the plane buzzed the runway several times, the pilot finally had to land in Manchester, about which there is little worth mentioning except it was there that I learned the English eat their fish cold and drink their beer lukewarm.

The next day we took the train to London, checked into the Savoy Hotel in the Strand, and I was ready to believe life would return to a schedule as close to normal as it could be when I was on "Judy time." Instead Lee Begelman showed up, uninvited and unannounced, checked into her husband's room while he was out, rested for a little, and then found out what room Judy was in—which just happened to be right across the hall—and knocked on the door.

Did Lee come to London to confront Judy? I don't know for sure, but I do know she was expecting to be invited in, because she was wearing only a nightgown with a light traveling bathrobe over it. Judy was also in a nightgown when she answered the door, and she had no interest in a little tête-à-tête. Clearly they hated each other. I couldn't see who landed the first punch from where I was sitting in Judy's living room. And by the time I realized what was happening, a ferocious fight was under way, and I couldn't stop it.

The women were trying to kill each other: kicking and clawing, pulling hair and clothes. Both were bleeding, gowns torn, now almost naked in the fifth floor corridor, which houses the exquisite river suites on the Thames side of the Savoy. Guests came out of their rooms. A crowd started forming. Neither woman was backing down, each fueled by hatred and resentment of the other—loathing that David had allowed grow—and both looked prepared to fight to the death. I was still struggling to break it up when the manager arrived—called up, I imagine, by one of the shocked spectators. With his upper-class British manners firmly in place, and looking beyond horrified, he boldly stepped in, but he, too, could do nothing. It was a vicious battle, and one risked serious injury by getting involved. In fact there were enough spectators for us to have acted in some united way to stop the fight, but everyone was too mesmerized to move. The manager was calling security when, by fortuitous coincidence, David came back and immediately stopped it. He did not treat his wife gently. Taking her upper arm roughly into his two hands, he dragged her back to his room and threw her into it. He then slammed the door behind them.

"I hope he throws her the fuck out!" yelled Judy. And she didn't mean simply out of the hotel, or out of London. Lee Begelman did indeed leave London within the hour. I retreated with Judy into her suite. She was in manic heaven. I listened as she rattled on and on: "She's a no-good cunt, that one," pronounced with a perfect English accent. Judy now expected to celebrate with David at lunch and started to dress for the occasion, deciding to wear black in honor of what she was sure would be the death of David's marriage. Soon David would knock on the door and come in to continue spreading his black confetti like so much fairy dust. He appeared to be in fine humor, but he had set himself up for the punishment of Lee's wrath and the threat of an expensive divorce.

CHAPTER ELEVEN

Vegas

I was a Vegas virgin (so to speak) when I visited in 1962. Back in the day, it wasn't just a place to go for fun and gambling. It was, I felt, one of the most glamorous places in the world. Men wore tuxedos in the casino, and women the most lavish cocktail dresses adorned with magnificent jewels. I didn't own lavish cocktail dresses or magnificent jewels, and I certainly didn't have a guy with me who would wear a tuxedo to the casino, but I had a good body that men noticed, and I noticed myself starting to look back at them. I wasn't yet ready to act on my impulses, but I was on the launching pad. Vegas was a loose place.

It was also the site of one of Judy's most terrible disasters— followed by a complete meltdown. What made it so awful? In my view it was unintended. Some might even call it an accident, but then maybe it was no accident, given the cause. As I counted out the days of what was to be a virtual imprisonment for me in this utopia, I wondered how many of these incidents there could be before she died? How many of these could Judy's body, already weakened by drugs and liquor, withstand? Would the next one kill her?

It happened as we were approaching the end of the second week of Judy's monthlong engagement, sandwiched into her schedule in between the films she was starring in. We'd been together a couple of years now, and she was back in the big time after a successful concert tour, happy to be appearing at the Sahara, one of the grandest places on the strip. The four-week engagement (which could be extended by another two) was worth hundreds of thousands, and it took more than a few concerts for Judy to earn that much. After an exciting first week, we settled into a routine. The contract was for one sixty-five-minute show a night, which, with any good fortune, got under way at 10:00 p.m. She, however, would usually come off the stage closer to midnight, and then one of two scenarios would be set in motion.

Scenario one: in which she showered and changed into nightclubbing mufti in preparation for the two of us going out on the town. I dreaded this one. Would that I could have gotten into it more, but I was always so exhausted. It wasn't just a matter of physical exhaustion. I was strong like a bull. It was mental exhaustion—the exhaustion of having to be on your toes all the time, never being allowed to relax, always on the edge of the ledge, worried about what might fall or fail.

On top of that I was not a party animal. Drinking was never my thing, and by three in the morning, I was usually dragging my ass, which was when we typically found ourselves, yet again, watching Frances Faye do her lounge act at the Thunderbird. Judy, however, was going strong and growing stronger pill by pill. I'm embarrassed to report that our third time there I fell asleep at the little cocktail table directly in front of the tiny stage where Miss Faye performed. Judy attempted to prod me awake; that is to say she gave me a well-deserved shove and in so doing pushed me onto the dance floor. I lay there, spread eagle in my customary fashion, apparently looking like I needed help from everyone present. And they all jumped in. I was carried into Miss Faye's dressing room, where a group of women with a strong sexual preference for one another started pawing at me—in my interest, of course—which woke me up fast!

Back to scenario one: It usually ended with breakfast at dawn in some diner on the strip, where Judy would chow down, usually on enough steak and eggs to satisfy a healthy truck driver. We were back at the Sahara by eight, and we'd both go to our rooms. Judy didn't have to get up again until eight in the evening. I had to meet the captain in the dining room at 10:00 a.m. to go over the guest list for that night. Then it was time to deal with thank-you notes, wardrobe, send out invitations, make calls to New York, and so on.

Scenario number two—my preferred ordeal—saw us retire immediately after the show to Judy's suite, which in this case (and almost always) was the penthouse. The two-bedroom aerie at the Sahara was furnished in contemporary style; the backdrop a virtual symphony in white that framed the white upholstered pieces, all of which were done in rich-textured fabrics and nestled into wall-to-wall white carpet. It was movie-star glamorous. Very Hollywood.

After Judy changed into a nightgown, we would sit on the couch in front of the glass coffee table and play gin rummy until she felt tired. Getting tired was a manufactured state brought on by the cocktail of pills she continued to take for about an hour. Reds, greens, yellows, purples, blues, and whites, bicolored capsules too, were all washed down with her wine. During that hour she often took twenty or thirty pills, believing that it would take that many to counteract the many pills she had taken earlier to get her up for the performance. In spite of wanting to sleep, she always seemed to be fighting it, fighting to make the day last longer. Her eyes could be at half-mast, and still she would order me to deal another hand. However, in scenario two, usually by 4:00 a.m., she would bid me goodnight, and I would go to my room a few floors below and collapse, most times fully clothed.

The night of the disaster—a scenario-two night—started off in the usual way with me growing terrified that it would soon be dawn, with Judy fighting sleep but finally laying down her cards just before the light crept in around the edges of the drawn drapes. Her tiresome goodnight was always the same: "I think I can get some sleep now"—my cue to leave. But on this night when she got up and took a step in the direction of her bedroom, one step was all she could manage. She went down like a stone, her face hitting the knife-edge of the rectangular steel-and-glass coffee table, which sliced through her skin so quickly I could do nothing but stare in disbelief. The corner of the table first caught her upper lip dead center, then went slantwise through one nostril, grazed the side of her right eye, finally exiting after making a long gash in her forehead. She fell facedown, and blood immediately started to pool around her head onto the white carpet. I bent over her in panic to see if she was breathing, way too scared to move her or even to touch her. Nevertheless I tried to take her pulse. I was so scared I could feel nothing. I had no idea if she was dead or alive.

Steadying myself, and with a calm voice so as not to stir concern in the hotel operator, I asked to be connected with Stan Irwin, the entertainment director of the Sahara. I followed Judy's instructions never to give out any information on the phone, as she was certain all operators sold dirt on her at a good price. When I had Stan on the line, I told him that Judy wished to see him immediately. A business meeting at that hour might have seemed peculiar anywhere other than Las Vegas, where life proceeds apace at 4:00 a.m. and nothing is strange. Stan, a kind and attentive man, heard the urgency in my voice and was there within minutes, dressed to perfection, because it was he who prowled the casino until the last lounge act wrapped.

I can conjure him up even now, in a wonderful tailored gray silk suit that complemented his head of salt-and-pepper hair with perfectly barbered silver sideburns. During his many years in Las

Vegas he had developed a kid-glove approach to talent, including troubled talent. He was intuitive in a way that gave one confidence that he had more than likely handled some hairy scenes, could be counted on in a clutch, and knew far more than he was telling. But I doubt he'd seen anything like this. When I opened the door to him, he wore a worried look that matched mine. He instinctively knew something was terribly wrong in spite of my feigned calm. I may have gone into some kind of functioning shock, for the hand Stan Irwin took into his in that moment at the door was like an icicle. A look that conveyed the horror of this event passed between us, and when he saw her it became chillingly real.

However, he remained as calm as I was, but less frightened. He found her pulse, and he assured me she was alive. My God, I was relieved! He didn't have to ask how it happened. The pill collection on the coffee table only confirmed what he already knew. He turned the unconscious Judy over, applied some wet towels I supplied as compresses to the wounds, stopped the bleeding, and called a doctor, and together we sat waiting for him to arrive.

We talked about how wonderful the audiences had been, but it was no more than aimless chatter meant to cover what was really on his mind. Who was going to step in for Judy? Who would bring in that kind of business? What about the thousands of reservations, and so on? The doctor was there in twenty minutes, and after treating Judy with whatever magic he had in his little black bag, assured us both that the cuts were superficial and would heal well in time. He suggested that I stay the night because Judy would be uncomfortable when she awoke. "Awoke?" I couldn't believe it. She's not unconscious? "No," he said, "she's sleeping."

The men carried Judy to her bed, and the doctor said he would stop by again next day to check on her. His suggestion that I stay with her was not a suggestion at all. It was an order. When I momentarily balked—and I did, telling both him and Stan that I needed to sleep—the doctor said he could get a nurse the next day to replace me, but he thought she should not be alone, just in case. In case of what? I worried. But I knew he was right and also knew it would be pointless to tell him that I'd been up with her for countless nights on end. He was brusque and wouldn't have cared. He pointed to the second bedroom and told me to lie down there. "She'll sleep for the next five or six hours at least," he assured me. "By the time she wakes up, I'll have a nurse here." Then the doctor and Stan talked privately for a few minutes while my mind ranged over a minefield of feelings—all of them bad.

Generally I didn't engage in a lot of self-pity, but on this night I found a wellspring of it and I jumped right in. I felt sorry for myself because I was so whipped. I had reached the end. I was tired of being constantly tired, of enduring her innumerable nightly overdoses. I had suffered her endless 3:00 a.m. phone calls for almost three years now (as had my husband), and in the process I had become hardened and judgmental. I held Judy responsible for tonight and for what she had done to herself. The well-known, well-publicized turbulent history that had brought her to this most terrible collapse was right on the money. I hated her for it and felt sorry for her at the same time. I worried about what would have happened had I not been there, and fretted that I couldn't stop her from swallowing a drugstore even when I was. I worried that I would be blamed if I allowed something to happen to her.

Judy's prescription-pill intake was terrifying. Somehow it was different than burning herself or cutting herself. How? Well, she only did those things when someone was around. If there is such a thing as a controlled burn, then that was what she did. It may sound stupid, but it's the way I rationalized it then. Of course anything anywhere can go dreadfully wrong. I realized that, but as long as I was there to put out the fire, or stop the bleeding, or call the doctor, it would all be okay. But pills, somehow, were different. She took them when we were together *and* when she was alone. She took so many. How much was too much? I didn't know. Never mind putting drugs together. I didn't think then about whether Ritalin went with Seconal. Who knew? I only worried about the number, and I worried about that a lot. I warned her about the danger of her consumption time after time. How simple-minded of me. How innocent. How naive. How stupid I must have sounded to her. She would tell me to "put it where the sun don't shine"—and she did, more than once. And now this! I didn't know if I was more relieved or angry she hadn't killed herself this time, as I looked at the huge stain left on the carpet.

I glanced at her in the bedroom. It was horrifying. I didn't want to be there. Well, that's not entirely true. Someone had to be there. Better the someone be me. Deep down I was grateful that I was the only someone around. I would not fail. If I couldn't stand on my two legs because of exhaustion, if I had to crawl, then I would do it. I would *not* lose my job. This seed in me called ambition would push through whatever frozen earth it found itself in. So, finally, at four in the morning, I decided I was more worried I would lose my job than I was worried about Judy Garland's welfare. I was frightened for her, she did engage my sympathy, but those feelings lost the battle raging in my head. Worrying about losing my job had won once more. I was not going to let that happen. No matter what went down, I would not be a quitter. I would stay the night. I was out to prove myself invaluable. I intended to succeed. I just needed to sleep.

Without asking anyone's permission—nor did he need any—the doctor swept all the open drug vials from the coffee table into his little black bag and assured Stan and me that everything would be fine. I knew it definitely would not be. I tried telling the good doctor that Judy would be out of her mind when she awoke if the pills weren't where she left them. I was direct, even confrontational. I told him I spoke from hard experience. I told him I was the one who "knew" her. Of course this annoyed him. He refused to take me seriously for even a minute. Who was I, after all? Some young dumb little assistant from New York who thought she knew everything. I saw myself in his eyes: stupid, thoughtless, and arrogant. His scowl conveyed it all. He fastened me with a disapproving look that reminded me of a stern Norman Rockwell country doctor straight out of a *Saturday Evening Post* cover. Someone in the portrait was questioning the doctor's judgment. Who is this young whippersnapper? the picture seemed to ask.

He would not allow an inexperienced nonentity of an assistant talk him out of confiscating the drugs that had caused such an awful accident, an accident that had come within inches of blinding or almost killing the great Judy Garland. But then, he did not seem in the least impressed with the fact that he was treating Judy, and I could see that he was dealing with her as he would any other patient. I reasoned that he must have been Stan's go-to guy for all star problems, and his been-there, done-this manner made me understand that this Judy could have had any other last name and his response would have been exactly the same. He was unlike the doctors, listed alphabetically in major cities, in my little black book whom I could call upon for late dates.

Now what remained was to finish up the business at hand. There was always that. Business. Judy Garland wasn't just a person: She was a franchise, first and foremost! Stan called David Begelman, and they quickly agreed that Stan would indeed have to find some big star to step in for Judy until she could perform again. A proper press release about vocal strain would be prepared. The public would be assured that with a little rest, Judy would be fine. She would then give the Sahara an additional two weeks by doing a 2:30 a.m. show every night. Two thirty in the morning? Omigod! Perfect for Las Vegas, and easy for those who slept all day. I dreaded it, but I said nothing. I sat on the couch, numbed, and waited for Stan to end the call. When the arrangement was completed, Stan was about to go back to work. I could see he felt sorry for me. Still, he found a way to suggest that I do something about the stain on the carpet before he was out the door. "We wouldn't want the maids to see that," he said.

So the main event of the night is now over, and I am once more dealing with Judy's blood, this time trying to disguise the stain, to make it look more like coffee was spilled. That is the best I can hope for; there is no way of getting the complete bloodstain out of the carpet. I am feeling bitterly sorry for myself. I am crying and asking myself, Why? Why am I doing this? Why do I care what the maids think? Suddenly I am sobbing hysterically, my tears falling on the carpet and mixing with the rest of the bloody mess. 'Is this only about ambition? What is wrong with my life? Who matters to me more? Me? Judy? I am cold and angry and sad.

At sunrise I passed out in the second bedroom and couldn't have been asleep more than an hour when Judy was standing at the foot of my bed pulling on my leg to awaken me. Regardless of the sunshine streaming in, Judy had turned on all the lights lest I miss something. "Look at me!" she screamed. And I had to. Dare I use the cliché "It was worse than your worst nightmare"? She was a ghoul. The Phantom unmasked does not come close. She was the Elephant Man, a total grotesque. Her lips were the most awful part, huge and discolored. One whole side of her swollen face was blue and green. "Let me call for some ice packs," I said. "The doctor said you should use them constantly until he can get back here."

"Fuck the ice packs. Where's my medicine? I need my pills, and I want them right now! Where the fuck did you hide them?"

"Me?! No! Not me. I swear it. The doctor took them. He didn't want you to hurt yourself again."

"Then call the fucking doctor, and get him back here right now. And I want my own doctor flown out here by this afternoon." It wasn't yet 8:00 a.m., and I didn't have a clue about how to reach this doctor at his home. He wasn't listed. I awakened Stan and begged him to make the call, but an hour passed and nothing happened. Judy was going berserk. She demanded I call all the area hospitals. I did so and got nothing. At nine I was able to reach the doctor's office and was told he was on rounds, the receptionist assuring me he would call as soon as he returned. It was a formulaic response, and no call came. Judy made me phone all the hospitals again. She was pacing, she was screaming, she was crying—and none of it was about the way she looked. It was only about her drugs.

By noon I had called the doctor's office at least a half-dozen times, now understanding that I was intentionally being put off by his staff. I was frantic, and the women I spoke with could surely hear the desperation in my voice; they did their best to calm me, but there was no way they could have imagined what I was going through, nor was there a way I could attempt to explain it to them. In their lives they surely had never felt as threatened as I did at that moment.

Finally they got a dose of it. Judy came out of her bedroom and was hovering over me, screaming in my ear, screaming into the phone. At one point she grabbed the phone and yelled out every obscenity she'd ever heard, probably many more than those on the other end had ever heard. In addition to using "fuck" every other word, "cunt" and "cooze" were two of her favorites, and I doubt the doctor's receptionist had ever been called either. Whoever was listening remained calm and acted as if they had heard it all before, for when Judy handed the phone back to me, the woman on the other end didn't seem rattled at all. But then, what could they do? I could only imagine the doctor not responding because he had not yet found a nurse.

By midafternoon Judy convinced herself that I was the one who had hidden her drugs. She went into the kitchen, took a large black-handled knife out of the drawer, and came after me with it. Would she have stabbed me? I don't know. She was a raving lunatic at that point. But I was younger, stronger, and way healthier. I wasn't going to get into a fight or try to take the knife away. I didn't want to risk either of us getting hurt. Terrified, I barricaded myself in the second bedroom. There was no lock on the door and I put my whole weight against it to keep it closed, while she did the same thing on the other side. Where did her strength come from? Was it fueled by some demonic adrenaline? I was managing to prevail, but how long could I keep this up? It was madness. I needed to get out of there. I needed a plan, and I formulated one. I would jump away from the door and let her rush in. I could only hope she wouldn't fall on the knife. I would then rush out the moment the momentum took her. And I did! I got out the door to the hall, ran down the stairs to my room, got the maid to let me in, and collapsed crying on the bed. It was over. Fuck ambition. I was not ever going back. One would have to be crazy even to contemplate it.

Of course I went back. In the late afternoon I was awakened by a call from David Begelman, who spent twenty minutes on the phone telling me how sorry Judy was. He assured me that she was feeling better now. He told me a new doctor had been in to see her and had given her some medication for her pain and some for her nerves. That was shorthand for "She's drugged," ergo everything's okay. David surely knew how to find those kinds of doctors. He said that Judy desperately wanted to call me to apologize. Wouldn't I just speak to her? He was actually begging me. I savored that. Although I had cried myself to sleep, now with seven hours in the tank, I was a new person; that is, the old me was back.

An hour and a two-hundred-dollar raise later, I agreed to have a conversation with her. I thought David's offer was generous, and I decided it was okay if I returned purely for the money. Not for him, not for her. I also thought that if I refused to go, I might be replaced. By late in the afternoon, losing my job again seemed like a bigger threat than losing my life.

Within two hours I had moved my clothes into Judy's suite, adamantly refusing, however, to give up my own room key, and for the next ten days I remained there with her. Of necessity she would not allow anyone else to see her looking the way she did. I was the waitress, the maid, and the doorman, always there to make sure that no one put so much as a toe inside. All management keys were disallowed. The days dragged on. Our boring routine hung on us like a curtain that admitted no light. Nothing went wrong, but then nothing was good either. In spite of my staying up late, my interior clock never changed. I awoke at the same ghastly hour of seven every morning, regardless of having played cards until three. I ordered room service and read. I looked out the window a lot, staring at people enjoying their freedom, wishing I had mine. It was obsessive.

At about noon I would hear her moving around in her room, but she rarely showed herself before three or four. Then she demanded everything at once. Breakfast might be French toast and a hot fudge sundae. Being indisposed was her opportunity for more than a bit of sweet self-indulgence. I encouraged it. Anything to keep her in what I called "a harmless place." I received the linens at the door and made up a fresh bed for her each day by five. I changed all the towels and wiped up the sink and tub. I vacuumed. We played endless card games and listened to her records. She had Frank's and Nat King Cole's sent in, but we mostly listened to her own. She admired her own ability above all. Sometimes she would sing along. Would that there had been TVs in the suite, we might have watched all day, but that amenity didn't yet exist. (It's somewhat hard to believe, but the early sixties were a time when shampoo in hotel rooms was just becoming a must.)

We talked about her affair with David Begelman ad nauseam because he was the common denominator in both our lives: her lover, her manager, and my boss. We talked about what she wanted in the future—how she and David would travel and enjoy life together. This was far better than hearing her talk about the past. For although the past was more interesting, revisiting it could send her into a tail-spin that often led to a plaintive diatribe directed at Louis B. Mayer. Mayer, the man who, as she had admitted on television, had had the greatest influence on her life, but also the monster who was responsible for overworking her, underpaying her, and starting her down the yellow brick road to ruination.

Trust me, I did not feel as though I was in on something divine, listening to the "voice of greatness." I was a prisoner yearning to be free. While David had turned the suite into a drugstore, guaranteeing that Judy had everything she needed, not a single one of my needs was fulfilled. No Vegas sunshine would touch my skin. Instead I learned more about who she was and more about who I was, and I didn't much like either one of us. She was willing to do anything to satisfy her habit, and I was willing to do anything for success.

CHAPTER TWELVE

Back in New York

Surviving a catastrophe has a way of making you realize your own worth. It was the end of 1962 and, after having lived through Judy's Las Vegas disaster and getting more than a few raises, I started to feel I was irreplaceable. Who would put up with the things I had? No one I spoke to. Certainly none of my friends! My mother thought I was crazy. My husband was beginning to believe the same. But it worked for F&D. Not having to be with Judy all the time had allowed them to build a business. I patted myself on the back and was a little cocky. I believed I was worth every penny of the $450 they now paid me every week. I was no longer expected to take dictation or type letters for anyone but myself.

Freddie Fields Associates had grown significantly. Freddie called it "the Tiffany" of management agencies. While talent agents were restricted to commissions of 10 percent, Paul Newman, Joanne Woodward, Henry Fonda, and Lauren Bacall were now clients and willing to pay FFA 15. There were two more agents squeezed into our space. FFA was well on its way. And Judy? She had done her job. The concert tour had been a huge success. *Judy at Carnegie Hall* was heralded as one of the best concerts ever in the entire history of entertainment. Hollywood was back in Judy's corner. Television was calling. The press was clamoring. Everything changed but Judy.

By then Judy and her children had been living for slightly more than a year in a lovely home in Scarsdale that I had found for her in in my role as FFA's real estate agent.

I'd originally put them into an apartment at the Dakota, a dark, dank, dreary eleven-room pad owned by John Frankenheimer, the brilliant and prolific film director best known for *The Manchurian Candidate*. All its apartments surround a quad that was eerie at four in the morning, which is when I usually showed up at least several times a week. "Wuthering Gothic," with a courtyard into which no sunlight ever filters, is the way I still think of the Dakota. The place scared me. I was delighted when Judy wanted to leave it.

She had no desire to replace it with sunny California. She seemed finished with her life there. This was a new chapter. She definitely wanted to stay on the East Coast. Would that she could have chosen a home in New York City! She said, however, that she always felt better in the country, so she had sent me out to find the ideal bucolic retreat for the family, a house large enough so that each of her children could have a room of their own. She needed something furnished because from all her homes over the years, Judy had salvaged nothing. Not a stick of furniture. Not a single memento from her brilliant career. No linen, no dishes, no silver. No precious possessions from all the homes she'd lived in in Los Angeles. She did carry a few pictures in her suitcases—like a homeless person. She came with nothing else. Nothing.

Once I identified a place in Westchester, Judy asked me to make the moving arrangements. She didn't ask to see the place first; I think she couldn't have cared less. But I cared. This was a real family home, like a family home in the movies. It had a staircase and bedrooms upstairs. If this sounds silly, so be it. It fulfilled my idea of the way things were supposed to be. It made me feel as if I'd done something good. After the family moved in, she asked me to buy new furniture for the children's rooms, but she took no interest whatsoever in what I bought. It mystified me. How could one not care, but the Judy I knew seemed not to care about things! Stuff wasn't ever important to her. Once all the arrangements were taken care of, I had to deal with a new realization. Instead of running across town to the Dakota, I now had to travel up to Scarsdale at four in the morning.

One night (meaning between 3:00 and 4:00 a.m.) I thought Judy sounded "different." It made me anxious. I threw on a sweat suit and called David Begelman after assuring Judy I was on the way. I knew I could call a limo and go to Westchester by myself, but I wouldn't do that when I was worried stiff something was wrong. The final Judy responsibility lay with David or Freddie; I was not ever going to be there alone if indeed she was dying.

I didn't ever call either of them carelessly because I knew their wives were not nearly as supportive as my husband. Both women fumed at the late night calls, and both spoke of it with me, more than once. Most of their conversations had an opener like "Just who the fuck does she think she is?" This night, however, I made the call to David. "I think something is really wrong this time," I whispered. Although these were words he'd heard many times before, he knew that if I called, he'd have to go. I was the poison taster, and the poison taster is never wrong. "I'll call a car and pick you up in twenty minutes." Those were the only times I ever saw David in store-bought polyester rather than custom-made worsted.

We got to Judy's house just before four. We found her sprawled on the floor next to the front door. This meant we wouldn't have to go upstairs and disturb the children. It smelled fishy. That she was beautifully dressed in a diaphanous gown with matching peignoir was the giveaway. Indeed, she wore matching satin slippers with a little heel and caribou trim, and her hair was perfectly coiffed. After only two minutes I knew it was a hoax. I told David what I thought. What an actress she was. She had sounded "different" on the phone knowing I would then want to bring D or F along with me. But David looked at her and told me he thought she was turning blue. Had he really swallowed the fish, along with the hook, the line, and the sinker? But then he added, "Her pulse is not strong, and she's very cold. Call an ambulance." I did it immediately, becoming scared that we might be looking at a suicide attempt that had actually worked. David was no drama queen, quite the reverse. He was a cool customer. He never exaggerated except when telling stories in the aftermath. Then he could go way over the top and be highly amusing. As we stood over Judy's comatose body at that moment, he was dour.

Fifteen minutes later, without our once having awakened anyone in the house, our limo was trailing the ambulance as it screamed its way down the Hutchinson River Parkway. Had Judy been dying, the forty-five-minute ride would not have helped, but then we could go only to her personal doctor, Kermit Osserman, who recognized the need to keep everything out of the press, and he could only do that at Mt. Sinai, the hospital he was affiliated with. Osserman was an elderly internist on whom Judy's late-night ravings took a great toll, but he was a trouper, wanted never to disappoint, and whenever called upon, this capable doctor and lovely gentleman was there on his marks.

With the limo on its tail, the ambulance raced up the ramp into the emergency dock, where four white-coated orderlies were waiting to transfer Judy onto a rolling gurney that would carry her inside for an examination and whatever other treatment was called for. At the very least I expected it would be another stomach pumping. Even before the brakes were set, the orderlies had the back door of the ambulance open, and in an organized phalanx quickly pulled the bed, on which Judy lay motionless, out of the truck. They lined it up parallel to the gurney, and then in one brilliant motion all four men grabbed the corners of the sheet on which she lay, yanked it up, and plunked her down on their rolling cot. Where-

upon Madam sat up straight as a ramrod and, in a tone indignant
with rage, spoke these memorable words:

"How dare you fucking morons handle me like a fucking side
of beef? How dare you! Get your fucking meat hooks out of me,
you fucking apes!" No comment from the astonished gallery was
possible. Judy then got up, and with as much dignity as she could
muster—given that one of the satin slippers trimmed in caribou had
gone missing—Madam limped, one-shoe-on, one-shoe-off, over to
the waiting limousine, got in the backseat, and ordered the driver
to take her home.

Poor Kermit! He didn't deserve to be awakened at four in the
morning. Judy was turning his practice into a water-cooler joke. He
was a man of great integrity, totally unlike the many Dr. Feelgoods
in my little black book who would prescribe unlimited amounts of
any drugs Judy wanted, for a fee. At one point I became so concerned about the handfuls of Ritalin Judy was swallowing that,
without a word to anyone, I decided I had to do something about
it. Looking through the Yellow Pages, I found a small pharmaceutical house in southern New Jersey and made an arrangement with
them to mill an identical sugar-water version. I imagined I would
be helping her, but I had no idea what I was doing. I replaced all
the real Ritalin in her vials with the placebo, which I purchased in
big canning jars, ten thousand at a time. Although after that I never
saw one iota of difference in her behavior, just doing it made a big
difference to me. At least I knew that she was putting less chemical
shit into her body, and that gave me a little peace of mind.

It seemed that most of the drugs were for insomnia. Her inability
to sleep was a nasty monster that stalked her. It lived in a black hole.
She teetered on the edge of that hole all the time. I imagined she
knew that if she fell into it she would go mad. Drugs kept the monster at bay. They helped her to quiet a mind that wouldn't be still, a

mind that made sleeping impossible. Judy cried about it. Sometimes she put her head in my lap and just wept. How sad is that? It made me wonder from time to time whether or not leaving her in peace, as she was before Freddie sought her out in London, would have saved her. If she had been allowed to veg out, eat, and do nothing, might she have survived? Finally I think not. I don't think vegging out was at all what she wanted. She knew she had options, and she chose what she wanted. She wanted the fame, the power, least of all the money—these things went into a cocktail she wanted to drink. She was as addicted to all those as she was to the prescription drugs. And once she came back, she needed as many drugs to get her up as she needed to go to sleep.

I knew nothing about drug addiction until I started working with her. Oh, I knew about alcoholism, about the falling-down drunks who populated my aunt's place on the Bowery, but I hadn't the slightest notion that anyone got addicted to prescription drugs. Bayer Aspirin is all that was found in the medicine cabinets in my home. Thrust into Judy's world, I was getting a fast education about a dozen different kinds of pills. I needed to know more, so I scoured the news for stories and devoured what I read about heroin, the drug that in the early sixties got the most lurid coverage. I could see that what I read exactly matched what I knew to be true about Judy and my experience with her—that addiction was a progressive disease that keeps increasing, as does the amount and the strength of the drugs needed to satisfy the craving.

Finally there are never enough pills. And so it was with Judy. As it was with Michael Jackson and other famous people. The more I understood her addiction, the sorrier I began to feel for her. It was tragic, and no one understood it better than David, who for his own pecuniary reasons had to keep her working. I will get back to that. David also understood she desperately needed a break, and he planted one into her schedule. And thereby hangs a tale.

CHAPTER THIRTEEN

A Vacation

Apropos of nothing, David invited me into his office one afternoon and asked, "How would you like to go on vacation?" I had now been working two and a half years with nothing more than the occasional Sunday off. I preferred to think of what I was doing as building my career, but what I was really doing was acting as an enabler and general handmaiden to a demented, demanding, supremely talented drug addict, while also being a doormat for one brilliant male narcissistic egomaniac. And I was totally whipped. I got all excited at the prospect of a vacation, forgetting for a moment that when a snake is in the grass, you can't always see it. I jumped at the opportunity. Then David added, "Judy is going yachting in the Caribbean, and she would like you to go with her." Can anyone make "yachting in the Caribbean" sound bad? David just did that, I said to myself. David offered me a thousand dollars extra to go, and I said I would. I didn't do it for the money—not that I disliked having it—I did it because I hadn't arrived at a point where I felt comfortable saying no. I wasn't yet sure what letting Begelman down would cost me. I hadn't developed enough confidence to take the risk professionally. However, that, too, was about to change.

I went home and told my sweet husband I was leaving for two weeks. As usual he was just fine about it, actually excited for me. I was always a tad less guilty when I wasn't home cooking dinner, which was not anything I did well, often, or had any appetite for.

So how does a non-yachting person get a yacht without having to rent it? One borrows it from a rich friend, of course, and Judy had a fine collection of those. Newport wasn't the only place where she knew wealthy people she could call upon. Charles Wacker was rich enough to have a whole avenue named after his family—as in Wacker Drive in Chicago. I assumed that Charlie—as Judy liked to call him—owned a lot of shares in the family's holdings on the street that bears his name. I've never been on Wacker Drive in Chicago, and I've never met the man, and I often wish I'd never met the boat.

The plan for the vacation with Judy was to cruise on Charlie's yacht from Miami to Nassau. When I heard that, things began to sound a little better. There might be at least some upside to go with what most likely would be a downer.

In my mind's eye I saw a big beautiful boat, something gleaming white with polished teak accents and oversize staterooms, a fantasy yacht made by Chris-Craft. Putting my marriage aside momentarily—which was getting easier for me to do all the time—I imagined stopping at glamorous yacht clubs and meeting handsome, debonair men, spending days with charming company as we glided over a silken sea. The fact that Judy was taking along a hairdresser seemed to confirm that possibility. Our crew would be uniformed, the cook world class; maybe we would have a madcap, wild, and wonderful time. I prepared myself for that, mostly at Saks Fifth Avenue. It was the season for cruise wear, and I treated myself well. I think I was ready for a little romance, but even if I couldn't find it on this trip, the consolation prize would be my new wardrobe.

Judy and I, along with a hairdresser named Orval Paine, who I believe hailed from somewhere in the Midwest, went directly from the airport in Miami to the docks at four in the afternoon. All the gleaming yachts were there just as I had imagined, each one tied up to its own slip. None of them was ours. Moored out in the distance was a very large trimasted, square-rigged sailing vessel that looked like a pirate ship. It had to have been salvaged from an old Errol Flynn movie, or maybe had once been a floating junk on the China Sea. It had on its prow a carved wooden bare-breasted mermaid with flowing golden locks.

Not that, I said to myself as I looked at the oddity, already knowing, without anyone having to tell me, that "that" was it. Gratefully I noted that there were no portholes with cannons peeking out. Somehow strappy sandals didn't go with this awful spectacle. Backless chiffon didn't. Gleaming white ducks didn't either. The beautiful luggage we had brought filled with lovely things didn't go with. A corncob pipe and a parrot went with.

I don't think Judy expected to see this huge hunk of floating junk either, for while she hadn't discussed her wardrobe with me, it was clear from her abundant luggage that she, too, expected something different. The four and a half inch stiletto-heeled Fiorentinas she was wearing were more than a bit inappropriate. However, she never once flinched, and after she set eyes on the captain for the first time, the boat could have been an old claw-foot bathtub and it wouldn't have mattered.

It was clear she liked the eye candy she was looking at. There was nothing not to like. Our captain was young, tall, slim, blond, blue-eyed, and attractive. Judy eyed him lasciviously and said, "Well, what are we waiting for? Let's get the hell out of here." She instructed me to count the pieces of luggage to make sure nothing was lost, which was only a reflection of her nervousness about the little white carry-on with the prescription drugs. Rest assured it had become an extension of my arm. Then she told the sexy sailor we were ready to come aboard.

The captain, however, had other ideas. He thought we had come down to the dock to look at the boat, and that's all he was prepared for. He hadn't even shopped for food yet. He saw that we would need a barge just to get our luggage out to the mooring, and he didn't happen to have one of those either. He would need the balance of the evening and part of the next day to organize.

"I'm sorry, Miss Garland," was what the captain opened with. "It's a really bad idea to get under way at night. I think you would enjoy yourself more if you rest tonight, especially after your trip. It will give us some time to load your bags," he said, looking at enough suitcases to fill his entire hold. "Treat yourself to a great meal in a good restaurant tonight, because it may be the last great meal for a few days." He chuckled at his own humor. I did not. "We'll leave by noon tomorrow." Uh-oh, I thought. No world-class cook? Uh-oh, issuing instructions to Judy? Uh-oh.

Judy, who knew better than the rest of us the difference between elegance and crap, was now going to spend two weeks on this hunk-ajunk so she could fuck the captain. For goodness sake! Sexual politics had not yet granted women permission to be avaricious takers. Judy was way ahead of the curve. She was the most promiscuous woman I'd met up to that point.

"We'll have dinner on the boat and leave tonight." Judy's response was definite, and slightly tinged with anger. She had already picked out her course.

At her command I waded into the wet and nasty dinghy that had brought the captain to shore. Judy waited until he carried her into the dinghy. Was this going to be the transportation for the bags too? It would take most of the night just to load them. My mood was sinking faster than the sun, and it didn't improve once on board.

The boat was ugly, all of it. My "stateroom" was an eight-by-ten dark, windowless closet with a double-decker bunk nailed to the wall. A dresser was its only other piece of furniture, and the unfortunate smell inside the drawers was reminiscent of what I thought Smee the pirate might smell like. I knew I would put no new clothes away there. The carpet in the living room looked as if it had been on a sinking ship, and the furnishings, such as they were, could generally be found on a curb awaiting the garbage truck. Where did I go wrong? I asked myself. The most obvious answer was: in Saks Fifth Avenue!

Orval—such a decent, kind, concerned, and likable man—and I had absolutely nothing in common except, of course, Judy. Conversation about her was off-limits. So there we were, chugging off into the dark, watery unknown with little or nothing to say to each other: one Midwestern hairdresser and one New York wannabe-sophisticate. He wondered if he had brought along enough hairspray, given the humidity, and I wondered if I would eat or starve. The best we'd been able to pull together in that department was cheese-and-mystery-meat sandwiches moldering in the ship's tiny fridge. Our first-and-only mate was busy with the equipment. Omigod! Where was the crew?

The handsome captain had disappeared into Judy's living quarters and was not to be seen again that evening. First-and-only mate was all by himself. I didn't know squat about sailboats, save for what I had seen in the movies, and what I had seen in the movies convinced a sailing moron like me that a staff of two on an eighty-foot boat was woefully insufficient. And now we were down to one. Didn't Errol Flynn have at least forty pirates with him? I started recounting the faces of the character actors I remembered in pirate movies—kind of like counting sheep—to occupy myself with something silly enough to keep me from being depressed.

Handsome C (which is what I will call our captain because I no longer remember his name—and he was not memorable, except maybe to Judy) wasn't anywhere in evidence the next morning either. At some point that night we'd put into port in a small marina at Bimini. Everyone was asleep, ostensibly, and since it didn't look like we were soon going anywhere, I got off the ship. I thought that if it suddenly left without me, that would not be the worst thing. It was now more important to try to find a muffin or a bagel. There were bikes to rent right across the road from the dock; I got one and ped-aled all three miles of the island from one end to the other with-out, alas, finding a town, a scone, or even a bread crumb. So far nothing on this trip was decent except the weather.

Judy called for Orval at three that afternoon. It had been smooth sailing, not that I had as yet seen one sail hoisted. Apparently it took two to do that, and our captain was still belowdecks. So we simply chugged along, using up our supplementary fuel, and I suppose Handsome C belowdecks was still doing the same thing. At four we pulled into a gorgeous marina with a yacht club, at the tip of an island called North Cat Cay. Finally a place that held some promise!

Hungry for more than just bread alone, I ran around the smallish island to see what it was about. Money! That's what. A haven for wealthy fisherfolk, but hardly what one thinks of as your little fish-ing village. I saw nothing but large estates scattered about, and the kind of gleaming boats I had dreamed of not long ago in Saks.

Returning to the yacht club, I was able to con a piece of pie out of a server cleaning up after the lunch crowd, hoping that it wouldn't be long before I would be sampling something more nutritious. Every step along this merry vacation seemed to be a problem. Not yet having had breakfast (or dinner the night before), I felt ready to do an unnatural act for the kitchen staff to get us something to eat. The name Judy Garland opened their refrigerator if not their warm ovens and hearts, and soon the five of us were gobbling up all the leftovers, the only patrons in the empty dining room. Oh, for some glamour too!

Handsome C's head was falling into the gazpacho. First-and-only mate was dazed as well. Orval was praising the hairspray he'd chosen, and Judy's coif bore the motionless proof. But she was smiling. I was too busy eating to care about any of them. Who could possibly know when, or even if, the next meal would appear?

At Cartier, one of a few elegant shops close to the yacht club, Judy bought the captain a watch. The thought crossed my mind that such a gift is generally awarded to a faithful employee after twenty-five years of service. I wondered if something even more substantial should have been given to our beleaguered Handsome C, who had likely done twenty-five years' hard labor overnight. He forced a smile in gratitude and made a shy thank-you in front of Orval and me, while leaning against the exterior wall of Cartier helped keep him upright.

I inquired if we could stay overnight at the yacht club, thinking there would be a swell dinner crowd and the strappy sandals would get their first outing. I saw the captain's face brighten a little. I'm sure he was grateful to be topside. Judy, however, wasn't interested. She was anxious to get going again. The break was over. Handsome C had to go back to work belowdecks.

Then we were again powering off into another sunset, now aware that it was the wrong time of day to get under way. Judy and Handsome C again vanished. Not able to endure another night talking about either hairspray or sea spray, I went below to spend time in the library, such as it was. The books were yellow with age, their bindings cracked and dried. I was in despair. I turned in by nine, knowing I would want to get an early start in Nassau the next day. Civilization! Sophistication! Food awaited me!

Sometime in the wee hours, maybe around two, I was thrown out of my bunk. Wacker's wonder was pitching and rolling, each roll sending me across the small room to collide with the nearest wall. It was almost impossible to stand, harder still to walk, but I had to get out of my tiny cabin before sustaining serious bruises and up-chucking the only meal I'd eaten in two days. I made my way into the living room, where I saw a yellow oilskin outfit lying on the sofa. No one had to tell me it was for me. I had a terrible time getting the pants on; I felt like I was inside a bottle being violently shaken. I had a death grip on the dining table with one hand, simply trying to steady myself so I could dress with the other. After I'd somehow managed to tie the hood tight under my chin, I climbed up to the deck to see where the merry vacationers were. The massive waves I saw overwhelmed me, but I had no time to think about being scared. I had to tie on to the lifelines first. That or go overboard.

Here comes the tall-sea-tale part. Even as I think about it today, I fear no one will believe it. But I do know what happened that night, and I'm grateful to be alive to tell the story.

Everyone was up on deck clinging to the lifelines while waves washed over our heads, leaving each of us gasping like so many asthmatics. It's over, I said to myself. This ship is going down, and we're all going to die right here, right now, tonight.

Suddenly the most insane thought washed over me along with the very next wave: the black humor of the dying. No one will ever know I was here. Headlines will scream: "Judy Garland lost at sea!" I hate my billing. I have no billing. There won't even be a single mention of my name. It will all be Judy. I looked over at her. She was shrieking nonstop. This time she finally had good reason to. My next thought: Judy, it doesn't matter if you strain your voice anymore. Nothing can save you. I remained calm and stupid. "Are we in the Bermuda triangle?" I screamed, aware of all the vessels that were lost out here and never found again. No one could hear me. Would they send out people to find us? Would the loss at sea of the great Judy Garland be made into a film? My mind danced around these stupid questions as I struggled to stay on my feet.

We finally managed to use up our fuel. No-longer-Handsome C and his first-and-only mate somehow got to the mainsail, and in trying to hoist it, bent the winch. No gas, no sail. We would toss like a little microbe in this maelstrom until either the storm was over or we were finished, and I thought the latter the more likely of the two.

But no—not what happened. The storm stopped—just stopped dead. It disappeared as quickly as it had arrived—from out of nowhere, back to nowhere. No-longer-Handsome C told us squalls like this suddenly popped up and then, just as suddenly, vanished. Nowhere on the horizon was there even a vestige of the storm left to be seen. The sky was cloudless, and our captain went about his business as if nothing had happened. Instead of being grateful to be alive I was angry that he was living. Why didn't you warn us earlier, you moron? It was a silent scream. There had been enough screaming going on without mine to add to the confusion.

The sea was now as flat as a tabletop, and we were resting on its smooth surface, motionless in a gently falling rain with one single cloud in sight. Right above us, of course. Looking east on the horizon we could see the glow from a sun that would soon show itself on what promised to be another perfect day in paradise. It was the most beautiful dawn I'd ever seen. There's nothing prettier, I thought, than watching the start of a sunrise through the rain. It was a spiritual moment deserving of an inspiring movie score by the likes of Dimitri Tiomkin or Vangelis. Judy might have appreciated that, but at the moment she could appreciate nothing. She was still shrieking.

Our hapless captain was finally able to get through on the radio to the shore patrol on the Nassau coast. Their coast guard arrived a few hours later with fuel and provided us with an escort into the harbor. We had drifted fifteen miles in the storm during the night, but we had survived. This part of our luxury vacation cruise was now over, thank God.

The beautiful Nassau I'd imagined, however, was not where our nautical escort brought us. The large cruise ships, gleaming yachts, and sailboats were all missing. We were in an ugly, heavy-duty commercial port where the freighters that normally supply Nassau were being unloaded. Big old rusted container ships were tied up to the large cement docks that jutted out into the harbor. As usual, our galleon looked ridiculous, and our silly appearance attracted unwanted attention. The longshoremen just beginning their day's work stopped what they were doing to stare at us as we tied up. We were an oddity in any port; I'd gotten used to that, but Judy's howling turned us into a freak show. I decided immediately that we had to get Judy off the boat and away from this island ASAP. Personally, I couldn't wait to get away from the boat. If I never had to look at it again, that would be just fine with me.

No-longer-Handsome C wanted to know the plan. His look was grim. I assume he was worried that we would want to stay here a little longer, or, worse, go somewhere else. "Get out of here as fast as we can," I assured him. It came out sounding as angry as I really was. I noticed that he did not offer to help; he just stood there waiting for instructions. I spied a dismal little hotel across the street and told Orval I was going to check it out. He said, "We can't take Judy to a place like that!" I could see that no-longer-Handsome C, too, was worrying that I would change my mind about the dump and decide not to leave his ship. Trust me, when I took a second look, I almost did.

The lobby of this dreary hotel was a haven being used by some nonthreatening derelicts to sleep off their drunk from the night before. I had a feeling that they'd been in the same chairs, rent-free, for the last twenty years. The desk clerk gave me the key to a suite on the second floor that was not only available but for which I doubted there had ever been any demand. I ran back to the boat, where Orval had brilliantly managed to calm Judy (with promises that he could save her hair? Mine was completely finished) to the extent that she was now merely crying—a notch down on the disaster scale from shrieking. Crying was manageable. However, Judy could not manage to walk. I grabbed her purse and the little white carry-on, left my beautiful Saks wardrobe behind (it didn't seem I would have any immediate use for it), and Orval and I, each holding Judy under an arm, literally dragged her across the street. Our great crew had disappeared below. I intended to come back to tie up the loose ends once we got Madam sedated and put down.

We dragged Judy into the lobby, and the desk clerk (and everyone else who came suddenly awake) looked at us with something between disbelief and disgust. After explaining to him that our "friend" was seriously seasick, we were able to schlep Judy up the flight of stairs to the second floor, and into the shabby apartment, where she swallowed the offered sleeping pills and fell on the bed.

Orval followed me into the ugly hospital-green living room so that I could tell him the plan. "We're not going to stay in Nassau," I said. "We'll let her sleep for a few hours so I have time to get on the phone and make some arrangements to immediately go back to Miami, where we can get some control over this mess." Orval quickly agreed because in his view I had debased Judy by putting her in this fleabag. Although he meant well, he had little else to offer besides extra very-much-needed male muscle. And one other thing: He was good company in this awful moment. He was unflappable and of sound mind, which I so appreciated. I asked him to return to the boat to start getting our luggage off while I made plane reservations and tried to find a car to take us to the airport. Off he went only to come back a few minutes later: "They're gone," he told me.

"What do you mean, 'gone'?"

"I mean the boat is so far out of the port they couldn't hear me yelling to come back." Our crew now had plenty of gas, and it was unlikely they were going on a lunch break. Most likely they wanted to see the last of us more than I wanted that very same thing.

I was nonplussed, perplexed, and paralyzed, but I didn't have the luxury of basking in those feelings because moments later there was a loud, aggressive knocking on the door. The desk clerk was standing there sputtering something in anger, all red faced and furious.

He pushed his way past us into the bedroom, where Madam was holding court in her underwear on the little balcony that looked down over Bay Street. This was no awful nightmare, it was really happening, not to her, but to me. Judy was crying and, at the same time, singing "Over the Rainbow" to a large group of big, beautiful, black, seminaked longshoremen below. Their number was growing, and they were hooting, hollering, and generally getting crazy. I doubt even one of them had any idea who she was—just some drunken woman who liked taking off her clothes and singing. They were going to enjoy it while it lasted, and it lasted a little longer than the desk clerk liked. Judy had a death grip on the wrought-iron balustrade that framed the little balcony. It took all the strength Orval and I had left to pry her fingers loose. We dragged her back into the room kicking and screaming, while the desk clerk told me in emphatic terms to get her out of the hotel inside of ten minutes. "Orval," I said, "sit on her if you have to!"

I couldn't take a chance on driving in this unfamiliar place with a crazy lady in the car. I needed a driver. The only vehicle I could find on short notice that came with a driver was a hearse. Seemed appropriate to me! Although we were not yet dead, we were still wrestling with a near-death experience. Orval and I managed to get Judy back into the aqua muumuu she had stripped off and, using a hold just shy of a hammerlock, got her downstairs again. Wacker's wonder was nowhere on the horizon.

In moments of extreme duress I react with efficiency while contemplating nonsense. Would I ever again see the strappy sandals, which I had had on my feet only once eons ago (three whole days) in Saks Fifth Avenue? Good-bye, floating chiffon! The once-gleaming white ducks, now stained and filthy past recognition, were all that remained of my purchases, and only because they were on me and had been from the get-go. They were now ready to be trashed. My clothes were sticking to me, and they smelled. *I* smelled. It's okay, I reasoned, still somehow capable of being momentarily rational.

Judy had admirers in the hotels where she had performed. Someone would surely save us. On the way to the airport, Judy's demeanor ratcheted down yet again to mewling and whiny, and although she was operating on shaky legs, they were her own. Things got even better once in transit. We were seated against the bulkhead of the all-one-class plane; Judy at the window, I sat on the aisle next to her and Orval across from us in the same row. Only a sprinkling of passengers behind us, and given that Judy was still whimpering, we were fortunate not to have autograph seekers streaming down the aisle. Maybe we could even get away without her being recognized.

When she asked me for her makeup, I rejoiced. The ugly episode seemed to be over. It appeared as though she wanted to look respectable when she got off the plane in Miami. She took her compact out of the travel pouch, looked out the window on her right, and then started to powder her nose. When she turned back to me, it looked as if blood was coming out of every pore in her face. She was cut and bleeding all over her cheeks, her forehead, and her chin. Blood stained the entire front of the aqua muumuu.

She had apparently taken the mirror out of the compact, cracked it against the window, and powdered her face with the shards of broken glass. She looked at me exactly as she had in the past when she cut herself; that is, with a sort of quizzical smile—I call it her Mona Lisa look—it says, Okay, feast your eyes on what I've done. Now what the fuck are you going to do? Will you abandon me? It was the acid test. The episode is made even more ghoulish when she grabs me and hugs me, so that blood is all over me too. I am talking to her, trying to reach her, but she does not hear me because she is once more in that dark tunnel beyond the sound of anyone's voice. And, frankly, what is there to say? I'm not sure what keeps me from screaming.

Judy and I had been through many bad scenes together, but never one like this. Little by little she was teaching me about self-mutilation. The stories about Judy in the press and on the tongues of the gossips were all about drugs and liquor. I had never read a word about cutting and burning. It was news even to David and Freddie. Did others know? I don't know. I only know what I saw, and what I saw convinced me that Judy cut herself when I was there because I could save her. Here again I found myself thinking, She will overdose on pills when she is alone, but never cut or burn herself in private. She needs both a witness and a savior, and sadly, it is me. And so it was during all the time we were together.

This episode went way beyond pills (not that they couldn't kill her; in fact, they did) and beyond slitting her wrists because it was so ghastly, grisly, so unexpected, and so bizarre. It shocks me when I hear about someone cutting themself. But Judy Garland?! That face! That fabulous face! Perhaps not one of the most beautiful faces, but certainly one of the most endearing. Dorothy's face. The face of our childhood. It didn't belong solely to her, it belonged to us all.

It was the most horrific thing I'd ever witnessed. I think, many more times than I would like to, about being twenty-six and sitting there while one of the world's greatest entertainers is slashing her face to ribbons right next to me. The plane was flying over the Caribbean, but Judy was a million miles from Oz, and my feet were planted in hell.

I sent Orval running to the stews for towels, water, ice, and first-aid—whatever they had. They knew Judy was on board, and they were excited. They all came running, empty handed, to see what was wrong. Wasted seconds—nothing to stanch the blood! I was frightened. Blood everywhere. All over her, all over her seat, covering her muumuu down the entire front to the hem, on her legs, all over my filthy white pants, my shirt, and my face. I can only imagine what a horrible sight it was for them. One quick glance, however, and they sprang into action, and, God bless them, they didn't ask any questions. They took care of her as well as they could, given the limitations. I promised them all autographed pictures. How lame is that? They would have terrible stories to tell. Would anyone believe them? My mind went there for a moment. It didn't matter anymore. Just get on with it. I was exhausted, and I'd stopped caring about Judy, about what anyone would think, about anything or anyone including myself.

We were able to get off the plane. The stews had packed her face in towels loaded with ice. One of them had a so-called coolie hat, and with its sash we tied everything into place. We tried getting some stains off her clothing and mine, but it was hopeless. We were both a mess. One of the stews spoke to the pilot on my behalf, and, following my instructions, he radioed ahead to Ben Novack, owner of the exquisite Fontainebleau, where Judy had performed.

I knew something about the dealings that Freddie Fields had had with Novack. Back in another lifetime, Novack had advanced Sid Luft, then Judy's husband, twenty-five thousand dollars for an engagement that Judy never played. Luft stole the money. Freddie settled the problem by having Judy do two successful performances at the Fontainebleau. Novack became a friend again—and Judy was a friend in need. Indeed!

Fortunately he responded to the call and, best of all, was able to arrange a limousine waiting on the tarmac when we arrived in Miami. With the cockpit crew, we carried her into the car, and it sped to the hotel. Novack was waiting for us at the back entrance by the kitchen, where Judy was quickly whisked up the service elevator to the presidential suite in the penthouse. Novack rode with us. It was a kind of insurance that none of the hired help would ever say a word to the press if they wanted to keep their jobs.

Like so many others who had done favors for Judy, Novack was extending himself to protect his franchise. Now he would always be able to book Judy and fill his nightclub. And what was I getting out of it? My salary was hardly enough. There wasn't a moment of Oh, poor Judy! left in me. I was fed up. I was finished. I had reached my saturation point. This last ugliness went further than I was willing to go. I started questioning everything. Did Judy's personal unhappiness entitle her to create so many problems for so many people? Was she worth all the trouble and unhappiness she caused? Maybe she was to the people she made a lot of money for, but I wasn't one of them. I was a salaried employee. I hated how my bosses were exploiting a sick woman, and I was helping them. And the longer I hung in, the unhappier I got. This didn't mean I was any less ambitious than before, but I started to feel that maybe I could serve that ambition without serving her. I would see this chapter through to the end, but, for my own survival, I felt I had to close the book on her.

The presidential suite that Ben Novack put us in was an expansive blue, white, and gold monument to luxury with many spaces: a huge living room, a dining room with a table meant to seat at least twelve, four bedrooms, and multiple baths. It was designed for entertaining on a large scale. It was decorated with expensive furniture upholstered in the finest fabrics, and offered incredible ocean views from almost every room. I didn't know such places existed.

There would be time to look, touch, and admire later. Now was the time, finally, to get a doctor who could take care of Judy, do whatever he could for her cuts, and put her to sleep for at least twelve hours. (I hated thinking of myself wanting always to put her to sleep.) Men like Ben Novack were able to accomplish virtually anything quickly. A doctor appeared and took care of business. First he pumped a horse-size syringe of Demerol into her butt, and she went out; then he went to work on her cuts. Orval and I chose our own bedrooms and said goodnight to each other knowing that, without our having much in common, we now shared a bond that could never be broken. I was so tired I was ready to go to bed dirty, but then I would have soiled the beautiful sheets.

A hot bath with fragrant bath oil, a shampoo, rich body lotion, a valet who took away all my clothes (including the filthy sneakers), a brand-new terrycloth robe that felt like cashmere to me, a king-size bed with exquisite linen—all mine! It was hard realizing it had only been three days since I'd left New York: three days that felt like a year, three days in which I felt I'd aged ten years. I lay back in the bathtub and thought about my next move while luxuriating in the glorious hot water. I would call David Begelman first thing in the morning and quit. I was ready to move on, and not a minute too soon. Let someone else carry the drug case all over Christendom; let someone else watch Judy pour a fruit cocktail of pills from myriad vials into her hand each night, washing them down with the awful swill she drank. I was sick of the pills, and especially sick of the goddamn wine, of needing a standing order for a dozen cases at a time. She left half used bottles everywhere she went. Let someone else buy her handbags large enough to carry two bottles of liebfraumilch—the 9 percent solution that she said was saving her life—on all the planes, trains, cars, and boats. The booze that was saving her life was ruining mine, and I was horrified by the self-mutilation.

I never slept soundly with Judy in the house. It was 11:00 p.m. when I finally turned in, and 4:00 a.m. when I awoke. I got up and slipped quietly down the hall just to make sure Madam was okay. I may have hated her after these last three days, and I definitely knew I was going on without her to wherever my future might take me, but at that moment she was still my responsibility. I wasn't sent to Miami with her for a yachting vacation, but to take care of her, and until I turned her over to someone else, I would fulfill that task. We had been through something terrible together. She had fallen apart. I was still standing. I knew I was by far the stronger of the two of us, and it was my job to help her survive.

The suite was dark and quiet; it felt normal for four in the morning. I turned on a light in the corridor and tiptoed to her door, opening it ever so slowly so that it wouldn't make any noise. She wasn't in bed. I could see from the illumination in the hall that her room was empty. I immediately looked at the bathroom door, which was wide open, the bathroom dark. I turned on the lights and went in. She wasn't there. I ran through all the open rooms in the suite. She wasn't in any of them. Finally I went to Orval's room and woke him up. "Judy's gone," I said. In his stupor it didn't register.

"Who's gone?" he asked me.

"Judy's vanished into thin air. She's not here! Orval, get up." He was now fully awake.

"She must be here," he said.

"Come look." He went with me to her room, and we started to do what I now think of as being one of the silliest things I ever did. We looked behind the drapes and under the beds in all the rooms. We checked out the closets and looked in the bathtubs. We got busy agreeing with each other that with the amount of Demerol that had been pumped into her butt, even standing up would be hard for her to do. Leaving, impossible! And yet she was gone. Finally I called the switchboard, asked for the desk, and inquired whether anyone had seen Ms. Garland go out. They gave me the answer they were instructed to give.

"I'm sorry, we don't presently show her registered in the hotel."

"C'mon, you and I both know she's here, except she's not—at least not at the moment, and I'm in the presidential suite with her, except she's not with me. Now you can see that I'm where I'm supposed to be. I have to find out where she is." The person at the desk steadfastly maintained that she was not registered, and the assistant manager on duty did the same. So much for that! I had no clue about where to look, but I did know what to do next: I called Begelman, filled him in, suggested he get his ass on the next plane to Miami and said: "By the way, I quit. If you're not here, I'm leaving anyway. This is your vacation now." I couldn't believe those words had come out of my mouth—including "ass."

I meant to make good my threat. I planned to be gone the minute I was dressed. Unfortunately I had to wait for the valet to deliver my clothes, and they didn't show up until 11:00 a.m.—at about the same time as Begelman. By the time he got to Miami, he knew exactly where Judy was: at some fleabag hotel on lower Collins Avenue (the part of town that's been gentrified and is now trendy South Beach). Clearly she had called him sometime during the night. It was impossible for me to imagine her moving herself around Miami Beach with dressings all over her face. And bloodstained clothes. What kind of place had she gone to? David told me she had registered as Mrs. David Begelman. She was delusional.

This "thing" with David (I could no longer dignify it by calling it an affair) was like some ghastly pas de deux, in which she depended on the sick dynamic between her and her controlling lover. David depended on it also. The moment one of them stopped dancing, the dance would be over. Neither one could leave the dance floor. They were equally addicted, and equally dependent.

I've concluded, at least for myself, that "dependency" is the operative word, as I was learning it is with addicts, and they were both addicts. He—an addicted gambler—depended on creating chaos. She—addicted to prescription drugs and liquor—depended on pain. They fed each other's illness. And I had seen more than enough of this bedlam to know that I now wanted no place in this picture. I was willing to tar myself with several brushes: ambition, dysfunction, neediness, but I was not an addict living with all the sturm and drang that comes with that, and I wanted no part of it in my future. Of course it doesn't always work out that way. But for the moment I believed I was growing up past the need to participate in what I thought was sick. Yes, I could become successful without living with sick people all around me.

So she had managed to stage another hideous drama to get David's attention. Although he was not fucking her at this particular time, it would come again. Meantime he was still manipulating her. He was the Svengali who hypnotized her, had her totally within his control—and he seemed to exercise this control easily as making mayhem was part of his nature. Maybe she was still in love with David. I wouldn't hazard a guess. It seemed to me, however, that with Judy, being in love meant being dominated and controlled. Since David was out at this time, there had to be someone who was in. There always had to be someone. It was Sid Luft. And there was no one more dominating than Sid. All I knew about him were the things Judy told me. I did not know him, or mix it up with him, until later. I'll get around to him. The brute deserves his own chapter.

By the time David arrived at the Fontainebleau, he had already seen her. He told me he put her in a hospital, and that I needn't be concerned about her anymore. I wasn't, and I thought he understood that I really was leaving. I felt so very finished, with him, with her, with the job, with anything that fit into that sentence. He absorbed that and then said, "I want you to come with me to something special."

"No!"

"It's really important. For old times' sake! You can still take a plane late this afternoon. I've put you on first class at five o'clock. Isn't that okay?" he asked me in his most plaintive way. I silently called it his bullshit tone. But finally I agreed to go with him after I extracted another thousand for the new/old/lost wardrobe.

He took me to an elegant luncheon at an estate on Miami Beach's bay side in an upscale part of town. It was a beautiful white-frame home with an imposing entrance, but it really sparkled when you walked through to the back. Floor-to-ceiling windows looked out on a large, manicured lawn that sloped gently down to the bay.

It looked to me as though the whole of Miami high society was politely partying on that lawn. I stood there for a moment looking at all the women dressed in poufy organdy dresses with matching picture hats, and I was embarrassed. I looked like Popeye in drag. David had done it again. I felt he was having a cruel joke at my expense.

David didn't have a decent instinct ever, ever, ever. He had already hurt me, hurt Judy, hurt Lee, and hurt many others he worked with. He was cruel, and I was in the wrong frame of mind for any of his "fun." Whatever wonderful charitable event these women were in the midst of participating in, it had nothing to do with me. David knew that. He also knew the chapter and verse of what I'd just been through. How could he be so callous? But that was David: always pushing the envelope. While his action might give him a few jollies, he knew it would make me angry. Why? I was vain about my appearance. I understood that I looked as if I had accidentally stumbled into the wrong place. I felt like all the women were staring at me, feeling sorry for me. Moreover, I had told David on the phone what I had been through, and he was both sensitive and intelligent enough to understand that this scene was completely inappropriate under the circumstances. It amused him. My anger amused him. How cruel!

Unfortunately for him he didn't realize just how furious I was. I made a fist, pulled back my arm, and with all the strength I had left in my weary body, I punched him as hard as I could in the face. He went sprawling backward into the table behind him, on whose fancy white cloth at least fifty set-ups were resting. The table went over with him on top of it. I don't think it was the force of the blow that sent him reeling; it was more likely the shock. I didn't wait to find out. I was out of there before anyone could ask: "Who is she?"

Back in New York I stayed home, allowing my anger to cool for a while, refusing to respond to David's calls. But after about a week, I knew I wanted to go back to work as long as it meant I would never have to work for Judy again. I was bored sitting at home. There was nothing for the "good little wife" to do, plus—I wasn't her. Although

I discovered reading again, I had much too strong a work ethic to curl up in a corner with a book during the working person's day. And when I questioned myself about looking for a job, the answer was always the same: Forget about that! I had now put three years into FFA. That, I believed, was my equity. I wanted to turn it to account for myself. I wanted David's job—well, not quite.

It was time for me to be an agent, a real agent, not a stage manager, not a dresser, not an assistant or a trainee. I needed to advance my career. I had to get back. I no longer had any fear that limiting my boundaries would cost me my job. My confidence had taken a huge leap. Freddie and David knew that they could always trust me to get the job done. Any job. And I knew that after what I'd been through in the last two years, there was damn little I couldn't handle.

I didn't learn anything about Judy from this episode that I didn't already know, but I learned something hugely valuable about myself: I was totally dependable, responsible, and capable. I could be counted upon in any situation to act with reasoning intelligence to bring things to a reasonable conclusion. Were these qualities always there, lying dormant, waiting to be tapped? I don't know. But I had now been tested time and time again, and I didn't disappoint myself or anyone else. Grasping this gave me confidence, and the confidence was brand-new. I would never feel threatened about my job again. I was "womanpower" worth having.

I met with F&D and made my demands. I wanted to be an agent. I wanted five hundred dollars a week. They agreed to my terms. They needed more manpower. (We weren't up to calling it womanpower yet.) The business was growing. Freddie was talking about opening an office in LA. "If you're going to be successful, you better remember this," Freddie said: "The business belongs in the hands of the people who sign the clients!"

CHAPTER FOURTEEN

One Kind of Husband

And now to Sid Luft. He was an ape! When we met, he was an attractive man in his late forties who was built like a truck. He was strong, with the kind of hard body that suggested he worked out. And he knew how to hit. Judy assured me of that. She told me on a number of occasions that she and Sid had gone a couple of rounds together, but mercifully, I wasn't on hand to see them. I wouldn't like to think of him, or any man, laying a hand on any woman, but that's not reality, and it wasn't Sid's. He was, however, responsible for one of Judy's great comebacks, having produced the movie *A Star Is Born* years after Judy was fired from MGM. But their marriage was fraught with difficulty, and they were not living together when Freddie signed her as a client late in 1960.

Sid didn't think twice about manhandling me. It happened on the very day that Judy was leaving for London to start *A Child Is Waiting*. After all Judy and I had been through together, David thought it was appropriate for me to bid Judy good-bye. "She wants to thank you," he told me. I was now a fledgling agent in the office. I had no clients, and I was just starting to learn how to deal in TV. I didn't have to go to the Stanhope that day, and I shouldn't have gone. Or at least I should have realized that there was something else going on. But I bought David's bullshit once more and went to the hotel (now an expensive Fifth Avenue co-op) where she was staying prior to flying out that night.

I arrived only to discover I had been summoned to be the reliable babysitter for the afternoon. Judy needed her younger children—Lorna, who was then ten, and Joey, seven—out of the suite so she and David could negotiate her departure with Sid Luft, who had a shared custody arrangement for their two children. Sid wanted to keep Judy from taking Lorna and Joe out of the country. He had booked a suite in the same hotel and was intending to stop her however he could. Judy asked me to take the children to Central Park and to check in with her in an hour to find out if it was okay to bring them back to the hotel. I counted the minutes.

I crossed the street with the two children and their attractive red-haired Irish nurse, who seemed to be kind and devoted to them. We took the Fifth Avenue bus downtown to the little zoo in Central Park, some fifteen blocks south. When it came time to make the check-in call Judy had requested, I could find no pay phone anywhere in the park. (Before cell phones, one had to go to a pay phone on the street, and chic Fifth Avenue never accepted such eyesores.) So while the children were enjoying the seal pool, one of the liveliest attractions in the zoo, I walked to commercial Madison Avenue, where, if I had a quarter, I could make the call on any corner.

I asked the nurse to stay exactly where she was. Even though the zoo is small, I didn't relish the idea of chasing through its various animal houses looking for her. David answered the phone in Judy's suite and told me to stay put and check back in another hour. Ugh. When I came back, the children were gone. No, they're here, I said to myself. The seals, especially at feeding time, are such a popular exhibit that they draw crowds two- and three-deep around their fence. I ran around and around the circular pool assuring myself that the nurse and children had to be somewhere in the crowd. But no! Then I ran like a crazy person all over the zoo looking for them. I checked all the bathrooms, and everywhere I went I asked strangers if they had seen this nurse, knowing one could not miss her fire-engine-red hair. But no one had seen them anywhere but at the seal pool. How strange is that? I thought. I was in a panic. I couldn't call Judy and tell her I'd lost them.

And then it dawned on me that the nurse had to be working for Sid. It was the only notion that made sense from the discussions I'd been party to, in which Sid was painted as a schemer and an opportunist. However, at that moment, it was also the only hook for me to hang on to. Given the battle then waging between Judy and Sid, it was the one scenario that worked.

In the taxi on the way back to the Stanhope I wrote a script for what might be happening. A kidnapping plot was afoot. Money for Sid the motive! The closer I got to the hotel, the more likely my scenario seemed. What made it possible were the two principals in the ongoing negotiation: David, a merciless extorter who would push anyone's back to the wall and then beat them down, and Sid Luft, about whom everything was said to be unsavory, underhanded, and slimy. But no more so than David!

When I got back to the Stanhope, the desk clerk could see how concerned I was, and, even though he was not supposed to give out room numbers, he told me where Sid was. I think the clerk saw himself as an incidental character in an unfolding plot. It was clear to everyone behind the desk that something improper was happening. Famous wife and sullen husband in suites on separate floors. The level of interest rises among the staff.

I went directly to Sid's suite. I knocked on the door, and when he opened it I could see the children playing on the carpet in the living room straight ahead. I confronted him, told him that Lorna and Joe were in my charge, and I wanted them back. Sid looked at me as if I were a total loony just before he slammed the door in my face. At least I knew the kids were safe. But that was hardly the point. I never for a moment thought they had come to any harm. What to do? I knew I must do something to get them back or face ugly consequences. Both Sid and Judy had vile tempers.

I knocked on the door a second time and appealed to Sid in some limp, whiny fashion, hoping that such an appeal would gain more traction. However, the reverse was true. This time he was far more annoyed with me and wanted to put an end to the nuisance I was causing. I never expected him to do what he did, which was to pick me up and throw me across the corridor. Literally. One hundred twenty-five pounds of me was like a paperweight to him. I bounced off the opposite wall and lay crumpled on the floor like a balled-up piece of paper trash.

My back went into some kind of spasm I'd never known. I was hurting badly and couldn't get up. Finally I crawled to the elevator and, using a tall sand-filled ashtray for support, pulled myself up with difficulty. The elevator man helped me limp into the old-fashioned phone booth that lived in the lobby, while behind the desk everyone stared, and without any alternative, I made the call to Judy. She went ballistic. I could not explain, given the screaming coming through the phone, that the fucking nurse was a no-good double-dealer. After listening to the stream of abuse leveled at me, I then told David what really happened. He asked me not to leave the hotel. Dummy that I was, I stayed, cowering on the seat in the phone booth.

How would David solve this problem? Well, he could always sell drama to Judy. They both feasted on it. So it had to be David's suggestion to hire hit men, and given his Las Vegas experience, he knew exactly whom to call. Goons were hired to break down Sid's door and grab the children. They were very effective, and I hope they beat Sid up in the process and left him on the floor in as much pain as he had left me.

As Judy rushed from the hotel with the children and David in tow, she saw me in distress sitting in the phone booth. At the top of her lungs, and she had lungs aplenty, she screamed some of her favorite curse words at me, "You cunt, you cooze!" and everyone in the lobby looked not at her but at me.

The next day headlines of the *New York Post* screamed: "Judy Hires Goons!" and it told the story of the kidnapping without ever once mentioning my name. But it was clear to me that David had concocted a script that was scandalous, in which I had played some traitorous role. My guess is that he'd told Judy I had conspired with Sid, and that's the reason she exited calling me every awful name I'd ever heard, and some that I hadn't. I could just imagine David embroidering the narrative as he conveyed it. So like him to amuse himself in this way.

My husband picked up the pieces and took me home, where I rested in bed for the next three days, but three days was my limit. Bored and less sore than before, I went back to work amid his protests. I was so pill-averse at that point that neither he nor anyone else could get me to take so much as an aspirin. But I was young and strong, and fortunate not to have sustained a permanent injury. The idea of suing Sid Luft never crossed my mind, and had I decided to do that, I wouldn't have gotten any support from Judy because by the time I set foot back in the office, she and Sid were good buddies once more. All I could draw from that idiocy is that if someone was willing to fight with her, she could then conclude that they must care about her. Huh? Weird logic.

F&D were unwilling to judge Sid, at least not out loud. They never once put him down to Judy. From their standpoint Sid was a savior, willing to put up with the hard time with her that they were not, and as I was no longer in the picture full time, having a body in place for her was worth more than money. Sid, on the other hand, hated F&D and wanted to take them to court. He was sure that they had stolen Judy's money, and I'm not sure he was wrong. I saw David endorse Judy's name on the back of many concert checks. He did it right in front of me. It was clear he was copying her signature. What I did not know at the time was what account those checks went into. I still don't. They could have gone into Judy's account just as easily as his. I had no paper trail and did none of the company's bookkeeping. Many years later, however, when David, by then president of Columbia Pictures, was knee-deep in scandal, having been caught forging Cliff Robertson's name on a check he cashed for himself, I realized that it was not only possible that he had cashed Judy's money but most likely that he had. And it was a lot of money, much more than the ten thousand he was trying to steal from Cliff Robertson, perhaps more than a few hundred thousand.

My feeling now is that he stole from Judy to get the money he needed for his and Lee's very lavish lifestyle. It's also possible that he used that money to settle his gambling debts, debts that he would have created with money borrowed in casinos using Judy's name, and paid for with Judy's earnings, for no matter how much David made—and he has to have made millions over the long haul—he never had enough. He was always deeply in debt.

If I learned anything from Sid, it was that there are men who like to live off women. They don't do any of the heavy lifting; they simply set themselves up in a cozy corner and call themselves advisers. In my opinion Sid wasn't fit to shine Judy's shoes. He was neither as smart as David nor nearly as charming. But they had a lot in common. Both were gamblers, hustlers, and liars. Sid liked horses, David, who lived like a pasha, liked expensive homes, the best restaurants, pricey jewelry and clothing. And each bet the farm on being a winner while they were both such losers.

What I most loathed about David—his cheating, his lying, his taking advantage of anyone who allowed it, in other words, his cruelty—had to be as apparent to Freddie as it was to me. I don't know why he was willing to put up with it, except to imagine that he didn't want to go forward alone, and as awful as David was is also as skilled as he was. A year or two before Freddie died, I visited him and we talked about David. I told him I thought that David had stolen huge sums from Judy. I sensed he agreed with me, but he didn't give it up. "Why are you protecting him now?" I asked. Freddie didn't have an answer.

CHAPTER FIFTEEN

Endings, Beginnings, and Endings

It was time to stop thinking about ending my marriage, and end it. It was so over for four years out of the five, and now I was becoming intolerant of the little things. I was sick of having to dine with my husband's parents once a week. They were refugees with one foot still in Germany, where they had lost many dear relatives to the Holocaust. They were sad, joyless people who doted on their only child, the light of their lives. I dishonored them by never being fully present at dinner. I desperately wanted to be alone. Immersed in self-delusion, I thought my dinners with Judy were more important. I could get Frank and Dean on the phone (for Judy). I was self-congratulatory because they knew my name. I traveled to places I never thought I'd see. Me at the pool of the Beverly Hills Hotel, me sitting at a blackjack table at the Sahara in Las Vegas, me at lunch in the Savoy Grill in London. Not me in a little German restaurant with bad food and a deaf waiter. I was so intolerant, so selfish. I thought I had earned the exciting life I was participating in. What was wrong with that? My perception was adolescent. My values the same. And the truth is that I was chasing after clients and hadn't yet accomplished anything to be proud of. My interaction with big stars came only because of Freddie and David.

Meanwhile, what I had at home was far better: the love of a good man. However, coming from my parents' home, I didn't know what a good man was. I had no role model. So without being able to see what really mattered, I ended the marriage and chose the fast-but-empty lane. In securing the divorce, I ran roughshod over my husband, which was easy to do because he was so patient and kind.

I've blocked out what I said to him. I do remember that he grew silent, made no protest. He didn't try to persuade me to stay. Tutored by his thrifty folks, he asked to keep all our money. The money didn't mean much to me, and I thought he was entitled for what he'd gone through. I agreed without once thinking how I would put down the security for an apartment of my own. I went to Mexico for a "quickie" in Juárez. The proceeding was conducted in Spanish, and I understood little, somehow an appropriate ending to a marriage I also didn't understand. The irony was complete. I hadn't heard the rabbi on the day I married, and I didn't understand the attorney on the day I divorced.

As well, I didn't realize I was developing a case of hardening of the emotional arteries. All I knew was that I had seen how the beautiful people lived, and I wanted all their trinkets: the houses, the cars, the jewels, and the clothes. When I think back on who I was then, it's hard for me to love that girl, but possible to forgive her. And I would have to forgive her a lot for what she did next.

I had an affair with David Begelman. I gave myself permission to do that because Judy was leaving to work at CBS. David would no longer have her in his backyard; nor would I. We both made it clear that we were staying in New York: he to run the East Coast office, I to take my place as an agent representing Liza. It was our excuse to shake free, if only temporarily. Judy, who had to have a man in her life, put Sid Luft back in place, and they moved into a new home in Brentwood.

With Judy gone, David's attention turned to me. I was flattered. He let me know—by the length of time he held my hand, by the way he appraised me, by his lingering and sometimes smoldering looks—that he was interested, but he didn't make a pass. I think he feared rejection. He was like the kid with his nose pressed against the candy store window. I thought about it a while before I let him know he could enter. And how did it happen? One day while at work I simply took the hand on my shoulder into mine as he stood behind me looking at a contract on my desk. He walked me into his office, locked the door, pressed the button to draw shut the mechanical drapes—signaling to his secretary that he didn't want to be disturbed—and undressed me. It was midday.

There was a lot about David I despised, but just as much that intrigued me. I was enamored of his intellect. He was a voracious reader who often had a nonfiction book in hand (he loved biographies of great historical figures), lest he find himself at the barber without some worthwhile reading. He was up on all the good movies and capable of discussing everything from the motives hidden in the plot to the work of the cinematographer. He was a newshound who took strong political positions. I admired this. It was the start of a political awakening for me. And he was articulate in everything he discussed, commanding a large vocabulary—in fact sometimes using words I needed to look up. ("Concomitant" comes to mind.) And I remember how he praised me when one day, unselfconsciously, I correctly used the word "keening" in a sentence. He was delighted.

I was the sexual aggressor here. I knew I was sending subtle signals—smiling when I might have looked away, lowering my eyes in an apparent come-on. I wanted to know what Judy knew. Yes, a part of my decision had more to do with Judy than simply giving myself permission to fuck him because she wasn't doing it at that precise moment. I wanted to be in bed with the man Judy slept with and raved about. I was sexually curious about him. I wanted a taste of what the shouting was about. I wanted to sleep with the man the great Judy Garland was in love with—from time to time. I wanted to feel her equal in that way.

With crazy logic I managed to persuade myself that as long as he was not fucking Judy, it was okay to have this affair even though he was very married. This is the dumbest thinking I was ever guilty of, and I regret to this day that I decided, in spite of knowing what a snake he was, to have my turn with him.

As to my affair with David, it's not worth much space. I'm sorry to disappoint you. Trust me, no one was more disappointed than I was. My mother used to say that you never knew anyone until you were either in business or in bed with him. That should have served as warning enough for me, as I knew full well who I was in business with, and although my powers of observation may have been slightly underdeveloped, they weren't totally useless.

The affair itself was anything but romantic. No candlelit dinners, no walks through Paris in the rain. It was about sex, plain and simple, and he was far from a great lover. The excitement for him seemed to be about where he could fuck me. On his office desk, in a ladies' room of the Pierre, in the first-class bathroom on an American Airlines red-eye from LA to New York—making us members, he said, of the "Mile High Club." My apartment was less exciting, although closer to a telephone. While "doing" me, David was also doing deals on the telephone. I was not amused.

If ever there was a sex object, I was it. I had no identity, and if I had eagerness for the act itself, I had no opportunity to demonstrate. His penis was present. The rest of him was somewhere else. Of course I wondered if he pulled the same ugly shtick with Judy, but I knew I would never be able to ask either the question. My husband was a gentle, tender, caring lover. David was none of the above. "Revolting" is the only appropriate word to describe sex with David.

I don't know whether Freddie knew about my affair with his partner. I took it for granted he did. I went about learning the TV business and looking for clients to add to my roster of one (for I had now signed Liza, and I was pursuing the rising actresses Joan Hackett and Jill Haworth) as if nothing was different, and I didn't discuss my personal life with anyone. I suspect David told everyone that had any interest in listening. I was noticeably with David all the time. He took me to meetings—ostensibly so I could take notes—and we traveled together for business. He didn't need me along, but he was interested in finding new places where we could "do it" while risking being caught, which was his thing. And his hypocritical in crowd, the Rudins, the Rosemonts, and the new guys at the firm, Marty Kummer and Danny Welkes, welcomed me as an insider in spite of the fact that they were friendly with Lee.

The longer I allowed the affair to go on, the more I hated him—and myself. I had to figure out a way to get him out of my personal life while keeping my job. He made it easy: He asked me to marry him. "No" came out of my mouth a bit too quickly, as I recall. And then I backtracked and spoke in clichés—about how flattered I was, and how special "we" were.

But we were not special at all, and I knew that and he did, too. He had proposed to Judy because she had implied early and often that they would be married. Talk of marriage was probably part of his stock ammunition. But after six months of doing David, the thought of being married to him was nauseating. My escape "pitch" came out of thinking about the dismal prospect of such a marriage. What I told him was no lie: that I couldn't go on knowing that his wife was sitting at home waiting for him. A month into the affair I was hugely uncomfortable being with a married man, and the feeling continued to grow until I couldn't handle it. "Guilt" was a word that he knew well and shied away from. I wasn't urging him to divorce her. Not at all! That's what he instantly thought, and he said he would get rid of Lee as quickly as possible. I was nothing if not sanctimonious when I advised him to repair his wreck. "No, don't worry, Stevie. I'm going to end this travesty," he assured me. It was lip service. "I hope I'll still be working for the company when you do," I told him with a smile on my face.

Since we both knew his divorce wasn't happening, I was careful not to let it sound like I was judging him. Thank goodness he couldn't afford a divorce! I told him we would remain friends, and we actually shook hands on it. Once I felt secure again, I asked myself some questions I'd been avoiding. Did fucking David improve my professional prospects? Was I trying to make it to the top on my back? I hated these questions, and disliked the answers even more, but when I finally had the breathing room to examine whether or not I thought the affair had helped my career, I knew the answer: You betcha! David felt he owed me.

Guilt was the currency David traded in. I got promoted instead of married. If I had been some complete dummy without any potential, I doubt the affair would have gotten me as much as a free pass to Radio City Music Hall. But because I was dumb only about inconsequential personal things, the affair gave me a leg up—so to speak.

However, once it was over and done with, he didn't delay (nor has any man I have ever known, for that matter) securing the next body for his bed. He moved on immediately. That sums up for me how much I had mattered. First he went a few more rounds with Judy, and when that was finally over after the London episode, he settled on the wife of his best friend, the real-estate magnate Lew Rudin.

I don't find it strange that all three of David's wives died of cancer, especially if there's any truth to the mind-body-connection theories. David brought misery to all the lives that he touched in a personal way, most notably Judy's. I escaped that, more than likely because Judy's exposure to him toughened me. I already knew who he was. He became my experiment rather than the other way around, and rejecting him let me know I was on the way to becoming the independent woman I wanted to be. I was pleased I did it with kindness. Having said that, I'm ashamed of having had an affair with a married man. It wasn't for me. I'm sorry I did it then, and I never did it again.

Nor is it at all strange to me that he committed suicide. And why? Because he brought misery as well to most of the lives he touched in a professional way, and it cost him. He lost most of his friends. He could send three, four, or more studio executives to bed believing they had a deal with him only to find out the next morning that not only didn't they have a deal, the deal they thought they were negotiating was no more than a figment of David's imagination. He persuaded himself that people didn't talk to one another, and he could say whatever he pleased. But people did talk to one another.

In a town like Hollywood where a rumor is old news within minutes, this wasn't good for the reputation of the company he was working for—be it FFA, CMA, or Columbia Pictures, nor was it good for agents in general. The executives in New York and LA knew he was a scoundrel, but he was their scoundrel. For a long time they closed ranks around him because of the important stars he represented (like Newman and Streisand), even when he put their backs up against the wall by making deals that were too tough— because when he finally did make a deal, he went for the kill. It wasn't necessary. The stars knew he was a bastard, but he was their bastard. So they, too, put up with him until they couldn't, until they caught him in lies or broken promises.

In the end everyone knew he was a louse, and the day he needed friends—well after he had left the agency business, and Columbia—they were gone. His debts finally caught up with him.

When he borrowed from Peter to pay Paul, instead of paying back people he already owed, he opened new accounts to support his grand unearned existence. He knew this would catch up with him. He would be punished. He needed that. It felt as if he intentionally drew a net of despair around himself so tight that he and everybody in the higher echelons of showbiz knew he was going down in disgrace. No longer his friends or admirers, the people he owed were coming at him from all sides. It would not be long before he was facing bankruptcy and, more than likely, jail. Thirty-two years after he was my bed partner, he ended his life alone in a bed at the Century Plaza Hotel in Los Angeles.

I have never again in my life run into anyone whose considerable charm and great intelligence, coupled with such ugly instincts, produced so much unhappiness. David was one of a kind, thank goodness. He was never able to put so much as one single toe on high moral ground, the only real estate that matters. Freddie and I talked about it from time to time. Freddie thought that one day David would slit his wrists in a warm tub. I disagreed. I thought when that fateful day came, he would blow his brains out. And so he did. His suicide was exquisitely planned and flawlessly executed. Just like every other awful thing he did. I did not shed a tear.

CHAPTER SIXTEEN

A Very Sad Day

The day Liza married Peter Allen ended the Judy Garland chapter in my life. It was March 3, 1967. I had now been representing twenty-one-year-old Liza for five and a half successful years. I am jumping ahead to include you in Li's wedding because I feel I can't move on until I put a period at the end of my involvement with Judy.

Mark Herron, a tall, thin, attractive gay man, became Judy's husband in 1965. They were traveling together when they discovered Peter and his friend Chris Bell, billed together as the Allen Brothers, performing in Hong Kong. Judy was impressed. She brought the two young singers to London, where they became her opening act, and she introduced Peter to Liza.

With Judy's blessing, Peter and Liza got engaged quickly. I never understood it, except to say that since the introduction came from Judy, it was paramount to Liza, who forever sought Judy's approval. However, like Mark, Peter was also gay, but perhaps not quite ready yet to own it. Still, Liza must have known. Even though very young, Liza was out there sexually. Way out there! One would have to say promiscuous. She was a healthy, strapping, beautiful (though not in the classic sense) young woman. She and Peter seemed blissfully happy in each other's company. They were inseparable; they ran all over town together. I found it hard to find her when I needed to. Were they in love? Was sex a part of it? I don't have the answers.

Both Judy and Liza each married gay men. I can understand why Judy Garland married the brilliant Vincente Minnelli, who is reputed to have shown up in Hollywood wearing purple eye shadow. Vincente made Judy feel beautiful, and he made her exquisite in every film he directed. Liza was their love child. There's that, at least, but that's all I can account for. There is no point in my dwelling on what I thought were weird mismatches. I asked my beloved gay friend Albert Poland, a great general manager in theater who started the original Judy Garland Fan Club, what this kind of marriage was about, and he couldn't come up with an answer either. (And, by the way, Albert knows many more details about Judy's life than I do.)

No one in Liza's immediate or extended family stood up and said they would give Liza her wedding. Judy couldn't afford it, and Vincente was not heard from. And no word from anyone on Peter's side of the aisle. I watched and waited, but there was only a shattering silence. I was heartbroken for Liza, and so I decided I would do it. Li agreed that my apartment—now a lavishly furnished pad on fashionable Park Avenue that my second husband's corrupt music money helped pay for—would be a suitable setting. Liza designed the dress she wanted to wear, she and Peter chose the man who would perform the ceremony, and I took care of everything else.

The day came, the guests arrived, and Liza never looked more beautiful. When all were assembled, Judy arrived. I opened the door, looked at her, and wanted to cry. The toll her life had taken on her was enormous. I had seen her last at CBS in 1964. Here it was only three years later, and she, at forty-five—in the prime of life—looked twenty-five years older. More. Fifty years. I don't exaggerate. Healthy women of eighty look much better than she did that day. She was wrinkled and pale and so wasted that I momentarily lost the ability to speak, to graciously welcome her into my home. Her elegant outfit could not hide how emaciated she was. I doubt she could have weighed more than ninety pounds. Drugs have to have been the reason she was this suddenly ancient-looking casualty. Her face was overly made up, the makeup accentuating the skeletal holes in her cheeks, just barely covered with skin. She was macabre, and had to be supported by Mark Herron, her husband, as she walked. I took her bony hand in mine, and she smiled as I led her into my living room. I imagined she was in pain.

The old familiar chill seized my body, turning my hands to ice. I took a bathroom break to run my hands under hot water and cry into a towel. Regardless of all she and I had been through together, it was devastating to see her in this reduced state. I blanked on the wedding. Fear and loathing and pity and despair all got mixed up together, and for the rest of the afternoon I operated on automatic pilot. It was an event fraught with so much emotion it blocks out my memory.

I do, however, remember trying to make myself see another Judy, willing myself to see Esther Smith, the girl next door whom I adored. I wanted her once again to be young and beautiful and back in Technicolor St. Louis falling in love with her handsome neighbor, John Truett, while I, a little girl of eight, was falling in love with her. That was a sustainable love that endured throughout my childhood and then some. And now, for the balance of that afternoon, I wanted the dream and not the reality. It had to be Esther who was here in my living room to honor her little girl; I needed to push away everything that was wrong with the world. I try not to think of Judy looking as ghastly as she did at Li's wedding. If I conjure that up, it still hurts.

If I once believed that I'd developed immunity to feeling anything at all about Judy because of what we'd been through together, I knew that afternoon that I was wrong. If I believed that the business had turned me into a hard-hearted Hannah, I was mistaken. Nor had David wrenched away the remains of some tender feelings I had for Judy. I found out that March day between the hours of three and five that I wasn't nearly as tough as I thought. And why was I grateful to know I still cared? Because it made me aware all over again of how important she'd been to me. She was the one— more so than anyone—who had made me aware of my life—what it should and should not be.

I was grateful that my chores as a hostess kept me wholly busy. But I also refrained from conversing with Judy because I feared she harbored residual bad feelings toward me. That was ridiculous, and I'm sorry I wasted my opportunity to be kind to her. At the end of the afternoon I again took her bony, damp hand into mine to congratulate her. Judy Garland, on the last day that I would ever see her in person, broke my heart.

Judy died not long after. Her funeral was held one city block away from where I live. I couldn't make myself go. I went downstairs in the course of my daily routine, and for two days saw a line that extended up Madison Avenue, turned the corner, and went all the way to Fifth. The line kept moving, but it never got shorter. What a tribute! How wonderful that all these people loved her and wanted to honor her. I thought back and was appreciative of her greatness, but that appreciation was larded with the memories of bad times.

I crossed Fifth Avenue at one point and watched the line from a bench just outside Central Park and pondered the same things I had wondered about so many times in the past—mostly when I was watching her perform. How would that audience feel if they knew what I knew? Would they then still be sympathetic? Why could I not mourn her now when I mourned her the day Li married, and she was then still alive? Would I always be stuck with this conflict raging inside me: loving her one day, hating her the next?

Had I allowed Judy to make me feel this way?' Who did I care about anymore? Could one, I wondered, be in showbiz, be hard nosed, hard boiled, pushy, and pushed around and still care about the people who did the pushing? I don't know. But those are generic questions, and Judy was a special case. For good or bad, there was only ever one Judy Garland.

CHAPTER SEVENTEEN

Sometimes

Allow me to take a moment here to indulge myself and simply consider how I feel about Judy at this moment.

As I said at the start, Judy Garland remains the lens through which I have seen, lived, and dealt with my life. But as I've gained distance and experience, I now view our relationship without the same emotional involvement. However, it's difficult to separate the person from the performances, which makes it hard to love Judy as I did when I was a child. My reaction today varies depending on the mood I'm in. The word "sometimes" is one that I can't be without when I describe how I feel.

Sometimes a simple thing I've done a thousand times will trigger some Judy ugliness—like picking up a bread knife. Sometimes I cannot be riding the Fifth Avenue bus as it passes the Plaza Hotel without thinking of putting out the fire Judy set to her nightgown there. And it was there that I pulled her off a high-floor ledge when she tried to go out a window. Let others debate her motives, I'm happy on the days when I pass by the Plaza and see only a building. It happens sometimes.

Sometimes when I see the old Carnegie Hall album featured on a Web site, it reminds me of the magnificent performance whose equal I have never seen again, but then sometimes it reminds me of Boston. Sometimes I can enjoy the old films when I'm channel surfing, but then sometimes I have to move on quickly because I know how different the image is from the person. I do not forget that sometimes I felt immensely sorry for Judy Garland. I remember her lying in my lap sobbing that she had worked so hard for so long and had nothing to show for it. But then sometimes I will see a limo on the street and remember the cars she would not allow me to dismiss, which waited, constantly changing shifts of drivers, outside her hotel for days. She tore my heart out with her tears, but finally my pity was engaged not because of the tears but because she simply didn't understand that the bad choices were all hers. The true sadness was that she didn't get it.

I don't discount that some choices were beyond her control, like the "monster bed" at MGM where she, Deanna Durbin, and other young players climbed in with company executives. If it's true, could I possibly feel sorrier for her? Then I ask myself: Wuz you there, Charlie? The answer is no. It's possible that the story was made up, told just to shock me, or maybe it was simply the ravings of a deranged mind. Judy knew how to lie, and exaggeration was her long suit.

The Judy I knew never wanted to die. But whether or not someone responded on that tragic night or not, her body could no longer withstand the abuse. Many celebrities who, like Judy, have died young remain young in our memories. For most Judy was old, perhaps because she had been around for so long, or perhaps because she looked so old when she died. She was only forty-seven. That still shocks me. And sometimes when I mention to someone else that she was only forty-seven when she died, it shocks them too.

———————

There are many people whom I owe. I owe Judy the most. She was the start of my start, and largely the reason I am a survivor. Sometimes I think I miss her, but in truth what I'm missing is that incredible time in my life, which was exciting, fun, scary, sad, tragic—somewhat in that order. One of the things I learned at Al-Anon, many years after Judy died, is that we're satisfied with happy endings, even if the outcome is different than we intended. They leave us with good memories. But when things don't work out well, we want a do-over. We may even create similar situations in order to try for a better result. So sometimes what I really want is to go back to that incredible time in my life, grab it by the throat, and change the ending. But only sometimes!

Part 2

Success

CHAPTER EIGHTEEN

The Liza Start-up

I began representing Liza in 1962. But I must start with Judy. Everything starts with Judy, who went to LA in 1962 to do the first of two television specials for CBS, leaving Liza alone in New York. I also remained in New York to start the rest of my life. But when an invitation was tendered to me to fly first class to the coast for the taping of the show starring Frank Sinatra and Dean Martin, I decided to put off the start of the rest of my life for a few days.

I was excited to see Judy back on top, working with the top performers in the industry, many of whom were now clamoring to be in the show, to shine in her reflected light. In the glare of that light I had another opportunity to see that top performers don't always do top-drawer things. Panic, a mode I was used to, had taken over the stage floor; Judy was rehearsing alone and had been all week because Frank and Dean could not be found. They were supposed to start work on Monday; it was now Friday, and the show was about to go on camera. I was so happy to be only an observer as I watched people ready for the dress rehearsal scurrying around trying to find substitutes, writers rewriting. George Schlatter, the producer, who had everyone in Southern California looking for the two superstars, was certifiable. I was on the stage talking to Judy when the two stars nonchalantly strolled in. Mouths could be seen dropping open in unison all over the stage. Frank took a beat and said to the awestruck group, "If you wanted someone reliable, you should've hired Eddie Albert!" (There should be a rim shot here.) Dean Martin did nothing except stand there looking beautiful. Frank and Dean then hit their marks, gave wonderful performances, and the show was nominated for four Emmy Awards.

There was a second special, and the success of both led to discussions for a series. Selling a television series is a windfall for any agency. A big-budget musical variety series with a star headlining it was, in the early sixties, the cherry on the sundae. For Freddie's little start-up, a sale like this would put the company into the same conversation as William Morris. Negotiations raged on for months, going at times from bad to worse. It was heavily rumored that James Aubrey, then president of the CBS network, was not a Judy Garland fan, which probably had something to do with his fight with Sid Luft years before. (Sid fought with everyone.)

However, finally Freddie prevailed and on December 28, 1962, Judy signed a deal for twenty-four million dollars, one of the largest in television history, not only in terms of money but also because it gave her full say as to whether she wanted to continue past the first thirteen shows (one season), and CBS could not cancel. Unfortunately, the show never found as big an audience as had been hoped, and it also became more than Judy could handle. There were endless problems getting her to the stage on time, if she could be gotten there at all. Imitating the wonderful set for *The Wizard of Oz*, the CBS crew painted a charming little yellow brick road lined with flowers that led to and from her trailer to the stage. But she could no longer meander down that path as she once had. I knew exactly what that was about, and I was relieved those problems weren't mine. That old bugaboo, "reliability factor," had reared its ugly head once again.

Back in New York Liza was alone. Judy took her two small children and was gone, seemingly permanently. Judy, who shed all her belongings but for the few framed pictures that she traveled with, was now shedding her daughter. So here is sixteen-year-old Liza, who adores her mother, in the big city. She doesn't have any money at all. Think about it. I certainly did. I know how much Liza wanted to stay in New York. She was mad for theater and hanging with all the gypsies on Broadway. I don't know if she had to plead with Judy to stay behind, but I know that if I wanted to leave home at sixteen, and I had neither money nor a place to stay, there would have been a mighty struggle, and I would have lost. Although Judy had no home, to Liza at sixteen, "home" meant being with her mother. Liza was now homeless.

I knew I had to make it work for Liza, or it would become an unmitigated disaster. I had helped to keep Judy alive; perhaps Judy figured I could now keep her big girl alive. Or maybe she didn't think about it at all. Still, without a word to me, she was in effect handing me the greatest responsibility of my early life, one that F&D wanted no part of. And I'll tell you why. Liza was a mess. Her waist-length hair often looked as if it might have been home to both animate and inanimate things. (The gamine haircut that became her signature style was still a few years away.)

Dirty and unkempt, she would come and hang out in my new office almost every day. F&D—to whom image was everything—weren't happy about it, but that was too bad. I felt so sorry for her. She was a sweet kid, modest, and very polite. I didn't have the heart to ask her to leave or even cut back her visits. She dropped out of school and didn't have anywhere else to go. And all she ever wanted, all she ever talked about, was getting into show business.

Most days she would give me a pep talk about how she was going to make it. She had enormous ambition, stars in her eyes, and determination in her pleas, but nothing in her pockets. I doubt she got an allowance from her mother once Judy was gone. It would have come in the mail, and there was none. Nor did I ask Judy for any money for Liza. That was not up to me. I gave Li what she needed, which wasn't much. You could buy her off with a burger and a quarter to get to wherever she was going to hang out next. Trust me, it was better not to ask. It didn't matter to Liza where she slept.

Nothing mattered to Liza as much as performing. She was sure that all she needed was for me to represent her. In spite of F&D, I was flattered. Finally one day I screwed my courage to the sticking place, went to them and said I wanted to help her. "Get papers with her, and get her some work so that she has someplace else to go," David ordered. Liza remained a nuisance to them until she started earning big money. (Then, indeed, they did come calling.) Liza was both vulnerable and sensitive, and she sensed how the guys felt about her. She steered clear of them, although she was always polite and enthusiastic when she saw them. She had a don't-make-enemies instinct that has always served her well. I suspect she developed it because of the need to tiptoe around Judy.

I can't claim that my earliest involvement in Liza's professional life was based solely on an appreciation of her talent. I didn't know whether or not she had any. I had only seen her kick up her heels to Gershwin's "Swanee" for a few minutes during a couple of Judy's concerts to allow her mother to catch her breath, and I'd seen her perform the leading role in a school production of *The Diary of Anne Frank*. It was a Scarsdale High School Drama Club presentation that so impressed a sponsor he paid for the students to tour Israel, Greece, and Italy with the play. Liza was especially good, but so was everyone, and that was school.

But now school was over for Liza, and this was real life. My two bosses thought that she was a waste of time and I was crazy. Nevertheless I signed contracts with her just in case there could be something there—and to shut David up. But it was mostly a sympathetic gesture. I knew what her life with Judy could be like from time to time because I knew what mine was like. But if I felt sorry for her, I can assure you she didn't feel sorry for herself. What was for me her parents' questionable behavior was for her her "normal."

I'm never sure what "normal" means, but I know for damn sure that what Liza was given, starting from the time I met her, was no warm and fuzzy home life. Not that either parent wasn't affectionate when they were with her; Judy certainly was, and I witnessed Vincente being affectionate in his way as well. I'm sorry I never got to know him better, because I was such a big fan of his movies, but whenever Liza and I stopped at his lovely house just off Sunset Boulevard—which happened only a few times—Vincente's wife, Denise, wore an expression that seemed unwelcoming to me, and my antennae were totally tuned in. She seemed to be treating unkempt Liza with a kind of disdain that, for me, translated into "Don't infect this house with your messy presence." There was never an invitation to stay for lunch, never a question about whether or not we were hungry or thirsty.

So while I have no doubt that both parents were very fond of Liza, parental concern for Li's education, schedule, diet, and structure just plain didn't exist. Parenting didn't exist, not only in a non-traditional way, but in any way at all. It may have been there at some point earlier in her life, but I wasn't around then. I only saw what I saw from the day I met thirteen-year-old Liza, and it was awful or totally absent. In fact, once Judy left for the series in 1962, she was absent from both our lives—if only on a temporary basis; someone else was getting the calls at three or four in the morning. And I don't know when she and Liza spoke to each other during those long absences, if at all. Yet she adored them both.

Once the ink was dry on the contracts, I knew I had to find Liza work, and I did—in theater. She won raves in *Best Foot Forward*, which I made the booking for, my very first in theater. Playing Ethel Hofflinger—a high school sweetheart dumped by her boyfriend (a very young Christopher Walken) so he could take a Hollywood star to the prom—Liza was brilliant casting and so real in the role. I found myself, along with the audience, watching only her. Of course I was interested primarily in Li's performance, but then one gets caught up in the play itself—if the play is any good—and all the actors seamlessly become a part of it. Liza blended in nicely, but she also stood out, and not just to me. Her energy was higher, her immersion as an actress total. I could finally see she had talent, but since I was not yet at all sure of myself, it took the audience reaction to convince me that she was the real deal.

Although there were some rumors that Judy and Sid had missed their plane (and I hope they were merely rumors), Judy may have thoughtfully attended the performance on the second night, knowing that if she came on opening night, she would attract all the press attention. No one was more grateful than I for her gesture, nor was anyone more proud than Judy. Within the limits of her capability, it was clear that Judy cared. The play launched Li's professional stage career and led to her being honored with the Theater World Award as 1963's most promising young actress. She deserved it. She had broken her ankle in rehearsal, and nonetheless just kept putting one foot in front of the other. She was the living embodiment of the title—putting her best foot forward.

While in the show, Liza was fortunate to meet a lovely young woman in the cast, Paula Wayne. They became friends. Paula was older and married with kids. She had an apartment on the Upper West Side of Manhattan, and she generously took homeless Liza in. This situation worked until I started to hear some grumblings. So I went across town to find out what it was about. I met an unhappy husband who didn't want Liza sleeping on a bare mattress on his living room floor. "Please get her out of here," he demanded. He was neither rude or even a tad impolite, merely (and justifiably) annoyed with an intolerable living situation that Liza wasn't able to see, and Paula was too kind to bring up. I told Liza to grab her things; I was taking her home with me. And it's not as if that took more than two minutes. She had no suitcases to pack.

And so Liza moved into the apartment I'd rented on East Fifty-fifth Street in Manhattan. It was a one bedroom and my first solo pad. She slept on the couch in my living room for the best part of a year. She co-opted my wardrobe, ate solid food from my fridge, and didn't have to struggle. With a lovely place of my own, I could easily share everything with her until she could afford her own apartment.

It was amusing what opposites we were. I was a day person; she thrived at night. When I left early in the morning to walk to work, she was fast asleep. When I came home at night from the office, she was gone. If I had to go out at night to cover theater or anything else, I would come home by midnight and she was still gone. Not my business. And I wasn't about to become a watchdog. I had no interest in assuming the role of nagging parent. I knew that wouldn't work because whenever I got on her case about anything (and I only ever did when it affected her career), it wasn't appreciated. I wanted to be helpful, and to give her a sense of security so that she could go out and do her job.

I wasn't dating much at the time, having only recently divorced my first husband. I simply wasn't interested in finding another husband right away. I figured if that was going to happen, it would. Going to bars or clubs with friends in order to meet some guy wasn't anything I had the time or taste for, so I never had to worry about embarrassing moments with men in the apartment. The grocer delivered food, the part-time maid delivered cleanliness, and life rolled merrily on without much more interaction between Li and me than we had when she still had a home of her own.

At least Liza knew that I was someone who cared about her enough to do this for her, and I hope the occasional hug was more than an empty gesture. Once I got her on a firm footing financially, I went out and found her a lovely apartment on East Fifty-seventh Street, a premier street in New York. It was a new building on the corner of the block I had lived on when I was married. I had seen a vacancy sign outside just before I moved. The apartment it advertised was perfect. We both loved it. That was a great day. We furnished the place a little at a time from the earnings that were just starting to come from television, the playground I was now becoming very active in in my career. Li's apartment was beautiful until Mate's first fateful night in his newly decorated home.

Li paid one pound ten shillings for a puppy she fell in love with at a shelter in London while visiting Judy, and she brought him home. He was her mate, which Li pronounced "Mite" with her new Brit accent. I could understand lonely little Li wanting a full-time companion. "But he's not housebroken," she told me. "What are we going to do?" I thought obedience school was the answer, but all I heard from Liza is, "I can't live without him. I love him." It was so very sweet, so very needy, so very Liza! However, she had a few upcoming engagements, her very first personal appearances in small clubs, and the dog could not go with her.

I found a training school that sounded perfect, and a gentleman straight out of Central Casting, costumed as a captain of the Luftwaffe, including the knee-high spit-polished boots, came to collect the dog. His "hello" handshake was designed to crush more than just the littlest bones. He assured us that within two weeks Mate would be totally housebroken. Looking at him was assurance enough that if Mate survived schooling with this man he would die before he pooped out of place. Off Mate went, and off we went about our lives. I forgot about Mate completely, and so did Li. After a long stretch, I got around to asking her, "How is Mate doing?"

"Omigod! I forgot all about him." This is the dog she couldn't live without. The spit-shined Luftwaffe captain returned with a dog that bore no resemblance to the Mate I'd met. This dog was tall and skinny and old before his time. Given where he'd been for the last seven months, I found that understandable. There was nothing about his face that a mother could love, but Liza loved him all the more. The captain then told us that Mate needed to be walked at exactly 7:10, 11:25, 4:30, and finally at 10:15. "And you will never have any problems again."

Perfect, I thought. This will fit right in with Li's schedule. He then presented Li with a bill for four thousand dollars plus for Mate's newfound obedience, and after we saw the captain click his heels for the final time, the two of us laughed until we hurt.

That very night, just by coincidence, Judy was coming for dinner. Liza's brand-new apartment finally was furnished—beautifully, I might add. She had a swell brown-and-white geometric rug on the living room floor, a great leather couch rested on it, and silk drapes hung in pools on the polished floor. Liza was doing fettucine Alfredo for Judy and the other guests. Dinner was only the start of any evening that Judy and Liza spent together. For that matter it was only the start of any evening that either of them spent alone. Nights went on until the last club closed. I, gratefully, was not invited.

If there was one thing Liza knew about me, it was that I needed to get my eight hours of sleep during the night, not the day. Beyond that I was keen to separate my personal life from hers. We both wanted our privacy. Sometimes I wondered who picked up the checks when I, or some other agent, wasn't around. Not Judy, and not Liza. I've since learned that when there's a celebrity present, there's always someone, some star-struck proprietor or friend who feels blessed enough to be in the company of greatness, who picks up the tab. From the owner's standpoint, it's good business and cheap publicity, but I always thought being a scrounger sent the wrong message. Not all celebs are freeloaders, but Judy and Liza were.

So on the very first day of Mate's return, Liza, who was busy entertaining, missed the dog's 10:15 p.m. appointment with the sidewalks of New York. In a show of appreciation, Mate christened every new surface of the beautiful apartment. Fettucine Alfredo and poop could be found in places both high and low—Mate was, after all, a tall dog. This two-dollar dog with the four-thousand-dollar education in manners had subsequent chapters, but those would be lived out with the greengrocer around the corner.

CHAPTER NINETEEN

Flying Solo

Now that Judy was gone, representing Liza was not the only thing going on with me. I loved having my own apartment and being alone. I didn't need anyone. I was willing to pay my dues, earn my way, and make it all on my own. My mother was frightened for me. She had so wanted my marriage to be a success, but when I told her it was not, she didn't take me on as I'd imagined she would. She quietly supported me. When the time came, she even helped me to move. I knew she was heartbroken—I could see it in her face, her sad eyes—but she did not give voice to her sorrow. There was a little resignation, yes, but otherwise she looked ahead. I would one day, not too far in the future, come to understand that a substantial part of her sorrow was due to her lack of courage to do exactly what I was doing. She quietly bore her suffering. I would not. I knew I had other options. She never thought she did.

It was 1964, and I was ready to confront the world without anything or anyone to lean on. I had toughed it out alone as a child, and I thought I had survived Judy. My experience with her had given me the armor to face the world. I wore a shield that protected me from most kinds of human emotions. I was hardened to human suffering. In any situation with complications—whether in negotiations or human relations—I figured I could clean it up and move on as I had with Judy. I gave short shrift to people who wasted my time and had nothing to contribute. I thought I was a good judge of that. I was certainly judgmental—about everything and everybody.

I persuaded myself there was nothing I couldn't do. I decided that I couldn't be put in the same sentence as the downtrodden women Betty Friedan was talking about because I was so far ahead of the curve. I was not only out of the house and into the workplace, I was starting to tap-dance on top of the glass ceiling. Look, world, I made it to agent! No longer the all-purpose schlep, file clerk, gopher, and babysitter.

By late 1964 I was making fifty thousand a year, which was huge compared to my friends, but then they were all women in secretarial jobs. I didn't consider comparing my salary with those of the men in the office at that point (but that day was coming, and sooner than I would have thought). The office was growing in the number of clients being signed. My office was growing: It grew a window. My wardrobe was growing, and so were my confidence and pride. I was, for the moment, riding high, and cocksure no one could pull me down.

My job was expanding to cover all of television for the clients we represented. My immersion in this new medium started with Liza. I had gotten my foot in the door booking Li, who was salable after her success in *Best Foot Forward*. F&D recognized this and asked me to handle the comics. My bosses had taken on several new associates: real old-fashioned booking agents, good friends from the MCA days. With them came a number of bookable comedians: Milton Berle, Jack Carter, and Shelley Berman—big earners all—who played the same clubs that Liza could go into. (And I was always thinking of Liza, still my only client.) F&D promised the comedians movie stardom. Not a one of them seemed to enjoy what he did: Each one wanted Paul Newman's career. Well, that was understandable. All they had to do was earn it. Television was their point of departure, and it fell to me to find them good dramatic roles in which they could demonstrate their fine acting ability. While the movie stars looked down on TV, comedians reached up hoping to grab on to it. I was now mandated to make that happen.

I woke up every day bent on figuring out how I could get Shelley Berman on *Ben Casey* or *Dr. Kildare*. I spent my mornings cultivating TV producers and their aides, who were snide, snotty, crass, and boorish. I spent lunch treating one or another of them to a better meal than they had manners for in the King Cole Bar at the St. Regis or the elegant dining room at the Regency. (No dating prospects here. These were not guys you'd want to bring home to mother.) By three or four in the afternoon, one of the comedians was usually sitting on the edge of my desk asking, "So what have you done for me lately?" Selling wasn't easy. It went something like this:

The producer of a new television series is on the phone. He has called because he knows my office represents Paul Newman. He wants Paul to star in the first episode of his new show to help get his series launched. Of course I'd like to help him because down the road, if the series gets picked up, I can sell him lots of clients. He thinks his new series is better than *Gone With the Wind*. (I've already read the script. It's not even as good as *Godzilla*.)

Meanwhile, back at the ranch, I am clear that I absolutely must nail a deal for one of the comics to star in a series soon or we're going to lose him and his big income from nightclub dates. Can't allow that to happen. Not good for business, not good for the bottom line. The comic believes he *is* Paul Newman, or as good as. However, once the producer knows he can't get Paul, I must go forward pretending Shelley Berman is, in fact, every bit as good an actor, and I must persuade the producer to take a shot with him instead. The producer then bumps me over to one of the boorish underlings, and I set up the next lunch date.

Truth is, there was a good net result. The lunch tabs I picked up on Shelley Berman's behalf probably exceeded his salary for one appearance on the TV series *Rawhide*, but then Shelley was a wonderful actor as well as a nice man, and the meals at the St. Regis were worth every penny. Besides, Shelley Berman supporting Clint Eastwood was a feel-good piece of casting.

The new agents and I worked closely together. The more I helped secure TV for their clients, the more they helped me secure good club engagements for Liza. They knew their way around deals in these clubs. They got the best money. I was a fast learner. "One hand washes the other" never proved truer than when I booked TV. As a woman agent in TV, I was an anomaly at the time. It gave me an advantage. Being a woman made securing lunch dates easy, if for no other reason than the curiosity factor. A woman selling comics who picked up the tab at the best restaurants on the East Side! That was new and different. I didn't think of it that way at the time, in spite of the fact that everyone I took to lunch remarked on it.

And so, finally, F&D gave me a secretary and I ran the TV department in New York, the home of every important buyer in that fledgling industry. Clients from Freddie's new office in LA were referred to me because I was now in charge of finding jobs for any clients interested in this growing medium, the medium in the middle between live and film, the medium that was about to explode, putting a television into every home in America, the medium that would establish Li's career, and practically end Judy's.

In the end I was treated well by TV. All the comics worked on dramas, but none of them ever became movie stars, except Dean Martin and Jerry Lewis. Only they weren't ours.

CHAPTER TWENTY

Starring Liza

Liza's success on TV made her a star, and F&D had shown me by example how to capitalize on this. Get a press agent. I hired a wonderful publicist, Lois Smith—a giant of a woman in every way—whose competence and take-charge attitude relieved us of the need to worry about press. She milked the interest in Liza, and then I booked her until her feet hurt.

Li did things the comedians couldn't do. She danced and sang, and did it well, and since it was the heyday of television variety shows, I had a playground that was enormous. *Kraft Music Hall*, *The Hollywood Palace*, *Laugh-In*, *The Carol Burnett Show*—all immensely popular shows—kept calling her back for several appearances. I booked her on *The Ed Sullivan Show* eleven times. I campaigned tirelessly to get her into the Academy Awards show as a performer, and very early in her career, 1966, she sang the award-winning song, "What's New, Pussycat?"

These appearances furnished her entire apartment and then some. She now had discretionary money, and her exposure made her a star. Besides making her known in every household in America, her appearances brought her to the attention of Hollywood and also helped create an audience for her out on the road. We both got it right.

Wherever she worked, back then she put out 100 percent. She was gracious, always gave credit to others, and never complained. Producers loved her. Directors were clamoring. The press was hovering. She ceased being simply "the daughter of . . ."

For me her ever-increasing popularity was heady stuff. Three years into my career as a full-time agent, and I was fortunate enough to be working with a rising star with real talent: a triple threat whose singing, dancing, and acting meant she could work film, television, concerts, clubs, and the stage. My calls were all picked up.

While it was essential that everyone in showbiz know who she was, within "my" industry, both network and some studio executives were also starting to hear my name. I liked it; wanted more of it, and I had nothing but time to devote to our cause. Without either a husband or children to concern me, and no immediate interest in a social life, the open road loomed ahead, and there was no traffic jam in sight. I could drive at top speed. Work, and more work.

Judy, now aware of Liza's popularity, suddenly became interested in Liza's talent. It was an asset to her. Although she had featured Liza on one of her CBS shows, that was more a "mother" thing than an acknowledgment of Li's stardom. But once Judy's TV show was canceled, and with no new films on the horizon, Judy went off to her once-again new favorite place to live—London—whence not so long ago she had come.

While there, she announced a concert exploiting Liza's fame that Liza had not approved. As if that mattered. As Li's agent, I knew that the concert having been announced, Liza had to do it. Liza understood that, too. And luckily, where talent meets with adequate rehearsal, good things happen. The Palladium was a great triumph.

For Judy, her brilliance so long recognized, her audience so ador-
ing, it was just another triumph. For Liza it was the first ovation
of that size and length. The overwhelming demand for tickets led
to a second successful concert that gave Liza a big leg up in that
market. She handled herself magnificently, and I think I was as
proud as Judy. Although far from being motherly toward Liza, I
did have enough of a strong impulse to protect her professionally,
and I could do that without emotional involvement.

Judy also wanted to protect Liza, but I could see, clearly, that
there was a competitive thing going on. It carried an edginess,
wherein suggestions from Judy took on an acidic tone. Any suggestions I made—whether about wardrobe or songs—were always in Li's interest. Judy wanted everything done her way, and it
came out disguised as suggestions. Liza had good instincts, but
Judy always trusted her own more than anyone else's. However,
bottom line, Judy very generously did share the limelight with
Liza. Liza's stock shot up, and so did mine.

I dealt with many producers on Liza's behalf in the early and midsixties, some of them buffoons, some blusterers, but each in their
own way taught me something about show business. The network
and film company execs treated me like a princess because I represented stars. Even though Freddie or anyone else in the agency
might have signed them, the stars were still my clients. Lest you have
any doubt, there's a correlation in showbiz between the amount of
respect one gets and the size of the talent one is selling.

I became skilled at oiling my way around a decent deal. I learned
when to be bullish and when to walk away. I developed, as my experience increased, an instinct for how far I could press in a deal
without losing it or hurting the other side. Someone recently asked
me how one does that. My short answer: There is no formula. Every
deal is a case of original impression. No two deals are totally alike.

One can use a musical metaphor and play the buyers like a piano. Sometimes one treads softly, pianissimo. Occasionally one bangs all the notes with force and vigor. It's a judgment call. My salary was not going to change if I killed someone in a deal. The 10 percent commission to the agency might be a few bucks greater, but if you angered the buyer, causing him to flee forever, it wasn't a victory for anyone. You either have judgment or you don't. I have never enjoyed putting anyone's back against the wall for a few extra dollars (as David did). And I don't believe it makes for a happy working situation for the artist. There are many who would disagree with that. They need to squeeze the last dollar out. They are bloodsuckers, and I don't like them.

Sometimes one gets lucky. The first deal I ever made on Broadway, I made with one of the legends on that street, and he was a prince: Hal Prince. He is a wonderful producer, a great director, and a man of enormous integrity. Such words are thrown around a lot, but Hal is truly deserving of each one.

Hal was in his thirties and already very successful when he produced *Flora, the Red Menace*. In 1965 his partner, the late great George Abbott, both the writer and director of the musical, was approaching his eighties. They were a magnificent odd couple whose names were spoken in the hushed tones of reverence. They put Liza through the wringer, auditioning her four times—which saw both of us sitting around the office waiting to see if there would be yet another callback. She got the role, and although she was magical in it, *Flora* was a flop. Maybe that's why she didn't get the role in *Cabaret* that she ultimately made famous on film and won the Academy Award for.

In spite of its failure, Liza did pick up the Tony Award for *Flora*, and she did it wearing my beautiful black floral print gown with spaghetti straps. She might have afforded her own at that moment, but it was totally normal for her to borrow what I owned. We had walked into my closet and selected the one and only.

Interestingly, Liza's very first musical act was, for me, the most memorable. I clearly remember her taking me to a cold-water rail-road flat on the West Side of Manhattan. It was as low rent as you could get in midtown Manhattan. We entered a dark hall that brought the mood, if not the intense cold, of winter inside. At the end of this cheerless tunnel was a kitchen where the stove was the only heat in the room. A young man sat at an old upright piano playing show tunes in his own wonderful way. He could play anything, in any key, in any manner or mode one requested: jazz, ragtime, boogie, or "give me 'God Bless America' as Mozart would have composed it." His energy and excitement were infectious.

Sitting at the oilcloth-covered kitchen table absorbing the warmth emanating both from her immensely talented son and the cast-iron stove was Mama Hamlisch. Her sunshine smile told me how she doted on her Marvin. Liza, too, could never resist the opportunity to show off when she happened to be in the same room with a piano and someone who knew how to use it. And as I watched these two great entertainers duet Gershwin, classic Broadway, marvelous old movie music, all great tunes that I loved, I knew I was witnessing something spectacular. Both Marvin and Liza adored performing, and an audience of two was enough.

"Marvin and I are going to do an act together," Liza advised. I'd certainly seen enough of his talents to think it was possible. Liza also rounded up Fred Ebb and John Kander, who had been lyricist and composer on *Flora*, to do the grueling work of launching these youngsters. All of them were at the beginning of spectacular careers. Fred became her lifelong friend; he designed all her acts and wrote her wonderful "special" material. With this remarkable team in place, I went ahead and booked the dates.

What came out of this collaboration was the most original and charming nightclub act I'd ever seen. Liza had two backup dancers: one very tall and thin, the other very short and fat, equally talented and wonderfully nimble. The dancing threesome was pure fun. You couldn't forget the act once you'd seen it, and you'd never forget the West Coast opening night if you were lucky enough to have been there. It took place at the Cocoanut Grove in the old Ambassador Hotel. All of Hollywood society turned out that night to see what Judy's little girl could do. The Kirk Douglases, the Gregory Pecks, the Gene Kellys, George Cukor, Vincente Minnelli, and Judy herself all sitting front and center. Suffice it to say it was a superglamorous, A-list showbiz night.

Liza's act was not unlike Judy's in that both started with an overture. Of course all the songs in Judy's overture were well known and closely identified with her. Some were songs that became famous because of her. Not so in Liza's case.

At the end of Li's overture—again, as in Judy's show—there was a drumroll, following which a voice would boom out on mike from behind the curtain to announce the performer. I was standing backstage with an excited and nervous Liza, and I, too, was excited. When the overture was done, the drumroll started, right on cue, heightening the moment. Then the offstage announcement came from the wings opposite us: "And now, ladies and gentlemen, Miss Judy Garland!" The man on the mike had clearly been more nervous than we. What a horrible mistake! A great gasp rose up from the assembled biggies. I was speechless and had no idea what to do next. Not Liza. With consummate grace she took center stage and said, "That's an act I could never follow!" Then she turned to her conductor, Jack French, and asked, "Can we please start all over again?" Jack raised his baton as Liza walked back into the wings, and the music that followed was drowned out by the applause.

Had the moment been staged, it could not have worked better. The star-studded audience gave her a standing ovation that wouldn't quit. After the grace she had shown under fire, she could do no wrong. And she didn't. She was wonderful not only on that night but on all the nights that followed. She was turning into more than a merely good singer; she was becoming a great showman. She not only had all the right moves, she had a beautiful slim figure with curves in all the right places that made her moves look like classy choreography.

The stars in my dreamed-of firmament of clients were all movie stars. I was obsessive about my career and oblivious to the world outside, a world filled with political upheaval. The Vietnam War was raging at the end of the sixties, and entertainers of all stripes were making their political points of view known. I did not hear them. I was wrapped in a cocoon where I could see nothing but my own activities and how they impacted upon my immediate world. I would never have dreamed of going to Woodstock or embracing its message. I didn't understand what its message was. I mention it because my own limitations at the time strike me as ludicrous now. My interest was only in signing the young filmmaker Michael Wadleigh, who was undertaking the monumental task of documenting the rock festival at Max Yasgur's six-hundred-acre dairy farm. The film, I thought, might make some money.

CHAPTER TWENTY-ONE

What Is an Agent?

Not many people outside the entertainment industry or media really know what an agent is. I was one, and I can tell you: An agent is a fraud, but a fraud with good intentions. An agent is someone who believes his or her own bullshit and can convince others of its value. An agent is someone with a great gift of gab and the ability to sell with deep conviction, even if one doesn't believe in the value. (But then one can convince oneself the sale is worthy.) An agent is someone who comes up with good ideas and allows her clients to believe the idea was their brainstorm. An agent is someone totally willing to sublimate herself to be the person the client wants her to be. Do you want me to be angry on your behalf? Here I am. Do you want me to be docile for you? Here I am. But regardless of what role-playing takes place, an agent must always maintain integrity and never lead a client knowingly in the wrong direction. An agent is a chameleon. I was one. By the midsixties I became a person who was agile on her feet, could see a strong wind coming, tack in a different direction, and maintain integrity throughout the process.

"The business belongs in the hands of the people who sign the clients." Judy had left me with the feeling that if I survived her, there was nothing I couldn't do. Freddie now left me with the understanding that signing my own clients is what I needed to do. In 1963 he'd moved his family to California, where the pickings were lush, and had opened an elegantly decorated office in very expensive real estate, Beverly Hills. Having made such a great success with Judy, he was quickly the new kid on the block, something Hollywood is perennially interested in, on his way to becoming the hottest agent in lotus land, with a reputation for signing the hottest clients. We were now a full-service agency with new call letters—CMA, short for Creative Management Associates (surely a twist on the old familiar MCA)—and he was primed to take over the greatest of all West Coast company towns.

I missed his voice in New York more than he ever knew. He had always been so good, so patient, explaining everything to me. He was a fine teacher. Now I only heard that voice occasionally on the telephone, but it was always with the same message: Sign clients, sign clients—it became my mantra. I had the chutzpah to believe that if I did it well, I would one day become his partner. It might take a few years.

In 1964, after four years with the agency, I was made a vice president. At CMA the title didn't come with a raise, it came instead of one. But it brought with it a soupçon of prestige. And I was now the head of the theater department, which was nonexistent prior to my grand elevation. It was also a department that had no activity whatsoever. I was told to make it happen. I was supposed to invest myself fully in the workings of theater and find the clients who would support this unit. CMA did have one client, Henry Fonda, who was willing and eager to perform onstage. Every few years Hank was sent a play he wanted to do. He was an experienced professional. Told that I was the "go-to guy," he called and told me the deal he wanted. No sweat. I then made the deal, and he went to work in a comedy called *Generation* that was directed by Gene Saks and ran for three hundred performances, or one season. He was wonderful, compelling on stage. During the run we became professional friends (as in "not at all close") and every so often we met for supper in Sardi's. That was big-time for me. He was always given one of the celebrity tables near the front, which helped secure a little recognition for me in theater. His lovely wife, Shirlee, was sweet and anxious to please; Hank was mostly silent and mysterious, not at all easy to get close to. I picked up the conversation and filled in the pregnant pauses. Hank picked up the checks.

When he gave me my promotion, Freddie told me the following: "The day you can walk into Sardi's and have the occupants of at least fifteen tables talking about you will be the day you've arrived in theater."

"What will they be saying?" I innocently asked.

"At one table they'll be discussing your latest lover; at the second table they'll be whispering that you're a lesbian. At the third table they'll be saying that you've had a child out of wedlock." I got the message, but I didn't have round heels. Hell—I wasn't even ambidextrous.

And so I worked all day and pounded the pavements at night, always on the prowl for the next big someone. I was highly motivated to distinguish myself as head of a department in an agency that was fast assuming a large reputation. I signed the brilliant actor Stacy Keach and two actresses with talent and ambition who worked in both theater and film: Joan Hackett and Jill Haworth. Joan, who had been working steadily before meeting me, was at that moment more interested in film. Submitting her for good roles in movies put her into competition with many rising young stars, some of whom were immensely talented, and some who simply were rising off the casting couches in Hollywood. Joan was an actress with special qualities. I read every script my associates in California could get their hands on, knowing that if I could get her seen, or better yet get her screen tested, she would have a chance because of her wonderful voice and a certain quirkiness that separated her from the rest of the blond beauties. Joan and I became great pals. We spent wonderful times together socially as single gals running around New York, and in the process she introduced me to Robert Redford, who was then starring on Broadway in *Barefoot in the Park*. Everyone in the industry knew that he was the "next" leading man. He'd already done his interesting breakout films, scored in dramatic television, and was now a success on Broadway. Hollywood was beating a path to the door of this new golden boy. What a coup it would be to sign him! He was exactly what I needed for a big reputation.

I had to get on line with much bigger players like William Morris to grab Redford's attention, but I had this huge inside advantage: Joan. She was a good friend of his, and he liked her. It was impossible not to; her energy and enthusiasm for life were infectious. She was always tooting my horn, and putting Bob and me together at dinner. I remember being invited to one at the home of the actor Richard Mulligan, who got so angry that I was pursuing Redford instead of him that he threw me out in the street in the middle of the meal. Bob followed me out to the car, trying to make me feel better.

In my effort to sign him, I chased Bob all over the United States and part of Europe as well, popping up at some location wherever he was. I was shameless. I never came on to him, nor he to me, adhering to one of Freddie's ground rules, "Never fuck where you eat" (if only I had listened to him where Begelman was concerned). Bob and I had no interest like that in each other, but he liked being courted and he was a pretty good tease, always implying that someday things might just work out if things worked out. What the hell does that mean? He had more than a little mischief in him, but I was up for the challenge. But what could I do to sign Bob that would give me a better chance than the next guy? At that moment I could promise him nothing but my interest, which I said would be far greater than the next guy's. I pitched the FF approach: "We are the Tiffany of talent agents. We only take the best, and we leave the rest. We are not interested in many clients, only a few wonderful ones." And I made Bob understand I believed he was one of the few wonders in the world of showbiz worth having. I sold Freddie hard, since he was the new Hollywood whiz kid. That wasn't lost on Bob, who had his ear to the ground. Lois Smith was also Bob's press agent, and she had an insider's view of FFA's success. That helped. But I needed a big carrot to hold out to the boy wonder, and I had the good fortune to have it land in my lap in the not-too-distant future.

Like Judy, who was so much fun to talk to when she was in her best of all possible worlds, Bob was smart, witty, and political. I never felt as though I was wasting my time. I always learned something about the environment when we had serious conversations. We got along well. We laughed a lot together. With Joan's blessing, I started inviting Bob to dinner without her whenever I found myself in the same town as him. (No one accidentally finds herself in Provo Canyon, where he lived, but I made it seem as though that was an entirely normal stop on the way to California.) Sometimes I felt like I was running in place, but I knew if I stopped running, someone else would be at the finish line. But let me come back to Redford the golden boy. In 1965 Bob wasn't paying any part of my salary.

Meanwhile, I submitted Jill Haworth for the lead in *Cabaret* on Broadway, and she got the part and an equitable deal. She would have *paid* Hal Prince to play Sally Bowles. Remembered for her work in the successful film *Exodus*, Jill was beautiful, delicate, and had all the right vulnerability for the starring role. She was a delight to work with. Still, truth be told, her stage presence nowhere matched Liza's. The defenselessness that Li projected on the stage came from a place one could understand only if one knew Judy. *Really* knew her. Nonetheless *Cabaret* was a success with Jill, and I was pleased for her because she worked so hard. It was another Hal Prince show, one he also directed. Hal was now Broadway's most sought-after musical director, and he and I were cooking together. If he was doing a Broadway show, I always knew I'd get my clients seen and carefully regarded.

Some very funny/awful things—all theater related—happened to me, and I would feel as though I were cheating if I did not talk about them. First and foremost came my experience with Mary Martin. Without doubt, mighty Mary had been the toast of Broadway for a long, long time. One of her greatest gifts was that she didn't age. In her sixties, she still looked like Peter Pan. Her name on the marquee didn't guarantee praise from the critics, but it did guarantee an audience, except for the show that I was peripherally involved in for five horrendous minutes.

My misadventure involved Eddie Albert, a Freddie Fields client who lived on the West Coast. You may recall my having mentioned that Eddie was the one Frank Sinatra had pegged with the gibe "reliable." And indeed Eddie was a workmanlike, dependable, featured actor who preferred to see himself as a leading man. He was the only one, however, who did. One generally found him playing featured roles on the TV playhouses of the day like *The Alcoa Hour*, *The Philco Television Playhouse*, and *Studio One*. The best role he ever had was as the photographer in *Roman Holiday*, in which he costarred with Audrey Hepburn and Gregory Peck, and in which he had slightly more to do than come along for the ride.

Meanwhile, Mary Martin, who was not a client, was suffering in Boston in a turkey called *Jennie*. Richard Halliday, Mary's husband, and the producer, believed the fault for the failure could not possibly be his wife's. It must, therefore, be the fault of the leading man . . . an oft-heard excuse. Mr. Halliday discovered that CMA now represented Eddie, and he called me with an offer for Eddie to fly first class from Los Angeles to Boston by way of New York to see the show in the hope that Eddie would step in to replace Barry Nelson, who was ruining the show.

Eddie accepted the offer, flew first class, spent a night at the Regency, all at Halliday's expense, and then went with me to Boston, where we decamped at the Ritz-Carlton—by no means a lucky hotel for me. Eddie didn't like the show one bit and refused to go backstage after. "Don't worry, Eddie, I promise I will get you out of this," I pleaded. "But you simply cannot refuse to go backstage after these good people have laid out a lot of money for your trip!" I begged; I insisted. No go. Only the cliché fits here: My words fell on deaf ears. No way I could convince this not-so-great star of stage and screen to walk with me into the dressing room and be polite—or to be anything.

While Eddie could refuse to go backstage, I had no such choice. And when I told Mary Martin that Eddie was not going to appear, Richard Halliday took out a sharp knife and gutted me from head to toe. "How dare you show up here without your client?!" I apologized again and again. I told the Hallidays how hard I had tried to get Eddie to come with me while assiduously avoiding telling them how ghastly a show Eddie Albert thought he'd seen. But they knew. "And you presume to call yourself an agent? Get the hell out of here!"

I went out into the bitter-cold winter night. No cabs, no transportation of any kind, I walked back to the Ritz completely sobered by the near-zero temperature and what had just happened to me. Did I know what I was doing as an agent? I was shattered and felt I had deserved being cut into small pieces. Halliday was right. I should have been able to deliver Eddie. Back at the hotel, I salved my wounds, crawled under the covers, and let sleep take me.

The following morning I fastened down my manners, called Eddie and told him I was taking the 10:00 a.m. shuttle back to New York. He said he wanted to go with me. He asked me to pick him up in his room, and when I got there he asked me to help him with something he was having trouble with in the john. Stupid me! I walked in through the open door, and there lay Eddie soaking naked in the tub extending an invitation for me to join him. In answer to the question: Was there anything worse than being cut into small pieces by Mary Martin and her husband? Yes, definitely! Having to see this ugly jerk lying naked in a bathtub! Would that I could have put my high heel on his flabby chest and let the hot water run. Frank Sinatra got it all wrong. Eddie Albert was not only unreliable; he was a prick!

And then there was Al Pacino. . . .

It was David Begelman in New York who got the early scoop on Al Pacino's brilliant performance in *The Indian Wants the Bronx*, an Israel Horovitz drama playing at a little off-Broadway theater way downtown. David suggested (more like demanded) that I sign him. By 1968 I had a wonderful associate named Sue Mengers, who had the balls of a blind burglar. Signing Al was going to be catnip for Susie and me. Together we were the slick sisters. David knew he could count on us to "wrap Al up." We went right down to the Astor Place Theater in SoHo, sat with Al after the performance, and told him how we would make him a star. Lines like "Al, you can do anything you want. You're that good" or "Al, is there anything you can't do?" always worked. An actor's ego is generally way too large to be defined by a single adjective.

Although he said nothing, it was clear that Al shared our conviction about his talent. And we truly thought he was good. He was as convincing in that play as anyone I'd ever watched onstage. But while signing contracts with Al was easy, talking to him turned out to be hard.

He came to the office for the "official" first meeting, whose headline should read: What do you want to do with the rest of your life? Every client endures this boring welcome to an agency, and for this presentation to our newer, elegant Madison Avenue offices, Al dressed himself as a homeless dirty schlump. We discovered quickly that this was no costume. This was Al, and he may have been wearing the only clothes he owned.

But if he looked awful, he sounded worse. In the many years that have transpired since I first met him, I trust he's developed more social skills. Way back then he was a grunter. "*Unh*," was his first answer to most questions, and while onstage he projected so forcefully, now I had to lean over my desk to hear what he was saying. I finally got it clear, however, that he was interested in doing a musical. There is for sure a reason why his career has thrived without his ever having appeared on the musical stage. Here it is:

Hal Prince was casting *Zorba*, a musical about the friendship between a Greek man and a young American. Given the play takes place in a Greek village, Sue and I thought there might be something in it for Al. He was, after all, dark and swarthy; he could as easily pass for Greek as Italian. Using my good professional relationship with Hal Prince to set up an audition for Al with a creative team that included Fred Ebb and John Kander, I advised Al that he should come to the theater prepared to sing.

On the appointed day Sue and I went to the Mark Hellinger, a huge Broadway house, to watch our budding star. All the appointments were set at fifteen-minute intervals, and at 10:45 it was Al's turn. The stage manager came from the wings and announced him: "Mr. Pacino at 10:45." Al shuffled out. He had his own special way of walking (hopefully that, too, has changed). He stood there for a moment in the key light while Hal Prince sized him up. "What are you going to sing for us?" Hal asked.

"'Luck Be a Lady Tonight,'" answered Al. At least he could be heard in the back, where Sue and I were sitting.

"Did you bring your music?" Hal asked.

"*Unh* . . ."

"Why don't you speak with the accompanist," Hal suggested. Al then schlumped upstage to the piano to talk with a man who could do anything asked of him. (Theater accompanists are an amazing lot. They can play anything you request in any tempo and in every key.) So Al and this accompanist chatted for about a minute, and then Al schlumped back downstage and again found his key light. We heard the intro. *Dada-da-da-da-da*, and Al started to sing. On key! Sue and I thought that was very hopeful. Here's what Al sang: "Luck be a lady tonight . . . Luck be a lady tonight . . . Luck be a lady tonight . . . Luck be a lady tonight . . . Luck be a lady tonight . . . Luck be a lady tonight." The lyrics had moved on, but Al had not. After the sixth repeat, we heard some pronounced slow claps coming from the seventh row, where Hal and his group were seated. This was not applause. "Do you know any other lyrics, Mr. Pacino?" Hal asked.

"*Unh* . . ." Al turned around and walked back upstage to chat again with the accompanist. A minute went by before Al returned to his key light. Again we heard *Dada-da-da-da-da*! And Al started singing. Here's what he sang: "Luck be a lady tonight . . . Luck be a lady tonight . . . Luck be a lady tonight . . . Luck be a lady tonight . . . Luck be a lady tonight . . . Luck . . ." The stage manager was now coming out with "the hook," in this case a heavy right arm with which he "escorted" Al off the stage and hustled him out the stage door.

Hal, meantime, was heading directly toward Sue and me. We had not only not been able to maintain our composure, we were just about on the floor. We were laughing so hard we'd nearly peed our pants. Hal walking up the aisle toward us did nothing to quell this. We couldn't stop laughing. "Is this some kind of a joke?" Hal asked me. Unable to keep a straight face, I couldn't even answer this wonderful producer-director for whom I had ultimate respect and admiration. "Don't bother to submit anyone to me ever again," he said, turning to head back to his seat. That was the end of my professional relationship with the great Hal Prince for at least a while. (Nor did it serve Susie well, who was about to follow me into the role as head of the theater department.)

Once we were outside, the fresh air sobered us a little, but only a little. Susie and I were still laughing but trying hard not to because we had to face Al, who was waiting by the stage door with a questioning look on his face. Al didn't have a clue. Without understanding why we were laughing, Al innocently asked: "So how do you think I did?" Sue and I collapsed in hysteria again. Finally I calmed down enough to be able to ask: "Al, honey, what were you *thinking*?" Al looked perplexed; Susie and I couldn't stand up straight. At last I said, "Al, I don't think a musical is your thing."

As it turned out, every other thing in theater and film did become his. He *made* it his. I had the pleasure of proposing him to Francis Ford Coppola's company for *The Godfather*, but that was little more than wanting to hear the sound of my own voice. Coppola knew Al's work from having seen him in a short-lived Broadway show called *Does a Tiger Wear a Necktie?* in which Al's standout performance gained him the Tony Award for best featured actor. Coppola wanted Al before I had opened my mouth. He wanted only Al for the role of Michael Corleone from the get-go.

There are reasons that great directors are great directors, and in my opinion casting is 50 percent of it. Coppola also fought for Al. He got heavy resistance from Paramount—who could not have been less interested—but Francis was willing to do battle. It was an uphill fight, and Coppola hung in and finally won when the suits looked at a piece of Al's brilliant work in *The Panic in Needle Park*. I had an opportunity to see something really special, when at a small film studio on the West Side of Manhattan, I saw Coppola screen-test Al four times in one afternoon. Each time the director asked for a different portrayal, and each time Al delivered what Coppola asked for. He was an actor of infinite variety and original talent. It was amazing to watch him go through his paces. I eventually lost Al as a client, having to do with a dustup with his manager. I will come to that later.

CHAPTER TWENTY-TWO

Moving On

Liza was thriving. Albert Finney, whom I hadn't met before he cast her in *Charlie Bubbles*, was the first to recognize and beautifully capture the wide-eyed waif on the big screen in 1967, and I thought she was brilliant. She was Oscar-nominated for her screen performance in *The Sterile Cuckoo* in 1969 and, as far as I was concerned, also deserved a nomination for her fine work in *Tell Me That You Love Me, Junie Moon* the following year. It was thrilling for me to see and understand that great directors like Alan Pakula and Otto Preminger wanted to work with her. They saw a special quality in her demeanor, notably her vulnerability.

I submitted her for roles in many films, and while she could definitely play a "love interest," she wasn't exactly your off-the-shelf ingenue. She fell out of the category of ordinary women's roles. Character leads were better for her, and they were often found in material that was not formulaic or predictable, but that's not always what arrived on my desk. It had to be a selective process. I was forever trying to get my hands on scripts chosen by the top directors to find the kind of role that would exploit Li's special qualities. Hollywood stardom was never going to work if she showed up in schlock.

With Liza now married to Peter, things started to shift perceptibly. Li and I grew apart personally. It was understandable. She had a husband and her own life, and that was a great thing. When her personal life interfered with her professional life, I stepped in, trying to be the mailed fist in the velvet glove. But it didn't work. "You've got to stop singing for free," I told her. "Barbra Streisand called me from out of the blue to complain that you sang "Happy Days" (one of Barbra's signature songs) in some nightclub. I don't recall booking you there!" (I'd never even heard of the place.) I might as well have been speaking to a wall for all the good it did. Li was anxious to help Peter launch his career. They often ran around to late-night clubs where they could perform together or where she could introduce him. "How can I get you paid for your work if you give it away?" I protested.

Many years later, when I met Hugh Jackman backstage while he was appearing as Peter Allen in *The Boy from Oz*, I told him that Peter had been a thorn in my side for exactly the reasons just mentioned. Peter, as we all know, went on to a glorious career both as a songwriter and entertainer until his untimely death from AIDS. His songs were made popular by many recording artists, including Melissa Manchester and Olivia Newton-John, with one, "Arthur's Theme," winning an Academy Award in 1981. I had a greater appreciation for him once he was out of Liza's immediate life.

I was learning that representing big talent allows you to be wherever you want. It wasn't necessary—as some insisted—to be in Hollywood. If I signed Redford, the golden boy, no one would care where my desk was. I finally got Bob into a meeting with F&D, and they dazzled him with their soft-shoe routine, talking about prospects and fabulous deals that would stir delight in the heart of any actor. Freddie was starting to discuss putting together the pieces for a company that would be called First Artists, whose mandate was to make it easy for artists to maintain creative control of properties they cared about. It was outside-the-box thinking. He would form a production company of stars mighty enough to persuade studio execs to financially support the artist's creative film instincts. The company would be in the control of the artists. What artist wouldn't be interested in that? Redford was listening.

Meanwhile, Liza continued earning big money and getting great reviews for everything she did. Important film scripts were coming to my desk. Important directors now called me about her, instead of the other way around, and my bottom line was profitable enough for me to insist that Freddie and David give me a crack at the film business even though I lived in New York and had no intention of ever living in Los Angeles. I wanted to raise my kids in New York City. I wanted them to use public transportation. I wanted them to have all this city's cultural opportunities and appreciate its cultural diversity. I love New York! It has always been the center of the world to me.

Film, however, was totally a male-dominated business in the sixties. The well-respected "literary ladies" who were known to have sold important books and plays sat quietly in New York, at home reading or behind closed doors in offices with lots of fresh flowers and potted plants. But they didn't do the actual Hollywood deal making. It was assumed in Hollywood that the only thing women knew how to do was to read and discover talent; negotiating deals remained a man's province.

One of the great literary ladies, Kay Brown, found *Gone With the Wind* for David O. Selznick, but she did not have the privilege of setting up the film deal with MGM. Another great agent, Audrey Wood, represented Tennessee Williams, many of whose wonderful plays were adapted for film. Miss Wood interested producers in these properties, and that's a huge part of it, but the guys in LA did the deal. Had I shown some predilection for the purely literary side of the business, I think Freddie and David would have been pleased. No one in the agency had yet filled that niche. The guys figured I would be a natural fit because of the Misses Brown and Wood who preceded me at MCA, but I was never going to be one of the hat-wearing literary ladies; I don't look good in hats, and I always wanted to go where the men went. I was sure I could. I didn't want to relinquish the care and feeding of my clients to the big boys. Oh no!

Having now been at CMA for eight years, I could look back over the many deals I'd made and know I had become a negotiator. Watching David, I understood that forcing the concessions necessary to close a deal was always his idea, but he was clever enough to make someone else believe it was theirs. One couldn't watch David oil his way around a deal without something rubbing off.

I lobbied my two obdurate bosses about my need and ability to deal in the front offices of Hollywood, and discovered I could plead as much as I wanted but nothing would change. I got angry and dug in my heels. I was going to make a start or else. Or else what? Would I leave? And then providence reared its head, and I received an invitation for lunch with an agent at William Morris. I did not tell F&D, and I did not go to lunch. However, word always has found a way of getting around fast in showbiz even without texting. Maybe F&D felt a little threatened. Thank goodness they decided they couldn't afford to lose me. If working in films was what it would take to keep me quiet and somewhat satisfied, they would open the door for me just a crack. But first they had to replace me in theater.

Enter Sue Mengers. Sue—a brilliant schmoozer, client signer, and irreverently funny woman—was the doyenne of the Sardi's set, hanging out at the "look-at-me" tables night after night with the composer Jerry Herman and many of the other leading lights of Broadway. She was an attractive world-class flirt, an overweight blond with a potty mouth and campy style that attracted every gay director and wannabe star on the Great White Way. Her antics, which included putting out the garbage naked (I wasn't there) and constantly lifting her skirt in public places to adjust her stockings (I was there), dominated her devotees' conversations, which made her the affectionate butt of their jokes.

She'd spent several years eking out a living at a small agency, selling respected stage actors, and doing it well. She was hired to replace me as head of theater, allowing me, finally, to concentrate on films, provided, of course, that either Freddie or David could then deal for my clients once they got the job. She was every bit as ambitious as I, and she, too, had wonderful clients to pitch, including Tony Perkins and Julie Harris (both big Broadway stars at the time) and eventually Barbra Streisand (who, while not signed by Sue, became a great pal of hers).

Although she and I were an unlikely pair—she playing cute, the seductress hiding her smarts; me eager to be the businesslike "brains"—we became good friends. The showbiz set in New York, having nothing better to talk about, bet that we would kill each other; but they lost their bets big-time. Sue and I were the winners. She made me laugh; in return I helped her with deals, and we schemed together as often as time allowed.

The film department in New York was headed up by a jolly man's man named Harvey Orkin, whom Begelman adored. He had lots of friends in the industry (which counts for something), but no muscle and no major clients of his own. His very existence irked Sue and me. We agreed he had to go down. I wanted the chair Harvey was sitting in, and both Sue and I wanted his salary (we both speculated figures for Orkin that were no more than figments of our imagination). I knew full well that the day I brought in signed contracts with Redford it would be over for Harvey.

And along came *Butch Cassidy and the Sundance Kid*, written by the hot screenwriter William Goldman, with the very hot director George Roy Hill at the helm and Paul Newman already cast as one of the leads. After almost four years of chasing him, I'd gotten a promise from Bob that if I delivered the role opposite Newman, he would be mine.

Redford needed only the right role to launch him into superstardom. I would be sitting in the catbird seat if I could deliver the movie. There was one little hang-up. Twentieth Century–Fox didn't want Bob. It wasn't a matter of disliking him, he was simply far from their first choice. They had a laundry list of stars they wanted more.

CMA, however, represented George, who shared my Redford obsession. Besides that, George was a little sweet on me and couldn't do a thing about it because he was both married and a nonpracticing Catholic still full of Catholic guilt. He could, however, hang out in my office for hours at a time, for days on end, conniving with me on how we could get Bob the role.

The studio's original intention was to put Newman and Steve McQueen on the screen together, which is why the studio was willing to pay then unheard-of price of four hundred thousand dollars for the script. But McQueen left after a dispute over billing. One down. Next the role of Sundance was offered to Jack Lemmon, whose production company, JML, had produced the 1967 film *Cool Hand Luke* starring Paul. George Hill didn't like this casting, and I pumped him up to call Darryl F. Zanuck and protest. This turned out to be unnecessary because Lemmon did not like riding horses, and he also felt he had already played too many aspects of the Sundance Kid's character before. Two down.

Warren Beatty was next on the list and was considered for five minutes, but getting Warren to say yes to anything took too much time, and given that a start date was already set, George was able to persuade Twentieth to move on. Three down.

Finally came Marlon Brando, whom George admired but really felt was wrong for the role. That was the hardest battle, and whenever George wobbled even slightly, I was there to urge him on. More than that! There were days when George was exhausted from the battle with Twentieth. I knew that whatever I had on my calendar would be canceled so that George and I could have one of our long, leisurely lunches together needed to fire up his enthusiasm again to the 100 percent level. I did it time and again, and it was worth every penny. Besides that, I adored George. Had he made the pass, I would have undressed on the spot. (I never found Redford sexy except on the screen; George was another thing all together.)

That he never once relented in his insistence that Redford play the part in the end got Redford the role. Meanwhile, I kept Bob clued in by phone, and, after months of machinations, when Redford was finally hired, I got my signed agency contracts. Bob later acknowledged that this film catapulted him to stardom and irreversibly changed his career.

When I delivered Redford's signature, my stock at the agency shot up sky high. F&D were ecstatic. I'd landed a client with legs, and not just the pretty kind. Talented new actresses show up every year; most hang around for a few films if they're lucky, and then they're gone. It takes only a new slate of pictures for producers to cry out, Let's find a new girl! But sign an actor who has both good looks and real ability, and you've managed a minor miracle. That actor can go on for forty years easily—as Newman did, as Redford has.

And now it was time to join the battle. Why should any of the men—Harvey Orkin in New York or Dick Shepherd, John Foreman, Alan Ladd, Jr., Mike Medavoy and Jeff Berg in LA—be paid

more than Sue and me? It was our clients—Redford, Pacino, Minnelli, Streisand—who were on top of every good director's list. I felt
as though I'd now earned the right to be the head of motion pictures
in New York, and Sue simply could no longer deal with Harvey
earning one penny more than she. So the two of us—both capable
of incredible mischief—staged an office coup. We hunkered down
in my office, locked the door, and set about changing the way our
world worked. Let me be abundantly clear about one thing: We were
not doing this in order to get on the women's rights bandwagon.
That wagon had already taken off and was gathering speed. We
never gave it a thought, although perhaps its existence helped fire
up our confidence. Truth is we locked my door that day primarily to
take care of ourselves.

Using the phones at my desk, we called the heads of every single
studio, men whose names were mentioned in hushed whispers like
Frank Wells, Richard Zanuck, David Brown, and Robert Evans,
with whom Sue later became close after signing Ali MacGraw. We
blindsided their secretaries with our name-dropping, and once we
got their bosses on the phone, we put them on notice. Deal with
us—and not Freddie and David—or forget about our clients.
Honestly, I don't know what recourse to action I would have had if
Zanuck called Freddie thereafter instead of me. But he didn't. He
didn't want to find out what would happen any more than I did.

Sue was funny. Typical of her wit was the conversation she had
that day in my office with Lenny Lightstone, right-hand man to
Joseph E. Levine, the clothier who founded Embassy Pictures and
had become one of Hollywood's most colorful characters. We
reached them together just by luck. Sue flirted with Lenny recklessly.
She had a little-girl way of making shocking statements sound cute.
"Lenny, I just love the way you talk dirty about movies. Let's talk
about movies together. Talk dirty to me!" What did she just say?

I could never. She made Lenny and Joe laugh while I made it clear that if they wanted our clients, they would have to deal directly and exclusively with us.

F&D of course found out what we were doing. How? We told them once all the calls were made. I remember David slamming his fist on the table (I had never seen that before). Freddie simply shook his head and said, "You shouldn't have done that." And then, remarkably, the conversation shifted in the opposite direction—pouring oil on the fire. Freddie: "You know that we always take care of you. . . ." David: "You two are the best. . . ." Uh-huh. Show us the money.

They were aggravated, to be sure, but what could they really do? We had them by the short hairs. It was Freddie who had said, "He who has the clients calls the shots," I reminded him. Change the "he" to "she." Susie and I were calling a lot of the shots now, but only about our clients, not the ones who belonged to any other agent in New York or LA.

Once we launched our campaign, we never looked back. We wouldn't let Freddie and David talk for us anymore, and they could do nothing more than grin and bear it. We had become too valuable. They couldn't afford to lose us. In 1968 I became a senior vice president and head of film in New York, and poor Harvey was kicked upstairs, which was the same as being kicked around. Sue was vice president and head of theater, which was highly successful and earned her a lot of money—more than Harvey—but not ever as much as she thought she deserved. Whatever!

I believe our persistence opened the floodgates for those women who became important film agents following us. I raise my hand and say that we were there first. I don't mind us taking that credit. While I was doing these things completely out of self-interest, I finally became aware of the repercussions my actions were having in the industry. By the end of the sixties the women's movement was in full swing, and sisterhood was in the forefront of our minds.

Sue never stopped making me laugh. "I think I'll sleep with Redford tonight!" Since all two hundred-plus pounds of her had bedded some of the top names in Tinseltown (I refuse to tell who), I worried as I laughed at her teasing. I didn't need her messing in my backyard, but then I knew Redford had the cold reserve of an infantry sergeant. It was unlikely she would get near Bob's zippers. Who knows? She may have tried. But then one day she told me he had too many moles on his face, and I understood immediately that she had gotten nowhere with him.

She was a card-carrying member of the gay theater mafia, and accordingly was invited everywhere the Broadway gays went. With her outrageous irreverent wit, she kept gay men in stitches, endlessly demeaning everyone on the straight side of the fence.

My favorite story starts with Jerry Herman, at that time the hottest composer on Broadway, who had a wonderful house in The Pines, the gay community on Fire Island. It was the only house there with a swimming pool, and Sue could be found there regularly on summer weekends lolling naked in the water. None of the guys were offended. They didn't care; they loved having her around. Oh, but it must have been a sight to behold! Humor by the pound; everything added to her vitriolic charm.

One day Melina Mercouri and Jules Dassin, then the toast of Broadway, showed up at the empty house and came out to the pool looking for Jerry or any other sign of life. Sue was the only living, breathing person around, and there wasn't a towel anywhere in sight. Without taking so much as a beat, she climbed out of the pool, wringing wet, her rolls of fat jiggling aplenty with each step as she ran up to the stellar couple. How I would have loved to see their faces as Sue made her approach. Grabbing Jules's hand and then Melina's, she gave each a vigorous pumping handshake and said, "Oh, Miss Mercouri, Mr. Dassin—I'm such an enormous fan. Allow me to introduce myself. My name is Stevie Phillips."

Sue told this story to *Vanity Fair*, and it appeared there first in a Sue Mengers puff piece. Sue loved the press. I used to walk into her office and find her on the phone with gossip columnists all the time. I was horrified. I thought press was for the clients, but she was forever burnishing her image and trying to get her name in the papers. She was a publicity hound, and I was naive. I never imagined having my name splattered all over would help me sign anyone, and when there was a photographer present—and there were plenty when I accompanied my clients to an event like a premiere—I moved out of the picture. Sue, on the other hand, moved in. It was the right decision for her, and it served her well.

Sue moved on to California in the late sixties, where for many years she triumphantly dominated the social scene in the film business. She was a brilliant hostess, and I doubt that many turned down her invitations lest they become the butt of her jokes. She wanted me to come to one of her dinners, and she invited Billy Wilder as my dinner partner. I was beyond flattered, and I had a good time. It was great bitchy fun. But I didn't need to go again (and who knows if another invitation would have been forthcoming). It wasn't for me. The dinner felt a little desperate, and after what I'd been through with Judy, mean was simply mean.

I did have lunch with Sue a few times at the house, of course (Sue didn't go out). I was thrilled that she used the Wedgwood I'd given her as a wedding gift. She said she loved it, and that made me very happy. Jean-Claude never joined us. It was not a loving household.

I was also asked to move to Los Angeles. Freddie approached me early, and David did so later on, but the longer I remained an agent, the less LA interested me. To me Los Angeles was a place where you looked in the mirror and no longer saw yourself; you saw what others were saying about how you looked, how you dealt, whom you were sleeping with, what you earned. Life in a fishbowl! It reminded me of the Sardi's plan, the plan that Freddie had encouraged me to follow when I first went to work in theater, and it had made some sense then. But as I got older, I discovered that the Sardi's plan was no longer my style, and Los Angeles was too easy a place to lose oneself in. I didn't want to dine out on the business at every meal. I didn't want to walk into the greengrocer and meet actresses I represented, or those I didn't. I didn't want to feel bad about parties I wasn't invited to, or attend the parties where I was asked and didn't want to attend. None of it was to my liking, so in spite of the fact that I thought it might be helpful to my career, in spite of believing that life on the West Coast was gracious and beautiful, I never gave it serious consideration. I was flattered when Columbia Pictures put out a feeler to me. I may have been the first woman they considered for studio head of production. It was not for me.

I was thrilled that Sue was a star in Southern California. She enjoyed her reputation. She got everything she wanted—except from Freddie Fields. When he sold the agency in 1975, she felt she deserved a big cut. Living in California, she'd persuaded herself it was she who built the agency, and there were enough yes-men around to feed her ego. Freddie gave her nothing from the sale. And I did not get a penny, but I was making $250,000 a year by then, and had been for a while. I was satisfied I'd been treated well, and had no complaints. Sue resented Freddie, and he knew it, for she complained bitterly to anyone who would listen. She was angry and unhappy, but then she was that all the time. Her wonderful wit came from a place of vitriol.

In the end she became by far a more famous agent than I, deserving her remarkable reputation. She had worked hard to develop a high profile. I didn't want that and found a way to continue signing important clients like David Bowie and Cat Stevens without it. Privacy has always been important to me. When I think of her, and I do very often, I remember a brilliant schmoozer and a fond friend.

There is a sad postscript to the Susie (I called her that) chapter in my life. After an unsuccessful stint at William Morris, where Sue was unable to meet expectations, she was forced into retirement—that is to say, she was fired. It was early in the nineties, and we had spoken only sporadically over the years. One day she called me and said, "Sue is depressed. What should I do, Stevie?" I did not hesitate: "Stop smoking those awful Gauloises and get the fuck out of bed." Sue loved to sit in the middle of her bed all day talking on the phone and smoking pot or those short, fat, foul-smelling French cigarettes. "Help me," she begged. "I need help." So I did some research and found her a trainer. Personal trainers were just coming into vogue, and I looked all over LA (on the phone) to find one tough little girl with enough strength to withstand Sue's mouth.

When I finally located someone I thought had the perfect personality, I sent her to Sue's front door with instructions: "See if you can get her to walk around the house. After a week, see if you can get her to walk around the block. Then drive her down to the beach and have her walk there. She hasn't smelled fresh air in years. Price is no object," I assured her. The trainer called me to say Sue fired her after only two days. I never heard from Sue after that.

CHAPTER TWENTY-THREE

Crazy

Freddie signed Peter Sellers, the great comic actor, at the peak of Peter's career in the early sixties. He was just about to start a film with George Roy Hill, *The World of Henry Orient*, which was to shoot mostly at the Astoria Studios in Queens. At Freddie's suggestion Peter phoned and asked me to locate a sizable estate he could rent on Long Island within reasonable traveling distance to the studios. Although we had never been introduced, Peter moved right past that and dealt with me as if we had been friends for years. Everything was "darling" this and "darling" that. He advised that he was intending to bring his family: two children, their nanny, his valet, and some pets. He required an "extremely gracious home." A swimming pool was a must; tennis courts optional.

I found the perfect place in Sands Point, and at the appointed time Peter and his troupe moved in. They were thrilled with the house and its lovely grounds, and for at least two problem-free summer months they enjoyed it.

Then, early one morning around three a.m., Peter rocked me out of deep sleep (why do stars always feel it's necessary to call at ungodly hours?) to tell me that the house had poltergeists. I didn't have the slightest idea what a poltergeist was. Steven Spielberg had not yet popularized the word, and no need for it had entered into my experience. "Uh-huh" I said. (David Begelman had taught me this all-purpose response long before. He said it could be used with many intonations and various voices. It could sound concerned, acquiescent; it didn't have to sound stupid.) "Disembodied feet are walking up and down the stairs, Stevie darling. Pictures are changing places on the walls. My man Bert is sitting right next to me, and he can attest to all of this." Peter then must have pushed the phone into Bert's face.

"It's terrible," Bert said. "Isn't it, Peter?"

"Terrible, yes," and Peter pressed on.

"Windows are going up and down by themselves." I then heard windows slamming shut. By this point the poltergeists and their talents were all too clear. "Uh-huh," I responded again, waiting to hear what my marching orders would be.

"By noontime I would like to be ensconced ["ensconced"?!] in the interlocking suites in the penthouse of the Regency Hotel. I mean *all* the suites in the Regency penthouse. You know the place, don't you? On Park Avenue." I got lucky. We often used the Regency for clients in from LA, and I had struck up a professional friendship with the hotel's wonderful manager, a lovely Englishwoman, Mary Homi. I even had her home telephone.

"By noon and not a moment later!"

"Certainly, Peter." Notwithstanding that stars feel just fine about phoning at outrageous hours, propriety dictated that I wait until at least 7:00 a.m. before making the call to Mary. I caught her on her way out the door.

The English are all so stiff-upper-lipped that they don't react with shock and awe to anything. Tell an American hotel manager that you wish to dislodge his or her clientele, and I reckon that if they don't hang up on you their reactions are bound to be more aggressive or even slightly more animated than Mary's was. "How do you think we can go about getting rid of our clientele?" she calmly asked me. "The penthouse is rather fully booked." Her tone was as cheery as her "Good morning, Stevie."

"Make them an offer they can't refuse."

"How much are you willing to spend?"

"Money is no object." We discussed her picking up the evacuees' entire tabs in order for them to accommodate Peter. "Bribe them," I said. "Whatever it takes!" for that's what Peter had told me. "I don't need to know. Just present the bill to Mr. Sellers when he leaves the hotel, and that will be that." I knew that Peter had an accountant-manager type who could be difficult. He would probably give Freddie Fields a heart attack over this one, but not my problem. Besides, the hotel cost would turn out to be the least of the expenses.

What I did not know on the night of the poltergeists was that it was Peter's first night back from a weekend in Miami, where he had gone to judge the Miss Universe contest. While there he had fallen under the spell of all the beautiful blond misses from Scandinavia, and had invited Miss Denmark, Miss Sweden, Miss Norway, and Miss Finland to return with him to New York for a wonderful time. (Indeed, the only thing that had been wrong with the house in Sands Point is that it had not come with sexy blond housemaids.) The voluptuous Scandinavians had all accepted Peter's invite, and by noon that day they were all comfy in the Regency penthouses, ready to enjoy a wonderful week of partying with Peter in glorious NYC.

Sadly all good things must come to an end, but I can only imagine each of the women rejoicing, for as Peter kissed each statuesque blond beauty good-bye she was presented with a large ruby ring encircled by diamonds. Harry Winston, the exclusive Fifth Avenue jeweler, rolled out a red carpet for me when he heard what Peter had ordered me to select for him. Each ruby the size of a dime, and the circlet of ten diamonds looked to be a half carat each. My popularity at the jewelry store didn't net me more than a thank-you, which is more than I got from Peter.

Peter eventually married the Scandinavian of his choice. Britt Ekland was as sweet as she was beautiful. Without any real estate help from me, the newlyweds found one of the swankiest flats in all of London and decorated it with the most exquisite furniture, occasional antiques, and the finest objects that money could buy. Peter was a rich man, and Britt had superb taste. One night in a fit of pique, or in the pique of passion, all their objects, including the artwork, became weapons. There was an epic fight in which lamps were smashed, tables thrown: assault by antiques—not exactly weapons of mass destruction. However, the destruction to their apartment was massive; not a whole lot could be salvaged, including Peter's reputation as a sane man.

I signed David Bowie hot off the *Ziggy Stardust* album (*The Rise and Fall of Ziggy Stardust and the Spiders from Mars*). I'd been campaigning to get music clients in London, but I had never met Bowie's manager, Tony DeFries. He called me out of the blue. Bowie was a rising star in the early seventies—unique, hot, and everyone producing concerts wanted his first American tour.

Bowie not only dominated the music scene when he arrived here, he totally changed it. Who was this person in these strange outfits with these off-the-wall lyrics? He created a new world, a whole universe of his own. I thought he was amazing. The manager was pretty amazing as well; a Bond Street guy in a Lower East Side world, a cool cat with shoulder-length hair as wide as it was long, not one inch of which went with his three-piece Savile Row suits and his conversations about arbitrage.

My understanding with DeFries was that I would try hard to get David work in the film arena, and in return we would book his first American tour. It was a coup. Bowie's upcoming tour was making entertainment headline news. It also made the head of the music department of the now-very-large CMA extremely happy because it would make his department very profitable for an entire calendar year.

Back in the day (and maybe it's still true today), when an important client had a personal manager, an agent mostly spoke to the manager; however, I knew that having a separate but equal relationship with the client was a good thing because of the volatility of stars. Anyone can be in one day, out the next. It felt, however, quite impossible to befriend David because I was far from being a part of his scene. I never became a groupie, never did strange piercings or body paintings, and never hung out backstage. My one real meeting with David was the day he personally delivered the representation contract to me at my apartment. We had "tea and sympathy" and precious little conversation. In the half hour we spent together he impressed me with his sweetness and his intelligence. Well traveled and aware of the political scene, he seemed to be a man of the world at a very tender age. He was soft-spoken and exceedingly kind and polite. That was the real meeting. The next was unreal.

While I was talking up Bowie to anyone in Hollywood who would listen, CMA's music department went to work to produce an eye-popping tour, breaking lots of ground by creating new perks and precedents the likes of which promoters hate agents for. The tour made geographic sense, financial sense, and all kinds of sense to Tony, the manager.

When the contracts were completed, they were sent to the promoters for signature. Upon their return, they would be presented to David for his countersignature. Many had already been signed and returned to us by the promoters. We were awaiting just a few more when Tony came to my office with the bad news: David was canceling the tour. I was practically speechless (I am never entirely speechless). I knew I was hearing straight talk. Tony DeFries was neither a drama queen nor a kidder. I still think of him as a businessman with an edge. He was all business now. He didn't waste any words: "I couldn't change his mind. He will not do it. I suggest you talk to him yourself. He's at the Beverly Wilshire."

It was already late in the afternoon, but I could still make one of the nonstops to Los Angeles at 6:00 p.m. if I left immediately, forgoing luggage and any other preparation. Screw what was on my desk—the unreturned phone calls, the other important deals. Screw it all. I told the head of music about the mess we were in. I told my secretary to get me a plane reservation. I told Tony to tell David Bowie I would knock on his door the next morning promptly at ten, and I was out of there. I had to succeed or the music department would fall off a cliff.

At the appointed hour, I was standing in front of Bowie's door at the Wilshire. I was shown into the living room of a suite decorated in some ersatz French Provincial style that was warm and welcoming. David was warm and welcoming too, but not to me. To the guy on the couch! He was sitting on the lap of an attractive black man, and they were in a lip-lock. They were both fully dressed, and I'm not at all sure what was going on between them as their lips remained sealed—to each other's.

"Excuse me, David. We need to talk." The lip-lock remained unbroken. Was this how I was going to have to talk to him? I figured it was (going over to the couch and pulling the two men apart didn't seem a viable option). So I made up my mind that despite what I was seeing I had David's attention, and who knows? Maybe I did. I barreled ahead, starting with a boring logical approach. "David, canceling this tour is a very bad career move. The promoters aren't going to sit still for it; they will all sue you." On and on I went for at least ten boring minutes. No response. What to do next? I hadn't a clue.

"David, talk to me. I flew all the way out here to see you, to talk some sense into you. At the very least, kindly acknowledge that I am here in this room." A no-change case! Neither man had moved nor changed positions even once. I was looking at a tableau, statue-like, a beautiful contrast in colors. David, whitish skin, strawberry-blond hair, pale-blue suit; the other man, a light-skinned black, white shirt and dark-brown suit. I was looking at a beautiful blend—at my undoing. My exasperation—nay, my desperation—was growing. What now? I tried reciting Lewis Carroll's "Jabberwocky." Bowie was English, after all:

> 'Twas brillig, and the slithy toves
> Did gyre and gimble in the wabe;
> All mimsy were the borogoves,
> And the mome raths outgrabe.
>
> "Beware the Jabberwock, my son!
> The jaws that bite, the claws that catch!
> Beware the Jubjub bird, and shun
> The frumious Bandersnatch!"

But then, when I looked over at the couch, nobody had moved an inch. I was riveted. I stared for a while. And then I went on to gibberish of the sensible kind.

"You know, David, something's definitely wrong with my life. Can you tell me, please, what it is? Where did I go wrong? Where did I take the bad turn in the road?"

By that time I was getting up in the wrinkled clothes I'd been wearing for the last twenty-four hours, and within a minute I was out the door. I wanted to peek through a keyhole to see what happened next inside, but no keyhole, so I moved on. What were my options? The way I saw it, I had only one: Go back to New York. Face the music. Only there would be no music. Had I been closer to David, perhaps I could have had a real conversation, but I doubt it. Their tableau had been too carefully thought out. There would be no music.

On the plane ride home I had a revelation. I started to believe that I'd been witness to a well-staged event. David knew I would come to California and attempt to talk to him. He would not refuse to see me; he was a polite, kind man. So he had arranged a setting in which he could be present and yet not respond. Call it a happening.

I decided I should be amused. I liked him. He also knew that by canceling he was putting me in a spot you couldn't sell to a leopard. Why would he do that? The answer has to be that he had his reasons, and I will never know what they were. And could he even explain his reasons to me? I was not a Martian. I would not understand, and he found an amusing way to avoid having to explain. Who would think of such a thing? Not I. But then I would never have convinced the world that I was a hermaphrodite, or that I had come from another planet.

By the time we were flying over Chicago I began to realize that David would not cancel the tour because it wouldn't simply ruin his career, it would end it. I reckoned he must have figured that out. He could, however, postpone the tour. That could make some kind of sense. If something important to him intruded on the dates originally scheduled, a postponement might be the solution. But he had not suggested the P word, and therefore he didn't have to defend it. The idea became mine, and I thought I could make it work. Promoters weren't in the business of suing big singing stars; they depended on them.

I decided over Chicago not even to try making sense of what had happened, but simply to go for the postponement and see if it could fly. I instructed the guys in the music department to come up with some new dates, ones that everyone could live with, and we would be home free. Why wasn't I smart enough to think of this before I left New York? For me, smart has always taken time. One plane ride does not smart make. I'm a little slow. Two plane rides— and I finally figured it out. Postponement worked like a charm. The tour was a mind-blowing success. His audiences were beyond thrilled—transported, I would say.

CHAPTER TWENTY-FOUR

Fun in the Sun

My mother and father were gone. My husband too. Judy gone. All within a stunningly short period of time, from 1968 to 1972. Time to move on. As the seventies opened, women's lib was in full flower, and I found myself marching in the feminist parade in DC with tens of thousands of other women supporting the ERA. Additionally, although I did not have a high profile like Jane Fonda, Judy Collins, or Joan Baez—politicized entertainers whom I admired enormously—I got on my own soapbox and protested the war in Vietnam whenever and wherever I could.

To F&D it looked as if I had suddenly emerged from solitary and discovered a great big new world outside. In truth my political awakening was not an overnight thing. It was very gradual. As the world of show business grew smaller to me, the world outside grew larger.

Of course feminism was an issue that had always been knocking on my office door, and I was determined to take care of number one. But also, as a true believer, I grew ready to run my bra up the flagpole if that became necessary to get equal rights and equal pay for all women. I championed the campaign and, as an activist, launched a small, one-woman campaign of my own.

I looked into the plummy old Oak Room at the Plaza Hotel—up until then totally a men's preserve—and decided it would be a lovely, and very convenient place to take clients for lunch. But management at the Plaza did not agree. However, the air was redolent with a make-it-happen attitude. Customs mired in the moss of old times were piling up in garbage bins. Customs at the Plaza needed updating.

Having made up my mind to persuade the management to take a view more consistent with changing times, I sat cross-legged outside the room at lunch and gave them the option to carry me out or allow women in. The assistant manager at the front desk wisely chose the latter after only one day of arguing and one day of begging me to leave. It was a small and short-lived campaign, such as it was.

But everything else was not that easy. Liza was not. She had started drinking, and rumors were swirling that she was doing cocaine. What I witnessed, however, was mild. Li ordered rum and Coca-Cola when we were together. It seemed harmless to me. I think she was mindful of the issue I made of addiction, and I did talk about it, but because I never saw anything much, it was easy for me to be in denial about her drugs. I refused to believe that this girl who wouldn't take so much as an aspirin when we first met, this daughter who at first hand had witnessed her mother's demise, would go the same route. But I was so wrong.

Reality may have been exactly the opposite; because she was Judy's daughter, she, too, became an addict. Was it genetic? So far as I know, nobody has yet found the gene for it. One hears that children of alcoholics are far more likely than other children to become alcoholics, but I don't know the answer. I hated when it happened; that I know for sure. I thought about how Judy might have helped Liza with her addiction.

Was there anything I could have done? Not that I ever was able to do anything for Judy. I have long since learned that only Liza could help Liza. I learned it the hard way when I discovered that supporting her addiction was more important than anyone in her life, including me.

Meanwhile, Liza kept on keeping on. She was my special province. No doubt I gave her much attention at the expense of others. But for me money was always a big part of the picture, hers and mine. I wanted Li to be wealthy. I didn't want her ever to have her mother's financial problems. And, at the same time, pressure from the agency was always present; I had to justify my own growing income.

And so when Li did big-money engagements in which part of the contract was a percentage of the gate, I was always present for her in the count-up room to make sure that she was never cheated. I counted the money along with the promoter. No one was going to tell me there was deadwood (unsold seats) because I checked out the hall at every concert, making sure members of the audience were taking their seats with actual tickets. No one was going to beef up the crew list, adding names of people that hadn't worked on the show. I was supercareful. The music business has always found a way to attract smarmy characters with their own accounting shortcuts and shifty tricks that deny performers.

I'll never forget the concert in Rhode Island where the foreman, during the count-up, insisted that there were forty guys on crew for the load-in . . . obviously a scheme he had gotten away with before. "Sorry, Charlie, there were only thirty. I was there. I have their names on this list," I told him. But the foreman had a different list, the one in his head. "There were forty men, or your little girl is going to be dancing in the dark in less than a minute." I called his bluff. He picked up the phone, and someone on the other end pulled the plug. All the lights in the arena went out. Liza was dancing on a pitch-black stage in a huge house without a single lit exit sign. Within seconds there would be panic. "You're right," I said, "there were indeed forty guys." The lights came on, and I paid the extra ten men he was shaking me down for, knowing I would get the money back from the promoter if he wanted to work with the agency again, and the promoter might be able to discuss it with the union if indeed those rednecks would be working for him again.

On the other hand, the promoter, too, might have been getting a kickback. So all bets were off. Time after time, in hall after hall, as I walked around, I found patrons in the audience taking their seats with pieces of paper instead of tickets. The real tickets would then be counted as "unsold," thereby decreasing the amount Liza was paid. Not on my watch. The cheating that went down in those situations is legend, but Liza rarely lost while I was there.

Outside the United States we had some grand adventures together. Sometimes making good money wasn't hard work. Marbella was one such case, and it provided comic relief. It started when my secretary buzzed me to say that a man from Spain was on the line with an offer for Liza to play Marbella. Not only hadn't I heard of the man, I hadn't heard of the place. "Tell him that Liza doesn't play abroad except with known promoters, and when she does leave the U.S. all the money has to be deposited in a bank of our choice three months prior to the engagement." Those demands were acceptable on the other end of the line. "Tell him that even if we decide to work with him we would need, as earnest money, at least half the negotiated price right now." That turned out to be acceptable, too.

Still not paying much attention, I casually said, "Tell him that Liza travels with her orchestra, and other personnel. We would need fifteen first-class airfares and as many hotel rooms, including two large suites." I kept trying to end the conversation, but nothing was a problem for this Spanish stranger, according to my secretary, who came back to me within seconds. "He wants Liza for a three-night engagement."

"Tell him Liza gets a hundred thousand a night." A conversation ender for sure! More than a million a night for some performers might be nothing now, but back then such an amount was unheard of. I was not eager to see Li go to Europe to play one lone-standing three-day engagement for some palooka I'd never heard of. If the offer carried any risk, there would have to be a big reward. Finished! I went back to shuffling the paperwork on my desk, but Joan got back to me again in practically no time at all.

"He's agreed to everything."

"Who is this guy?" I wondered, and I picked up the phone, suddenly willing to give him my full attention. Señor Banus introduced himself, and I asked him very specific questions about where Li would be playing. I had no reason to expect him to be a liar, and if the money showed up, well, it was thirty thousand dollars' commission for five minutes of my time. Finding his replies satisfactory, I sorted out the final details. All the money and airline tickets came exactly when this caballero said they would. The contracts were signed, and on the appointed day, we were off. I wasn't going to miss this one. Once I knew where Marbella was, the sunny south of Spain sounded just wonderful to me.

The rich and famous always find spectacular waterfront real estate with expansive views, sugar beaches, great food, and interesting activity before the rest of us. Would that I could have googled him; I might have found that Señor Banus was Generalissimo Francisco Franco's right-hand man. The administration he served had treated him well, and now he was attempting to turn this paradise he'd earned into a first-class resort. He had the money for development; all he needed was a little publicity. He needed Liza. This is a measure of how important she was then: the Beyoncé of her time. Banus knew her endorsement could establish Marbella as a world-class watering hole.

As things turned out, it was fortunate I'd tagged along, because when we got there I saw no hall, no arena, and I quickly found out there wasn't even a small theater anywhere within a hundred miles: No place to play the date. Marbella, however, was exquisite. Sean Connery was looking very relaxed as he played golf on the beautiful links adjacent to the hotel. I noted a few shops and a disco opposite the marina, where a few smallish yachts nestled in the slips and beautiful people strolled around in expensive casual clothes. Not much else to see, but in whatever direction one looked, one saw the name "Banus." It was emblazoned over every store, on every street sign, in big letters that welcomed the world to Marbella. Puerto Banus, Disco Banus, Banus shopping mall. *B-A-N-U-S* in bold letters everywhere. I developed an ardent curiosity about this man's provenance. Everyone spoke in hushed tones. I couldn't wait to meet him. He was standing by the door of Hotel Banus.

Liza, tired from the trip, retired to her suite while I got the tour from the wealthy señor, a portly man not short on confidence. "About the hall, Señor—"

"Every tree that you see had to be brought from my vineyards up north," he told me, making a grand sweep with his arm over the tree-covered vista.

"Excuse me, sir, where is the hall?"

"It will be here," he said, and then he went on about the future expansion and the new luxury shops that were coming soon.

"What do you mean, 'It will be here'? It is not here."

"Don't worry, it is coming."

"Huh?"

"You must not worry. The hall will be here by tomorrow at two." He was trying in his best English to give me every assurance, but it all sounded nuts to me. I immediately warned Liza something was funny, "But we have the money, all of it—every last dollar is in our hands! Let's just wait to see what happens." I wasn't about to let Liza do a shoddy show.

The next morning, a caravan that stretched back to the horizon descended on the golf course. The trucks carried risers, bandstands, generators, lights of all kinds, red velvet bunting, a piano—everything needed to create a stage out on the beautiful lawns. Peons by the dozens set about assembling all these pieces with a professionalism that would have embarrassed concert personnel back in the United States. It took but a few hours to complete the magnificent stage, and then, as a final gesture, they put a large trellis behind it that served as a cyclorama. The coup de grâce came when additional trucks laden with hundreds of thousands of roses arrived. The laborers threaded the roses through the trellis to provide the prettiest backdrop one could have wished for. Setting up stages in parks is commonplace today; back then it was almost unheard of.

"But what about the audience, Señor Banus? There are no seats."

"I'm taking care of that now. You must not worry." I then watched in mouth-dropping awe as employees from the hotel brought out a dozen large tables, all ten-tops, and set them with the finest gold-trimmed china and silver dinner service, adorned the tables with elegant centerpieces, and retired, only to be replaced by liveried servers and stylishly turned-out footmen. It was like a fairy tale. Actually it *was* a fairy tale, because for the next three nights Liza performed for almost all of the so-called royalty of Europe.

Sr Banus and his portly wife—on whose ample bosom reposed some of the largest emeralds I'd ever seen—had the pleasure of escorting Liza around to meet all the invitees. We dined with princes and princesses, nightclubbed with queens and kings forgotten by history—all of whose names had at least five hyphenated parts—and discovered that not every titled individual was as scintillating as one would have imagined from their smiling faces in fashionable magazines devoted to the madcap life. Liza and I giggled a lot. She was on her best behavior, charming and willing to do for Banus what the Señor and his rotund wife wanted. The concert went off without a hitch. We were having a grand time.

On the last night some wealthy stranger, reputed to be the pharmaceutical king of France (I never got to meet him), gave a party for Liza at his hunting lodge up in the mountains behind Marbella. "Hunting lodge," for some reason, conjured in my mind's eye a Gothic mansion with lots of dusty trophies and musty old rooms. I'd seen too many movies, or maybe I was just so insular I didn't yet understand that rich Euros know how to live exceptionally well. The lodge was a low-lying sprawling place as current as tomorrow, with lots of glass, suede, and leather, and accents the color of a Santa Fe sunset. I felt like Daisy in *The Great Gatsby* as I walked around touching the soft baby-calf cushions, admiring the pastel silks, sinking into the luscious rugs scattered over the Spanish terra-cotta. Three different orchestras, each on different lawns, played different styles of music. What's your pleasure? the whole enterprise seemed to ask. I got my comeuppance when I retired to powder my nose. Lined up at the room-length mirror were many of Europe's most gorgeous models. I like to think that they were there on scholarship to various rich men. And me in my little pants ensemble, the shrimp in the crowd, no beauty either. I vowed never again to go out in public with flats on my feet.

And then, there was Rio in the early seventies.

Liza was going to be the main attraction at Carnival. We were excited. "Copacabana" and "Ipanema" to me were the names that dreams were made of, and nothing we saw dispelled that illusion when we got to Ipanema beach. It was even more beautiful than the French Riviera. The samba was a heady perfume wafting through the streets, putting you into a different frame of mind.

Everything was bursting with sensual life: The girls were golden, and the men bronzed gods.

Liza's nightclub appearance was but a single night at a large hotel. That was easy. What was more important was that she stayed a few extra days to see the samba parade, giving them millions of dollars in free publicity. Invitations arrived every day: to loll in the shadows of Corcovado on a two-hundred-foot yacht (this exquisite boat was longer than a city block and seemed to have more servants than guests—a far cry from Charlie Wacker's washout), to elegant dinner parties attended by the rich and beautiful, to Carnival balls and posh nightclubs. There were photographers everywhere. *Hello* magazine would have its pages filled.

No one I met seemed to have anything on his or her mind but dating and mating, dressing or undressing, and staying out all night. It was party time, and it was irresistible to me in a way like never before. Rio's sensuality got under my skin, into my very soul, and the message it conveyed was relax and enjoy. It was as far from my normal as I'd ever been, and since I thought it unlikely I would ever again see anything like it, I surrendered to it. I bought floaty scarves, diaphanous blouses, and string bikinis; I had my hair washed in mango shampoo; and I fell in love with a beautiful man. He was my dinner partner at a party in Liza's honor given by a wealthy entrepreneur to introduce Li to Rio society. How lovely, I thought.

I'd been divorced for several years, had done some dating, had had quite a few affairs; the one with David that was a disaster, one or two others that were heartbreakers. One of them was with a music mogul who had it all. He was gorgeous, brilliant, rich, charming—and drunk. All the time. It took me a while to figure it out because he was high-functioning and so successful. Another heartbreaker was with a concert promoter who had unlimited potential that would never be realized because he was controlled by his upbringing. He could not see beyond the Midwest. These affairs were disappointing, and they hurt me. And then there were a number of affairs that were bores and not worth a sentence. No one mattered at the moment. Go for it, I told myself.

To start with, this man was beautiful: tall and slim, with a playboy appeal minus the tackiness. He had perfect clothes, a perfect Porsche, perfect manners, even the latest, most perfect tapes— Helen Reddy, Al Green, Rod Stewart—to play as we drove into the mountains to look up at the favelas, and down at the lights in the skyline that framed the beach. We covered all the ground in conversation: from politics (Brazil was fertile ground for that) to sex. After four glorious nights spent dining in lovely restaurants and dancing in chic clubs, it was time to know him better, but I couldn't give myself to him. This perfect playboy will break my heart, and it isn't worth it, I decided. I wasn't liberated enough to be a man's one-night stand. Hell, I wasn't brave enough! It was my survival instinct. I decided to test him. If he came to New York, I would rethink the matter.

He did come to New York, and he looked as good on our shores as he did in Ipanema. Again I was a gutless, spineless simp, scared to be hurt. I was imagining I would be merely another notch on his bedpost, and I hadn't as yet come to the mind-set that wanted him as a notch on my own. In personal matters my feminist ideology was still fighting my upbringing. He was the one that got away. One good thing: He will always remain perfect.

Liza was the fount of my fun perks for the first four years in the seventies. It was like working with Lady Bountiful. I got off on it as long as nothing interfered with the work. It was important that every engagement start on time, and that in each performance she give 100 percent. And she did. However, the fun gradually did start to interfere, and I watched the balance between us change. We were going in different directions. She was always on her way to a party. Sometimes I couldn't reach her for days. I began believing the party mentality was getting in the way of her judgment. That was no fun for me. The uh-oh moment came when her conductor confirmed Liza was definitely using cocaine. No longer a rumor, it helped to explain why everything was becoming more difficult, why she would disappear, why a week of phone calls went unanswered.

One night I collected her at Halston's apartment to take her to a meeting. The great designer was now doing all of Liza's clothes. I remember chatting amiably in his living room filled with people and tall white flowers. No one there made any sense. They were all happy, however, even though their feet weren't quite touching the ground.

In Paris we stayed at the grand Plaza-Athénée, where I met Charles Aznavour, who was occupying every minute of Li's free time. Although Liza didn't discuss her affairs with me, and I didn't try to peek, I was told by members of the band that Li and the French troubadour were a hot item. Unlike me, Li had no difficulty climbing into bed at the drop of a hello. Neither had Judy. They definitely had that in common, and I was just starting to be in awe of women who could do that.

In Berlin the American ambassador invited us to dine. In Hamburg we were given a grand tour of infamous St. Pauli, the red-light district. In Vienna I drowned, delightfully, in hazelnut torte *mit schlag*. I felt like royalty: Li was the new princess on the scene, and I was thrilled to be a lady-in-waiting. But my princess didn't need much attending to during the day, so I was more like a lady of leisure. I went to wonderful restaurants for lunch and shopped in fabulous stores while Liza slept in. She was happy to hang out in the hotel. Sightseeing wasn't her trip, but she knew the city by night in a way I never would. It was the nightlife that made her tick. The rest of the clock could get stuffed. After performing, she never lacked company to run with, to drink with, or to sleep with if she chose. She continued to be "in like" for one night at a time with our musicians, and some that were not ours. If the performance was good, I had no reason to complain. Her shows continued to sell out, and everywhere we went, audiences adored her. It was first class all the way, including my travel, which was paid for by promoters happy with their profits. For a latchkey kid from Washington Heights, this was living large.

The good thing about Europe was that once our plane departed, the new friends that came backstage waved good-bye. It was different touring in the United States. Once we got into big arenas and big money, she had constant traveling companions. We were on groupie overload. I was never able to manage the freeloaders, glad-handers, and hangers-on that showed up on our chartered planes.

I had negotiated an arrangement with one of the airlines to fulfill all our touring needs; excellent for them because they had planes to deadhead back to points of origin, for which we more than paid the gas bill; excellent for us because there was always a plane waiting for us on the tarmac at 1:00 a.m. after a concert.

These charters accommodated approximately seventy-five people. With the orchestra, hairdresser, makeup artist, and other necessary personnel, we filled forty seats, but usually the plane was close to maxed out. Who were these strangely dressed people with us who were loaded all the time? Were we carrying drugs? Or transporting minors over state lines? The airline was happy to have our business, and they asked no questions, but I worried—a lot, for I knew the answer to every question was yes.

I had become a spectator at a movable feast. The party started at the beginning of a tour, and three months later it was still going on. I didn't cause Liza to drink or do cocaine; I couldn't control it, and I couldn't cure it. I knew that. I'd learned that with Judy. But with Judy I tried to change things. Granted, I couldn't. But at least I tried. With Liza I didn't even try. And we both paid the price.

CHAPTER TWENTY-FIVE

The Success Effect

Lucky me! I had two personal clients gracing the covers of important national magazines: Liza on the cover of *Time* and *Newsweek* in the same week, and Bob Redford on the cover of *Life*. Life was good. I was representing two of the most sought-after stars in America. Boy, was I full of myself! Enjoy the moment, I told myself; it won't last forever. Was that prescient! But for seven years, beginning in 1968, I did enjoy it. I milked it. I accepted congratulations and patted myself on the back all around the industry. How much of it was I really responsible for? Bearing in mind that I was not the one with a talent for anything but organization, I would have to say that the answer is Not very much. However, I have observed that people who do nothing don't get lucky often. I worked hard for my luck. I scoured the pages for source material: newspapers, magazines, books, treatments, and ideas—anything that could be put into development.

The good times continued to roll professionally because my clients were talented. Liza and Bob Fosse, a client of Sue's, collaborated on the extremely successful TV show *Liza with a Z*, which won every kind of Emmy Award. All I can boast about is that I brought

Liza, along with her hard work and considerable talent, to a place where the sale of this show could profitably be made. The show itself was a delightful song-and-dance program that showcased all of Fosse's signature moves, and I loved sitting in the audience of a Broadway theater all day long and watching this remarkable performance as it was being filmed. It was remarkable as well that the invited audience was also willing to sit there all day—eight hours with only a few breaks—in fact grateful to be there. They got their money's worth without having paid admission.

Fosse knew all the great dancers in New York, and to the last they clamored to work with him in spite of the fact that he was an extremely hard taskmaster whose withering glances and scorching remarks—all delivered in muted tones—could reduce even the best dancers to ashes. He could look at a dancer giving her all, and observe in an offhand way. One example of his largesse: "We'll wait while so and so discovers where her feet are!" Killer remarks like that.

I wore my clients' enormous success like a label sewn outside my clothes wherever I went, and as a result of the reputation I was acquiring, decided this was the moment in which to make my assault on the music industry. Rock-and-roll clients were now ripe for the picking. And it was the last unbreached male bastion. I realized that since there were no women in the front offices of the record business, I would be a novelty. There was an intriguing conversation to be had about music stars writing film scores and maybe even playing featured roles in films. Now, in the seventies, this was a far more tantalizing conversation for musicians than that of, say, Premier Talent, which could only offer tour booking. Mention major motion pictures and every rock star's manager's tongue started to hang out.

Socializing with people in the new rock and roll brought me to a party where I met my next husband. He is not worth wasting too many words on. The music business, I discovered, was a place where managers were skimming off the top, taking from the bottom, and squeezing the artists in the middle. It was corrupt, and so was the handsome devil I married, who was in the thick of it. It wasn't long after I discovered suitcases stuffed with money coming home from concerts that I also learned my latest love had embezzled from his company, Premier Talent, and his partner did not take kindly to it. Freddie insisted I utilize the negotiating skills of the law firm CMA retained to keep my husband out of jail.

As if that wasn't humiliating enough, it got worse as he watched me thrive while he continued to fail. I held on as long as I could because of the two children we'd had, but after he tried cheating Uncle Sam I threw him out.

Alas, I'd given my children a crook as a father, and that has resounded throughout my life. In the midst of all the good times, he was one of the worst mistakes I ever made, and I've suffered for it. Sometimes what the universe so generously gives with one hand, it selfishly takes back with the other.

Having said that, I can't complain about how I was treated by the rest of the music crowd, either in New York, where the record executives resided, or in London, where the music managers lived. With CMA's client list on the tip of my tongue—Newman, Redford, Pacino, Streisand, Minnelli—and having been married to a rogue in the music business, a lot of those folks knew who I was. They had used me and my marital problems as convenient gossip. It was my entrée. Well, whatever works! And it did.

Besides Bowie, I harvested another big signing: With the help of a friend and agent in our music division, Vincent Romeo, Cat Stevens became a client of mine. Before becoming Yusuf Islam, a prominent convert to Islam, he recorded one hit album after another in a soft style uniquely his own. I loved his work, and I never got a chance to tell him so in person. In the music business one mostly dealt with the managers rather than the clients. Stevens had an amusing manager, Barry Krost, whom I enjoyed spending time with whenever we were on the same coast. Krost had droll comments on everyone's style in the music industry while affecting an eye-catching style of his own. Little did I know that he would one day end up representing Liza instead of me. Still, though it might sound improbable, I think of him fondly.

And then in 1972 Liza won the Academy Award for *Cabaret*, and she was, for a showbiz moment, the biggest star in Hollywood. She was stunning in the role of Sally Bowles. Although the song "Cabaret" is its hugely popular number—due largely to Liza's rendition—it is the song "Don't Tell Mama" (not included in the movie version) that for me epitomizes Liza, for in real life she was the child-woman who worried about what her mama thinks. Never for me was there a song that more perfectly fitted the play— and also the girl playing the role. It was completely true to her character in real life. Liza, masquerading as a grown-up—doing grown-up things, both good and nasty—while beneath the facade is little more than a lonely little girl, a lost soul.

For this movie, although my contribution in the larger sense was minuscule, I feel as though I can take a little bow. By the time *Cabaret* came along, I'd been involved in the negotiation of dozens of motion picture contracts and knew them as well as I knew my name. I wouldn't be allowed solely to do those negotiations now; whole squadrons of attorneys are now in place to do what I did, but back then, once I had wormed my way to the inside, negotiating deals was not a problem. It was my long suit.

I've never had any difficulty practicing law without sanction of the bar. I did it for all my clients, and passed the contracts on to house counsel to review. So on *Cabaret* I negotiated the impor- tant star deals, and the film's producer, Cy Feuer, allowed me to coach him on his deal with the studio. Feuer was basically a Broadway guy and a good professional friend. I'd made a number of actor deals with him in my theater-agent days, and I loved his spirit, his smile, and his tough-guy attitude. He was a little bulldog with a rumpled shirt, and he spoke straight. Trust me, there weren't many like him, certainly not in Hollywood.

Ray Stark, a megaplayer in Hollywood, was as unlike Feuer as oil is unlike water. Ray, the überproducer, was only one of many who wanted to do pictures with "ordinary Bob." I won't go on about the films I negotiated for Redford. He worked in one after another. He worked on the development of his own material with different writers (*The Candidate, Jeremiah Johnson, Downhill Racer*); he had a strong sense of what suited him—playing interesting Americans from different walks of life—and he chose well. The only film I ever talked him into was *The Great Gatsby*, and it wasn't good. I did all his deals, which saw him jump from three-hundred fifty thousand for *Butch* to a million for *Willie Boy* before *Butch* was released. Representing him and doing his deals helped burnish my image, and nobody cares today but me. I don't even think about it anymore. It's more fun and more revealing of the industry both then and now to talk about the silly things that went on, and, as you already know, I love silly.

The Way We Were, a Ray Stark production, was one of Redford's biggest successes. I urged Bob not to do it because when he had to sign his contract the script wasn't ready, and he was upset about it. "If it's not on the page, it won't be on the stage," I said. Words of wisdom someone else wrote, surely out of hard experience. But Sydney Pollack, the film's director, was a good friend of Bob's, and Bob decided to go forward in spite of any warning from me. The way it was on *The Way We Were* was that the script was rewritten nightly before each day's shoot. This was at first unacceptable to Ray Stark, who liked the script he had purchased and didn't want to see it changed.

But to explain what happened on *The Way We Were*, I have to go back to a little dustup in my office that should never have happened.

Stark tried to renege on a cheap script-development deal with a young writer, Steve Tesich, he had contracted for a mere fifteen thousand dollars. The deal was for a treatment based on Steve's original story idea. The writer delivered the treatment under the terms of the contract, and Stark didn't like what he had written. However, Stark owed him the money. For Ray the amount was nothing, but it would mean food on the table for a year for the writer's family. Marian Searchinger, a lovely woman in my department, came to me in tears, begging me to intercede on behalf of the fledging writer who was a minnow in the pool where Stark was the shark. Stark was also one of Begelman's best friends, and we did lots of business with him. Too bad! I made Stark pay what he owed by being terribly nasty, threatening never to allow the film department in New York to work with him again, and he relented, paid the bill, and never forgave me.

This happened just as Redford was starting to film *The Way We Were*. The other unrelated thing that happened in the same month was that I broke my leg badly in a skiing accident. Oddly enough, my broken leg, the young writer, and Bob's concern about the script on *The Way* all came together in a gesture of uncharacteristic kindness from Ray, who sent me a dozen yellow roses with a sweet note. He had suffered a similar skiing accident a couple of years earlier, and the note was your run-of-the-mill "from one skier to another," wishing me a speedy recovery.

I was pleased that Ray was willing to put the bad feelings away, and I wrote a similarly mundane thank-you for the roses he'd sent. Ray then took my thank-you note and scribbled the following on the bottom: "Dear Sue, we really should have shot her!" (Referencing what one does to a horse with a broken leg.) Sue Mengers, who how lived on the West Coast, was also a good friend of Ray's, and it was she who had persuaded Ray to send me the flowers in the interest of burying the hatchet someplace other than in my back.

Unfortunately Ray Stark's busy secretary made a mistake, and instead of sending the note with Ray's scribble on it to Sue, she accidentally sent it back to me. Suddenly I'm looking at my ordinary thank-you bearing Ray's addendum, knowing how Ray really felt: that he preferred to kill me flat out. I took this awful note and sent it to Redford, who was busy filming and hating every minute of Ray's interference on the set. He was known to show up with different hookers in tow from time to time—hookers whom he put on the movie's payroll.

Redford and director Sydney Pollack decided to order Ray removed from the set—permanently. Ray's response was to send a case of good wine to Bob, hoping Bob would relent and let him back in. Bob now took my thank-you note for the flowers (with Ray's ugly addendum), and he scribbled on the very bottom of it, "Dear Stevie, let's shoot the gift horse instead." And he had his secretary send it to Ray, along with the unwanted case of wine.

God bless producers who talk a good game and then don't pay up. I reaped the benefit of just such a mistake. It arose out of Bob's quest for interesting original material. Bob was a serial developer of scripts, and early in the seventies he saw a six-page photo spread in *Life* about a man who was single-handedly trying to save the bighorn sheep in the mountains of Montana. He thought it would make a good movie. The savior, an environmentalist named Jim Morgan, was an interesting character and by no means an ordinary mountain man. He held a doctorate in ecological studies and, while living in the mountains, was also busy filing impact statements with the EPA in Washington, DC. Redford asked me to get the rights to Morgan's life story, and off I went in hot pursuit. Not an easy man to find—even using Redford's name liberally wherever I called. I finally got a callback from Morgan, who found one of the messages I'd left at a diner in Idaho Falls. When at last I heard Morgan's voice on the other end, I introduced myself and told him the reason I was calling. But before I even got Redford's name out of my mouth, he interrupted with: "Are you one of those Hollywood cocksuckers?"

"Well, yeah! I am." He then told me that he had already granted the rights to another producer whom I happened to know, Edgar Scherick, and he hadn't gotten paid. Boy, was he angry! "Why don't you send me the contract?" I suggested. He took down my address and then hung up. I was surprised when the agreement arrived, a one-page, two-paragraph contract, handwritten in pencil on grease-stained yellow legal-pad paper, and it was airtight. I called Edgar, whose offices were just down the block from the agency, and suggested forcefully that he send the check over immediately:

"Edgar, you dine out on more than this each week. You're depriving a man that's trying to save America for you and your children. Aren't you ashamed? Send me a check for two thousand dollars [the full amount] within the hour, or I'm going to embarrass you by telling this story in places you'd rather not have your name mentioned in the same sentence as 'thief.'" The check came within the hour, and I forwarded it to Morgan immediately. He was so grateful he said he was determined to "do something wonderful" for me, and I let him.

He asked me to put together a group of my friends—as many as I wished to invite—and he would host a float trip for us down the Salmon River, otherwise known as the River of No Return. I collected eleven buddies—the most famous of whom was a producer on *60 Minutes*—and on the appointed day we showed up, as instructed, in a cornfield near Idaho Falls, where we were picked up by small planes belonging to the Idaho Fish and Game Department. We were then flown at a thrillingly low level through the magnificent Snake River Gorge and dropped off in Salmon, where, that night, at dusk, we were led on horses to a scenic overview that "breathtaking" doesn't begin to describe. It was all about the light; "purple mountain majesties" is right on the nose.

The next morning we rendezvoused with the guys from Idaho Fish and Game at the Salmon put-in, and started the float. They brought everything. The entertainment was provided by Morris Morgan, Jim's older brother, a real mountain man who hunted for his food, built his own shelter, sewed all his clothes from animal hides, and had wonderful campfire stories.

The River of No Return: long placid pools and horrific rapids. Close to the onset of fast water, you could hear the rapids' intimidating roar as loud as a jet plane just overhead. The object of the exercise was to brave it in a McKenzie, a tiny rowboat with a flat surface underneath less than two feet, created so that it could easily be swiveled into a channel by a strong "river rat" capable of reading the current in advance. I'm proud to say that I went over the Salmon River Falls in a McKenzie rowed by the head of Idaho Fish and Game, and I lived to tell the tale. This amazing experience opened up a new world of rivers for me, and in later years I ran the Middle Fork River, the Upper and Lower Rim of the Colorado, and the Arkansas, Roaring Fork, and Animas Rivers. The film about Morgan, incidentally, never got made.

Nothing is forever, as we know. And I knew that representing two out of the top five or six stars in America could not go on forever, but I did not expect it to end the way it did.

CHAPTER TWENTY-SIX

Betrayal

Freddie told me more than once that they all move on. Every client—every star, and actors not yet stars—all ultimately believe they can be better served elsewhere. No matter how hard you have worked, or how well you have succeeded for your clients, they eventually find it difficult to refuse all the good meals at great restaurants that are accompanied by strong selling from the next agent in line. In a business where one's only commodity is one's own self, selfishness rules. And when a star is being courted by competition that uses flattery and promises—the great tools of our trade—it is hard for the star to resist the overtures. There is some loyalty in showbiz, but one has to look hard to find it. I'm still looking, and basically I'm an optimist. Freddie did sign many more clients than he lost, and when he lost them he took it in stride. I didn't.

When I lost Redford in 1975 I was heartsick. Bob was straightforward and honorable about leaving. He met with me and told me he wanted to move on. I knew I couldn't hold on with all the rumors flying around—that is, with Sue Mengers bitching and moaning on the phone every day that Freddie had sold the company and sold her out—all long before any announcement was made. I always knew that part of Bob's attraction to CMA was Freddie Fields, who would no longer be there. It was speculated that Freddie would head a studio or make an independent-producer deal at one. And then there was also a new kid on the block. Mike Ovitz, trailing heat wherever he went, was forming a new agency with the top young agents at William Morris. The buzz was all about Ovitz, who was seen holding hands with every important star in Hollywood. It took Ovitz four more years to get Redford, who went to William Morris first.

I thanked Bob for seven wonderful years. Truthfully, his career only got better once he was gone because he added another gem to his crown. He started directing, and first time out he won the Best Director Oscar for *Ordinary People*, which I thought was brilliant. I dropped the ball by not knowing he wanted to direct, by not pushing the envelope with him. Directing may have been his idea, but it should have been mine. He was doing everything during our representation of him that directors do except calling the shots. He was always on the hunt for good material and good writers, he worked on the development of the movies he starred in, he conferred on casting and locations—it was clear what came next, and I didn't see it.

I hold myself responsible for not coming up with the first directing project before anyone else. That might have saved the day. I did not introduce him to enough new writers or find source material that was fresh. I was on automatic pilot. I wasn't thinking. I wasn't one step ahead of the next guy, which is where I needed to be to hold on to an actor as intelligent and thoughtful as Bob. And that, after seven wonderful years, was the end of my professional relationship with "Ordinary Bob."

However, Redford gave me the American West as a present. I skied a thousand runs, hiked a hundred trails, climbed a number of Colorado's fourteen-thousand-foot peaks, did horse-pack camping trips in the high-country wilderness, fished for trout in uncharted mountain streams, and fell in love with the Navajo and Hopi cultures because he showed me the beauty of that part of our country for the first time. I owe him. Some of my favorite Redford films—*The Natural* and *Out of Africa*—were made soon after he left. And it's still heartbreaking.

Losing Pacino was less straightforward. CMA did not lose Al Pacino, only I did. But I learned a big lesson that would serve me well: The blame game is not worth playing. It's a waste of time. To start with, Al and I were not pals like Bob and I were. We did not speak on the phone three or four times a day like Bob and I. I'd always found Al difficult to talk to, and consequently we never grew close. Al had a business manager, Martin Bregman, who handled Al's money and that of other clients, like Barbra Streisand, Alan Alda, and Liza Minnelli. He and his good buddy Begelman worked together on a one-hand-washes-the-other basis. They brought each other clients, and that enriched them both.

Bregman got involved in some tax shelter/cattle scheme and invested lots of his clients' funds in the deal. Bregman was attractive and smart, and I don't think he had any evil intent here; however, some deals work, and some are losers. This one turned out to be a scam, unbeknownst at the outset to Marty. But while the clients lost lots of money, Marty lined his pockets with the commissions he got for putting his clients into the deal. "No bloody fair," I whined, and pulled Liza away from his management. It was easy to do because Liza was upset at the loss of her money. So was Streisand, and she, too, left Bregman. In return Bregman took Al away from me, which he was easily able to do.

The whole mess left me wondering how much Al knew and how much money he lost. He wasn't yet as high up in the earning ranks as Liza and Barbra, both of whom lost tens of thousands. Had I kept my mouth shut and left Liza with Bregman, I could have maintained my representation of Al; I would have been able to continue talking for him, and looking for material on his behalf. But there was no integrity in my not informing Liza. Besides, it went right along with the slimy way Begelman did business, which might have been to let Marty fast-talk his way out of it, promising to get it back in the next investment, and so on. I owed it to Li to speak up. However, I believe that, had I thought about it more, I might have found a better way to handle this mess. There was a compromise in there somewhere. I couldn't see it then. Everything was so black-and-white to me. It was a good object lesson. Moving on!

The rumors about the sale of the company that year turned out to be true. The new owner, Marvin Josephson, also came from the agency world and was very successful, but he wasn't anyone I knew. I had followed the Fields plan, which was to keep my head down and not bother about what other agents were doing. Meanwhile, all my associates knew Josephson but me. I was uncomfortable. I had grown up with F&D. In a way Freddie was my surrogate father. I didn't want a new environment. I didn't want even to give it a chance. Besides that, having lost Redford and Pacino, I would now have to prove myself all over again, build a new client list, and maybe even take a cut in salary. Who knows? I did a lot of speculating. Of course there was still Liza, at the pinnacle of her career. Liza! Yes! I decided on a new life plan: Liza and I would go into business together.

In spite of cracks that were now showing up on the well-paved road to Liza's fame, I thought everything would be okay. I looked at my Liza, the brilliant and lovely young woman who, upon winning the Oscar for *Cabaret*, showed up a day later in my office with a basket of flowers three feet high. She needed help to put the huge arrangement on my desk, and then came the best part. She handed me a card that said, "We did it."

I truly cared about Liza, and I believed in her. Although I knew that her voice was not as good as her mother's or Barbra's, she worked hard, very hard, to win over audiences, and her quirkiness, her please-love-me desperation seduced them wherever we went. She was a good actress, and a great entertainer. I had enough confidence in her ability and in my own to imagine that together we could build a successful independent production company of our own. I believed that I knew how to turn her great success into greater profitability, how to make the deals work for her, how to make it all happen for the both of us. And if we worked closely together, I thought I could keep her straight. Boy, was I wrong!

It would start with a simple three- or four-picture deal tied to one of the studios. It would give her a chance to develop her own scripts, ones she could star in and maybe one she could produce for someone else. Of course the films would have to be successful for the escalations in the contract to work, as well as for the options to be picked up. There were deals like that going all the way back to Bette Davis, and there is no question that this kind of deal was available to Liza. It was an easy setup for me, and worth taking a chance on.

I imagined creating musicals utilizing the talents of Li's buddies Fred Ebb, John Kander, and Marvin Hamlisch; I imagined developing dramatic vehicles with good writers and directors, scripts that would exploit Liza's specific strengths. I spoke to Li about it with great enthusiasm. She got excited, too, and agreed that it was the way to go. And so, after fifteen years, I resigned from CMA. I told my new boss, Marvin Josephson, that I would be gone in less than two weeks. I told my lawyer to prepare an agreement with Liza. I had one foot out the door, and I was very excited about the future, truly looking forward to a new kind of professional independence. That's when I got the call.

It was a phone call from a man whose name I had only ever heard just in passing: Mickey Rudin, a powerful entertainment attorney in Los Angeles who was known as Frank Sinatra's mouthpiece. It was he who answered the questions about Sinatra's gambling interests and underworld acquaintances. In dispatching me, he was nothing if not totally direct; brutal is more like it: "Liza will no longer require your services!" And he hung up. It took him fifteen seconds to relieve me of everything it had taken me fifteen years to build. I started to get nauseous, thought I would throw up, and the hand holding the phone shook so hard I almost dropped it. I hadn't made a single response. He didn't give me time to make one. I sat there staring for a long time, not moving—not *able* to move. My body temperature dropped, like in the old days with Judy. My hands were freezing. I couldn't focus. I couldn't make myself move. I just sat there. I was in shock.

And where was Liza? Nowhere to be found! I knew she was in California. She had a new love in her life: Desi Arnaz, Jr. She was spending a lot of time with him and his family. I can't recall ever meeting him, and I had had no inkling he would have such an impact on me. I didn't know how to reach him. I called Li's father and all the people we knew in common; I left word for her all over the West Coast, but there was no return call. Liza knew how to disappear when she wanted to, and she never did it better than in the few months following my firing. Did she know that I was now out of work, that I was jobless, divorced, and supporting two children? My physical shock lasted less than an hour. The shock to my psyche lasted more than a year.

For days I was too depressed to move. My children, who were five and six, had no patience for that. I had to give up self-pity to play with them. How could Mommy be home and not play? They wouldn't allow me to feel sorry for myself. But then, self-pity hasn't ever been my trip. When I started to come around, I instinctively knew I couldn't win a battle with Rudin. Thinking like an agent, trying to estimate where I would come out if I took him on, I figured I'd be the one with the short straw, because I understood that Rudin could not have made that phone call if Liza had not given him the authority to do so. And, of course, hiding out was Li's usual response to such circumstances.

Banging around in my brain was what Freddie had taught me years before when he first instructed me: "Agents, lawyers, and accountants—they're only just advisers. The client is the principal. The client is the only one that makes the decisions." Rudin was a wealthy attorney with unlimited resources and a reputation for being nasty. I would have had to hire legal counsel, and, at best, my grounds were questionable. I hadn't yet signed a contract with Liza for the new company. I felt I had an oral agreement, but then it was Liza's word against mine. I was bleeding. I licked my wounds and talked to nobody.

Worse, once I was gone from the agency, it was okay for Liza to stay there. Josephson changed the call letters from CMA to ICM, and it continued to be Liza's professional home. Had I crawled back to get myself a paycheck, I would have had to face the humiliation of no longer representing her. How calculating of Rudin! It was beyond cruel.

Hardest to accept was that none of this could have gone down if Liza hadn't wanted it to. I kept repeating this to myself like a mantra: It was Li's decision. But while my head knew this was true, my heart didn't want it to be. We had won the Triple Crown. And for this I was fired, summarily dismissed, a disgrace in the company? What heinous crime could my associates imagine I'd committed? Had Liza really considered all the ramifications of her decision? Did she even know what happened? Probably not. She was as self-absorbed as any other star. She was busy being in love again. Somehow I was able to keep moving, but not able to let go of my denial—that it was Liza who did this to me in the nastiest way.

For a time rumors about Liza beat a path to my door. There was no avoiding them. Everyone I knew in show business was anxious to tell me whatever he or she knew. Mostly I heard how Mickey was going to make Liza rich. She was already rich, but maybe she wanted a lot more. Her mother, after all, had died broke. That had to be pretty scary. If that in fact was Rudin's promise, he made good on it. He kept Liza touring all the time. It's easy for me to say he should have used her success as a launching pad to further her film career. That wasn't, however, what he was capable of. He wasn't about to turn his back on his practice in order to harangue literary agents to find appropriate material for her. He put Liza in the hands of inexperienced agents who weren't capable or connected. They weren't film packagers trained by Freddie Fields; they were merely order takers. What they *could* do was follow Mickey's bidding, and that was to keep her on the road. They wanted to keep Mickey happy. After all, he also represented Frank Sinatra and Lucille Ball. If they did a good job for him, might they now get into the Sinatra business?

Mickey did package Liza with Sinatra. Frank and Liza in Atlantic City! It made lots of money, but in my opinion it was a crime. It didn't mean a thing for her career. The longer she stayed out on the road, the more the Hollywood interest in her diminished. Her movie life went into the toilet. It was a giant missed opportunity. Mickey Rudin made her richer than she then was while lining his own pockets in the process. And while on the road, where permissiveness and bad behavior are as commonplace as tacky hotel rooms, it was rumored that most of Liza's earnings were going right up her nose.

It was at least a year before I got a call from her. I'm not sure why it came, and I didn't ask. I simply accepted the invitation she offered to lunch. We spent an empty hour and a half on inconsequential small talk. Though it may be hard to believe, hardest of all for me to believe, I still hadn't completely processed what had happened, hadn't yet located my anger, and I wasn't prepared to join any issues with her. And it wouldn't have mattered. Liza doesn't confront issues. She has always passed the buck to someone working for her. I understood that. I taught her how to do this during all the years when I was pleased to be the "heavy." Had I had the presence to open a real discussion with her, she might have sent me back to Mickey Rudin. But I didn't, and she didn't. Instead she treated me like an old friend, hugging me when she saw me, jollying me. "It's *so* good to see you. How *are* you?" It was bullshit.

Finally at the end of the meal, it having accomplished nothing toward personal redemption, I decided to look at the luncheon as an opportunity to find a softer way back into her life. I told her I wanted to write a screenplay for her based on one of her songs, a piece of special material Fred Ebb had written for her entitled "Liza with a Z" about her name, which was continually misspelled and mispronounced. The idea just popped into my head. She was delighted. Maybe she saw it as a way out of guilt. I have no idea if she had any.

I was winging it, but as a result of my ad-lib, I got myself a deal at United Artists. In the script I conceived, the misspelling leads to all kinds of other complications. The script was a piece of crap, and when I turned it in, that was the end of it. I considered the payment my severance for fifteen years of work. Now that we were "friends" again, I got a Christmas card with a small gift for the next five years.

It was while doing a benefit concert at Radio City in 1990 that something telling happened. She phoned from backstage as she was about to go on to say that her good friend Halston had died, and that she was in terrible pain. She was sobbing and couldn't get herself together. "What should I do, Stevie? Tell me what to do. I'm hurting so much. I can't stand the pain." I found the nicest possible way to tell her that the show must go on, and made some suggestions for honoring her friend after. Why me? Why had she called me instead of all her other powerful friends? Because I had been the most stable person in her life. We both knew that.

In 1991, when she was appearing there again with a new act, I arranged a pair of tickets and took my Jenny, now twenty-two, to the show. We went to the greenroom after the show, and when Liza entered she gushed over us, ignoring everyone else there, including Baryshnikov.

Perhaps the continuous touring, the endless concerts, Halston's death and, most of all, her increasing addictions sent her into the tailspin that prompted the next call, about a year later. She was now in the kind of pain that was beyond her endurance. She said she couldn't get out of bed for days at a time. She told me that she had trouble differentiating colors. Everything hurt. She was so totally lost that her voice barely resonated.

My heart hurt for her. I never got over feeling sorry for her, but she needed more help than I could give. I urged her to go to Alcoholics Anonymous, and encouraged her to make a permanent commitment to it. She did that, and was open in the press about seeking rehabilitation. At her request I even attended a few meetings with her. But during this period her career went further into the dumpster. At this point we were in totally different places. She was suffering, and I was back on my feet. When she got back on her own, perhaps I could help her once more with work.

I thought the remedy for her career might be found in television. In the eighties important careers were being made on TV. With the assistance of Jim Watters, the former entertainment editor at *Life* and *Time* magazines, and a good friend of mine and Liza's, I developed a comedy series idea that was, at least in my opinion, salable. Liza had a wonderful sense of comic timing. If she showed any interest in the idea, Jim and I would secure the best writers, the best show runner, the best of everything needed to support her.

I went with Jim to Los Angeles to visit Liza, who was now in recovery and feeling more like her old self. She was resting and trying to find her Hollywood land legs again. She was sharing a house with a good friend and living a healthier lifestyle. I approached her with the series idea tucked under my arm. It was definitely self-serving, but the concept was strong, and if I could take it to market with Liza starring, it would put her back on her feet at a time when her career was still salvageable. By then, my having produced successfully on Broadway, my career was thriving, and I thought my success could serve her.

However, the world she was living in at that moment was far from any reality that I understood. She boasted in our meeting that she was working on four new films and that she was going to direct them all. What notable project had she ever directed? What film existed to display her work? It was nonsense. But it was also clear that she understood she had missed out on an important film career; however, the moment when she still could have grabbed on to a film life, and held on if she did any good work, had long since passed. Comebacks in film don't happen often. Judy was one of the lucky ones. Her daughter was not.

Although it took at least ten years, my denial of Liza's betrayal finally vanished. I had to deal with understanding that I'd been unceremoniously dumped by an actress who could not have cared less, by a performer who may have been too self-absorbed to understand, even to realize, that she had once left me out in the cold. In time my anger disappeared, and I realized that Liza was sadly stuck with the choices she'd made. She owns those decisions, and like Judy, she's made some really bad ones. She has hurt herself and her career more than anyone else ever could have.

I never told Liza any of the terrible episodes that I endured when I traveled with her mother. I would never have spoken of these things then. We had both been children. What did I, at twenty-four, understand about self-destruction? I was anxious to protect her from all that. And Liza never discussed with me anything that went on between her and her mother. My own experience informs me that bad stuff had to have been going on, but there was this code of silence that served neither of us. I gave it up long ago.

I finally heard—twenty years later—an explanation for my

dismissal that rang true. A mutual friend of Liza's and mine told me that it was Desi's mother, the great Lucille Ball, the mother-in-law-to-be, who told Liza to dump me. She suggested to Li—firmly, I suspect—that if Liza was going to be part of the family, using the family representative, Mickey Rudin, was the way to go. If, after all, Rudin was good enough to call the shots for her and Frank Sinatra, he was good enough for Liza. Stevie who? is what I imagine Ms. Ball asked. Perhaps Liza simply got tongue-tied. Perhaps Liza agreed. To Ms. Ball I was nobody. But back then, I was somebody who cared. Of course most every story has a footnote: Both Lucille Ball and Frank Sinatra eventually fired Mickey Rudin.

There is a postscript to all this. In 2001 I was taking care of my mother's youngest brother, who was at the time ninety-six and failing. I'd made a sort of assisted-living arrangement for him with a woman he had a crush on; she'd been one of his caretakers while he was still able to live independently. (Uncle George was proof positive that the male "thing" is never over.) He continually spied on this woman having sex with a succession of lovers in her home until the day he slipped on one of her seven shih tzus' dog shit, and it was all downhill from there.

The love nest in West Palm Beach was not far from a house Liza was renting while recuperating from a bout of encephalitis. She called me in New York to say that she had to see me. "Please come, please!" It sounded dire. And I cautiously told her I would come on my next visit to West Palm. Would I have come if she had called from Seattle? I doubt it. I bundled Uncle George and his walker into my rented car and drove to Li's house, where a tall, casual-attired beefcake ushered us into the living room, where we all sat waiting for Li to appear. He and I stared at each other without anything to say. I had no idea if he was the boyfriend, the body-guard, the friend, or the neighbor.

Finally Liza appeared, leaning heavily on her own walker. She dragged one foot, and her speech was slurred. She spoke slowly and worked hard to form words. It was easy to see she was suffer-ing. "Look, Stevie, I can walk. And the doctor says I'm going to be fine. I'm going to go back on the stage before you know it." I intro-duced her to Uncle George. He said hello, but she did not. "You will help me, won't you?" That was all that interested her.

"Li, honestly, honey, I haven't represented anyone for years. Truthfully I don't even know the buyers anymore. Do you have all the medical help you need?" She looked at me. It was finished. The interview was over. She said, "Excuse me, I can't stay any longer." As she turned to leave, I noticed that some department store's plastic security tag was still attached to the printed chiffon blouse she wore. On the car ride back, Uncle George—who was of sound mind—said, "I can't believe that was her." Neither could I.

It was Liza who finally taught me the lesson Freddie had tried to teach me years earlier. Loyalty in show business doesn't exist. I know people who would protest this statement, and perhaps a few might be right. But for most it's easy to believe one's partners are loyal when all is going well. It's when the sun goes down that one usually finds oneself standing alone in the dark.

Part 3

Maturity

CHAPTER TWENTY-SEVEN

A Different Kind of Whorehouse

What makes a comeback? Here's my theory: Hunger. Not for money but for the chance to show you've still got what it takes, that you can't be kept down, that you don't accept defeat. Confidence. Just forget about starting a business without it. You must have unwavering faith in your own ability. And eyes. Preferably those directly connected to your brain, so you can recognize an opportunity when it's put in front of you. I've watched a lot of people let such a moment blast right past them. Why don't they see it? Are they too comfortable in their misery—or too scared to grab life by the balls? When Judy opened the door to her flat in London in 1960 and saw Freddie standing there, she saw her chance and grabbed hold of it with both hands. It was a life lesson for me. It planted a seed that took root in a deep place. I saw my chance and threw caution to the wind.

It came by phone: a last-minute invite from Bill and Eileen Goldman, good friends, to join them at the Actors Studio to see a musical in progress being worked on by mutual friends. They feel sorry for me, and they're just being nice, was my first thought, which was probably correct. Unattached, underemployed, unappreciated, and feeling generally unloved, I had very little desire to go out that night, but no reason not to. Because they were such kind and caring friends, I got up off my butt, got dressed, and met them for dinner followed by a play at the Studio. I didn't know what I was going to see and didn't much care. But once the play started, everything changed. By its end I knew I wanted to produce it on Broadway. I'd never produced anything before.

After brief encounters with solar energy and social activism, the results of a little interlude I had with a guerrilla architect I'd met through Redford's consumer-advocate wife, Lola, I'd hurried back to show business, where sunshine radiates in the smiles of the few winners, and wind power is what comes out of the mouths of those who dole out the dollars on either coast. Ned Tannen, then president of Universal, was willing to pay me a small retainer to look around the company to determine if I could make a contribution somewhere. What he really wanted was for me to utilize my prior connections with big stars for the studio's benefit. He had reason to believe that I could attract Redford into a Universal film. But he wasn't quite that blunt. Instead he urged me to evaluate the possibilities for myself within Universal and then let him know what interested me.

I looked first at the television division. In California it was a male-dominated bastion with a lot of little fiefdoms, not one of which would I want to inhabit. I saw women sitting at all the secretarial desks not able to do more than answer the phone and deliver the coffee. No one, surely not the self-important feudal lord of this boob-tube kingdom, was going to give me an opportunity to show him squat. It could remain an all-boys' empire as far as I was concerned.

I looked next at the movie division. Movies, my drug of choice, were as wonderful to me then as they had been when I was a child, and as they are now: a wonderland of escapism, entertainment, and pure joy. But again, everyone in movies had their butts in a chair at 100 Universal City Plaza in LA, and I didn't think I could make packaging movies come to fruition from New York; at least not easily. Getting actors into movies didn't interest me nearly as much as putting movies together.

So, as I had imagined, my being appreciated at the studio came down to delivering the talent whose private telephone numbers I possessed (quite a few!). I was at the point of admitting that to myself. My retainer after a year was running out, and soon I would be out the door as well. And then the universe spoke. What I saw on the stage that night at the Actors Studio changed everything.

Peter Masterson was directing his gorgeous wife, Carlin Glynn (an excellent actress), in a musical about Texas that they had put together with two people I didn't know, Carol Hall (the composer) and Larry L. King (on whose *Playboy* article the show was based). Texans all. It was an endearing story about hypocrisy, not about prostitution, and what was so terrific about it was its authenticity. It looked and sounded like Texas. You could smell the barbecue.

I'd never seen a musical about Texas (*Oklahoma* was one state removed), and from the first delightful song I thought that this could hit. The book was charming and very funny. Without my having the slightest assurance that Tannen would step up to the plate, I went backstage afterward and offered to option it in Universal's name. You need two things to do that: a lot of balls and then a bathroom close by to throw up in.

I met with the authors and sold myself. (That confidence I never lacked.) I told them Universal would option it for twenty-five thousand immediately. Although there were a few other producers interested, the authors conferred quickly and went with me. I think they believed the show—if a big studio were to be involved—would really happen. They liked the instant cash, until much later when the show was a huge success and Universal exercised the option to make the movie.

I called Tannen and told him I'd finally found what I wanted to do and described what it was. He took a beat, and I held my breath. "Don't you want to get Bob Fosse or George Roy Hill to do it with you?" Ned asked, remembering the important director relationships I had. I've got the deal. Ned's going to do it! I knew it in that moment.

"Overkill," I answered. "These guys are doing just fine, and they're the ones that made me love it."

"But what the hell do you know about producing?"

"If you'll stake me, we'll soon find out."

"How much?" he asked. In 1978 I thought we could do it off-Broadway for about $250,000, and he was agreeable—but only because that was so little compared to the telephone numbers he dealt with on a daily basis.

"Are you sitting down?" I asked him. "The title of the show is *The Best Little Whorehouse in Texas.* Can you deal with that?" I didn't have to wait long for his answer.

"I like it; we'll go with it." It was a title worth millions, and he knew it right away. Not every big exec I knew would've gone along. He asked me to send the script out to the studio lawyers to read. For the amount he was spending on it, it wasn't worth his taking any time to read it himself.

Before long I got a call from a lawyer in the business affairs department at the studio. He asked me the sixty-four-dollar question. "Are the characters in the play based on living people?"

"Yes, sir."

"Then please immediately send along the rights contracts you've got with them for us to look at." My pregnant pause provoked a practiced response from the attorney. "No contracts, no production!" With that, Larry L. King, who was able to track down the real madam on whom the musical is based, and I were off to Dallas.

I'm not quite sure how Larry was able to dig up Edna Milton

Davidson, because at the time she was hiding out from the IRS. But Larry, one of the "good ol' boys," was well plugged in in the Lone Star State, and when we arrived in Dallas, there she was, my first madam. Believe me, she was unlike anything anyone would have expected. No makeup, nondescript wardrobe, and a so-so body . . . no one would ever pick her out of a crowd. She was plain. She'd come off a dirt farm in "nowheres" Oklahoma, where, as a young girl, she'd had her feet stepped on by so many cattle that she walked funny. We sat down to talk in the lobby of the hotel where we met, and I made her the $37,500 offer that Universal had authorized. She grabbed it as fast as she could say the letters IRS. It was her bailout; she knew it, and she wasn't about to argue the amount. I'd brought a contract with me, and she signed it immediately, no questions asked, no lawyers needed.

I told her we would also need such rights from the sheriff and asked if she could possibly help us. "You wait right here," she said, and I saw her go into a phone booth not far from where we were seated, while Larry went to the bar. (Oops!) She was able to reach "the man," and she made an appointment for us at 1:00 p.m. that very day at the Cottonwood Inn in La Grange, Texas, not far from where the Chicken Ranch whorehouse had once thrived. I got plane reservations to Austin (the nearest airport to La Grange), reserved a rental car, and we were on our way—until it started to snow. Snow in Dallas? Not likely and not often. A half hour later the ground was covered with the thinnest possible layer, and the airport closed. Traffic ground to a halt. But Miss Edna knew something good when she saw it, and she wasn't about to let it get away—or as Larry L. King so aptly phrased a similar moment in the musical: "She saw a bird's nest on the ground." Edna surely wanted all the eggs in her basket. "I'll just go get my Buick," she said, and before long we were on our way to Austin despite the bad conditions, which seemed not to bother Edna at all.

After some idle chatter about Texas weather, Larry passed out in the backseat, and I knew he was "in the bag." As we made our way through sloppy streets leaving Dallas, I wondered if I was going to be working with yet another alcoholic. Did it really matter?

I brushed the question aside because I now saw my chance to find out everything about whores and whorehouses a girl like me just might want to know.

"Where did most of the girls at the Chicken Ranch come from?" I asked Edna.

"Mainly country gals. They're the best kind. They know how to listen. I don't like those big-city types." I wondered if that judgment included me, but it would be unproductive to explore that, and besides I was extremely curious about how much the women got paid, so I plunged right ahead and asked. "The girls got 60 percent and the house kept 40," she told me.

"Okay, but how much did they turn tricks for?" I asked her.

"Ten dollars mostly; fifteen for something special!" I decided I didn't really need to have her explain what "special" in a Texas whorehouse meant.

"Did they work every night?"

"Day and night, six days a week."

"That's a lot."

"Well, we were always very busy, sittin' in the middle of so many colleges like we wus. The girls got time off for their monthlies," she told me, as if to say it wasn't hard work at all—plenty of time to relax. Meanwhile I did some fast mental calculating.

"So I figure that they made about four or five hundred a week." I thought my figure was high, but Edna looked at me as if I were some kind of idiot.

"Any girl who couldn't keep three to four thousand as her share was out of the house in a week." I was so stunned I kept my mouth shut for at least ten miles. Finally, though, my curiosity kept driving me nuts, and so I pressed on: "I just don't know how a girl could earn so much money in a week doing *that*." Edna took a beat and—without even bothering to look over at the ninny sitting next to her in the front seat—said: "Grease and slide, girl. Grease and slide!"

It was becoming clear we were going to be not only late, but very late. The drive was turning into a marathon that looked like it would last at least six hours. "The sheriff will be long gone by the time we get there. I hope you know how to reach him."

"Oh, he'll be there, all right," she assured me.

"But we're gonna be more than three hours late."

"I can see you know nothing about men!" That shut me up. I knew truth when I heard it.

Indeed she was right about T. J. Flournoy. Sheriff "Jim" was waiting at the Cottonwood Inn just like she told me he would be. He was a lot to take in all at once. This ample man stood an intimidating seven feet tall in his bare feet, and seven feet two with his boots on. Add the cowboy hat, and he was a mountain. He had a red bulbous nose as large as my entire face, and it bore evidence of having enjoyed much good liquor every now and then—probably more then than now.

He, like her, was no spring chicken. He was still, however, a big bad guy with a big bad reputation. Looking at him, no one would want to mess with him. Larry told me he was reputed to have killed his own brother. I could only imagine the Texas-size circumstances (I was quickly beginning to understand that everything in Texas was outsized) in which that incident took place. The tale about the "brother" may be apocryphal, no more than part of the Flournoy legend, but the story upon which the musical is based is absolute truth.

When Marvin Zindler, the well-known TV consumer advocate from Houston, came to La Grange to shut down the whorehouse, Flournoy picked him up by the seat of his pants and put him through the plate glass window of the department store he'd been broadcasting in front of. The crash sent Zindler to the hospital for weeks. While it would have been great fun to explore these memories with Flournoy, that's not what I was there to do. I had to make the deal, and so I cut off the small talk. The little I learned about TJ that afternoon, however, came as a delightful surprise.

Notwithstanding how intimidating he appeared, he was as sweet and polite as a well-mannered child, and he was clearly happy to see Miss Edna. When he said he'd waited lunch—given that it was now past five—I realized for certain that she knew a whole lot more about men than I did.

We all sat down for a meal of the house favorite; a fattening feast of chicken-fried steak. It had enough thick white gravy covering each piece of meat to wade in up to the ankles. Fortunately I was talking so much I didn't have to get the whole meal down. After explaining the plot of the musical, and how, as the sheriff, he functioned in it, I got around to making him the offer. He looked at me as if I had just fallen out of a tree. "Are you talking about givin' that kind of money to me?" he asked.

"Sure," I said. "We think that's a fair amount for using a character based on your life." To begin with he couldn't believe anyone like him was going to be in a musical show. From his modest conversation I could tell he did not think he was interesting, regardless of what anyone else thought. I noticed that one of his hands mostly remained under the table. It could've been in his lap, but it wasn't hard for me to imagine it in Miss Edna's instead. (Both of her hands were aboveboard.) He looked a bit twitchy, and reflecting he was uncomfortable with accepting money, I offered to give it to his favorite charity. After thinking for a minute or two, he looked directly into my baby greens and said, "Well, ma'am, I just cain't possibly take that money. Y'all should give it to this little lady sittin' right here next to me." I sat stock-still. I needed to make sure I heard right.

"Are you sayin' [I was now talking like him] that you want me to give the entire amount to Edna?"

"You heard me right." And that was that. For Edna this was more than just the bird's nest. The whole aviary had just landed at her feet. She had made seventy-five thousand that day. Better pay than the whorehouse.

"Okay, we have a deal," I said. Flournoy and I shook hands on it. My long fingers got lost in his baseball-glove-size mitt.

I did in fact send him a script, and he sent back a letter approving it, telling me that was contract enough for him. He didn't need to talk with an attorney. Edna had endorsed the project, and he was willing to go along with anything she wanted. Also he foresaw no political trouble for accepting a contractual fee for the rights to his life story. That had nothing to do with his refusal to take the money. The sheriff simply wanted to give a wonderful gift to the woman he had loved. This had been speculated in the play script. His gesture ended all speculation about whether or not there truly was a love story between them: This happily married man loved her still.

After lunch, Edna took us to the La Grange hospital, of all places. There, on a brass plaque, was her name, above all the others. In the funding of a new hospital for the town, she had been the biggest contributor. The whorehouse had also paid for the Little League uniforms and contributed to all the worthy causes in La Grange. Edna was shrewd, and she had been anxious to be the town's best neighbor. She didn't want any trouble when her girls came to town for a manicure or a meal in a restaurant. How many of her contributions amounted to bribery, and how many came from the deepest and most charitable place in her heart? We can guess, but we'll never know for sure.

In real life, at the end, the consumer pest Marvin Zindler won, and the Chicken Ranch was closed, much of it destroyed. But on the ride up to La Grange, Edna told me that there was still a small part left standing. As long as I was already there, and the whorehouse was near, I wanted to see it, stand in it, and try to imagine what the girls felt when they were standing there. Edna picked up her head housekeeper so that we could all go over to the place together. The woman lived in a once-thriving black community that had sprung up on the outskirts of town to provide the support personnel the whorehouse needed. The Chicken Ranch had been a cottage industry responsible for lots of good-paying jobs.

The diminutive woman Edna collected was every bit as delighted to see her as the sheriff had been. She got into the car, and within five minutes we were at the place where so many famous lawyers, doctors, state senators, and politicos of all stripes had come for relaxation and entertainment.

The housekeeper took me into the only remaining bedroom. It had a double bed with a chenille coverlet. There was a nightstand by the bed with a cheap lamp on it, with one of those frilly shades tied with a thin red velvet ribbon. And there was a sink. "The girls would wash every customer beforehand," she told me. "We wus very healthy about the place," she said with pride. She opened a drawer in the nightstand, from which she took a thin, scrawny-looking cotton rug. "Look at this, look how beautiful. This rug set right here by the bed." And she made me hold it so that I could savor it and understand its luxury as she did. I was touched. Then we sat in the kitchen (the only other room left standing) reading Edna's rules of the house, which were still posted on the wall. I include them here for your amusement, and because I love them:

1. Absolutely no narcotics are permitted on these premises—if any are found, the Law will be called Immediately.

2. Drinking is not permitted during visiting hours, and anyone doing so will be asked or ordered to leave. In short, DOPE-HEADS,

PILL-HEADS and DRUNKS are not permitted to live here, regardless of who they are.

3. Thieves, liars or robbers are not wanted or needed here.

4. Beds are not to be wallowed in. That's what hogs do.

5. I don't want any Boarder to receive more than one phone call per day—and that is from home. Three (3) minutes is sufficient time for anyone to talk concerning their family business. MONEY is not to be discussed on the phone at any time.

6. As I have said this is not a "white slavery place" and it never will be, as long as I have anything to do with it. Therefore I will not have a Boarder in my house with an excess amount of bruises and a lot of tattoos on their body. Cattle are branded for identification, tattoos are much the same as brands. I can remember my name without them. Can you?????

7. Boarders are permitted to see their lover or pimp only one night a week. Phone calls are subject to be Monitored. Remember— don't let your mouths overload your capabilities.

8. Long, sad faces look like hell to me, and I don't like them in my parlor. A smile doesn't cost anything but it could prove expensive not to smile.

9. When you go to town dresses worn should not be shorter than two inches above the knees. Pants or shorts prohibited in town.

10. Filthy talk can wait forever.

I rescued a red oil lamp sitting on the kitchen table to bring home. I would have stayed longer simply soaking it all in, had not Edna warned us that it was getting late and we still had a distance to drive to get back to Austin.

We decided to stay in Austin for the night and fly directly out of there to New York in the morning. We offered to put Edna up because it was a long drive back to Dallas on the endless unlit Texas roads. Edna said she had to check with her husband to see if that was all right with him. When she came back she told us she was leaving right away. I imagined then, and I believe to this day, that she went back to La Grange to thank the man she had once loved for the very generous gift he had given her that day.

Somewhere in the process of putting the show together, I decided that it would be a publicity bonanza if Edna came to New York to do a walk-on in the show. She'd only ever been in Texas (and Oklahoma, where she was born), and she said yes right away. Every newspaper was anxious to have its chance with her, and if she didn't turn out to be quite the scintillating madam of their imaginations, she did manage to satisfy each interviewer's curiosity. What was printable got as much space as it deserved. Unfortunately it wasn't long before she thought she could play the leading lady's role, and it was easier to send her home than to talk her out of it.

There wasn't a thing about Zindler that hadn't already appeared in the press, so he was considered public domain by the legal eagles, and accordingly wouldn't be entitled to any payment for life-story rights. I spent an hour with him, just for the hell of it, and I was persuaded of two things; one: He was the world's greatest authority on every subject and, two: a sizable portion of his ample earnings had gone to some bad cosmetic surgeons.

CHAPTER TWENTY-EIGHT

Broadway Gets a Whorehouse

"You better hire a good general manager," my theater friends said, "because you don't know what you're doing." So I hired Joe Harris. They all told me he was one of the best. I told him what I wanted to do, and he said, "You don't know what you're doing." So I fired him. More balls than brains, but listen—he wanted to go the conventional tryout route, Boston or Philly, and I wanted to open in a big old movie house off-Broadway. I thought it would save money. If it worked, we would move uptown quickly with sets and costumes already made to fit a Broadway stage.

Well, it worked. We saved a million dollars. I'd like to think it worked exclusively because it was a great show, but it was definitely helped to success because Jacqueline Kennedy Onassis showed up on the third night. When our press agent, Jeffrey Richards, received a call that she was coming, he arranged to have cameramen there. "Don't bother her," I told Jeff, but he was smarter. We got a shot of her under the theater marquee, which of course had the word "whorehouse" in it, and it was a press bonanza. After that we were golden. The carriage trade, rank-and-file theatergoers, and anyone who was anyone wanted to see the show. If you wished to be up on your cocktail conversation, you *had* to have seen *TBLWIT*. We were a hit.

Many producers put up their own money and come to opening night with their friends. Having done nothing but provide financial backing, they all rush up to the stage to collect their Tony Awards in June. They're known as checkbooks. I want to be a creative intelligence, a voice in all the choices that are made in production, casting, script changes, and so on. I like to negotiate all my own deals with everyone involved in a show, and I'm willing to hang in with the dry cleaner week after week. Trust me, there's more than one reason he's called "dry," but he and the others who service a show are a good part of what producing is all about—watching the expenses, making sure the set floor is mopped, keeping the crew happy. Bottom line: *TBLWIT* paid back in three months. That may be a record. I'm not a checkbook.

Tommy Tune is terrific—brilliant and smart and charming and fun. He's a great entertainer, and he knows how to make things entertaining. I loved his work from the first moment I saw it in Buffalo in a show called *Sunset*. So I met him for lunch with his agent and told him I would make him a rich man. I was moved to say that when I saw he was wearing pants held at the waist with an oversize safety pin. I didn't know if it was a fashion statement or simply that he couldn't afford pants that fit his six-feet-six frame. The show needed better musical staging than Pete Masterson, a fine actors' director, had offered at the Actors Studio, and, for me, TT was the answer. I hired him first, and told Masterson, King, and Hall after. That was doing things backward, and they could have refused but they didn't. It was Tommy's first directing job on Broadway, and he shared the credit with Pete, who was as gracious about it as anyone could be. Tommy, who got a percentage of the box office, did get rich. They all did.

It was my first time casting—and it was so much fun. In the late seventies there were no reality shows like *American Idol* and all its imitators, and so the process of talent elimination seemed unique to me. Hundreds of talented actors read the ad in *Backstage*, and it seemed like thousands showed up to strut their stuff. From the masses we would cull a chorus of eight men and eight women. The creative team and I auditioned them forty at a time. First they danced. That usually eliminated at least thirty out of the forty. The remaining ones sang. That usually got rid of another five. Anyone left got to read.

When casting was over we had "whores" who were each individual, and guys who looked like college football players.

Casting stories are legend. Here's my favorite: After a run of a few years, every show develops a revolving door. Actors move on, and our show was no different. It seemed like we were always advertising for new "whores." Many of the women we saw felt obliged to do a striptease for us. This was never asked for. One of the girls, however, found a way to go beyond even that: After she'd taken off all her clothes, she took out her teeth.

Rehearsals can be hell. I would sit in the orchestra watching the musical take shape, there only to give my support and encouragement, and to keep the lines of communication open between my authors, who fought with each other over everything, starting with "Good morning," which was never good when they were hungover.

Once you decide on your creative team, you have to let them do their thing. But as it turned out, I didn't always like their thing. Tommy and the three authors devised a big production number called "Two Blocks from the Capital." The underlying message was that around the corner from our seat of government anyone can buy whatever diversion or perversion he wants. The point was valid, it was a good song; the lyrics were funny and right on the money, and the cast member performing it was terrific. But in my opinion the staging was way too edgy. Chorus girls feigning sex onstage with animals and tickling each other's asses with feathers just didn't work for me. I couldn't imagine inviting the Universal top brass to see it without total embarrassment, without risking my future. It had to go. My creative team was most unhappy, especially Tommy Tune, whose brainchild this had been. They stood together against me, but I would not be moved. I called an end to rehearsals until they agreed to dump the song. "Go home," I told them. "Rehearsal is over until the number is gone." No one was willing to risk the entire production. The number was gone. I felt vindicated.

Okay, unions. I think they're both important and necessary, *but*— and here comes my big butt—they caused me problems, expensive ones.

1. When we moved from off-Broadway to the big time, I had to pay for the set to be "repainted." This involves neither paint nor brush. The union (International Alliance of Theatrical Stage Employees) simply stamps the set "approved." IATSE's seal of approval cost us $400,000.

2. The show happily ran off-Broadway for six weeks with four stagehands. When we transferred uptown, we needed fifteen men to run it. Same show, same set, nothing had changed. The good news is that the union guys were never again short a hand for the backstage poker game.

3. We had a nine-piece band onstage. On Broadway, however, we paid the AFM for twenty-five musicians, and we paid it for almost five years. Some of the guys we paid were retired and living in Arizona, and some were playing their trombones in heaven. We never once laid eyes on them. But that was the agreement the union had with the Forty-sixth Street Theater, and I had to be good with

it until we moved to a smaller house, the Eugene O'Neill, where its contract called for only fifteen musicians. The union muscled me, saying, You'll pay what you always paid. Big mistake. I fought them and won. But it got nasty. Not one other producer stood at my side in the grim battle, so when I was not able to turn my victory into a precedent to benefit all of them, I shed no tears.

We couldn't use the word "whorehouse" in newspapers or on TV. No way could we persuade the venerable *New York Times* to take our ads for important preopening publicity, and we needed those badly. What to do? We did the only thing we could: We went topless: No media marquee. It was a first, and the press we got out of the story made up for the loss of our "good" name. For the TV market we showed a big production number with lots of boots, cowboy hats, dancing, and singing; and the message was, Y'all come down and have a foot-stompin' good time!

The *Times* finally relented, and so did the other media in New York, but the name was always an issue wherever the show traveled. My favorite moment came when I submitted a list of potential ads to the agency that makes the ad buy for the MTA buses that span the city. From a long list of possibilities—all rejected—they finally agreed to put banners along the sides of the buses that read: "Come to the Whorehouse." Whoopee! The hierarchy of St. Patrick's Cathedral that had just annihilated us in the press had to stand outside the church watching the buses pass by.

We had a first national touring company, a second national touring company, a bus-and-truck company—all the accruals of success. Our brand was known nationwide. We were a megahit. Universal had no problem deciding to make the film, and spared no expense attendant upon doing so. They exercised their cheap option, and we were in preproduction. That's what I'd given the studio in return for immediate financing. Back then the authors were jubilant that they could go to work on the show immediately, and they would not have been able to do so without our giving Universal the option. But now they were stuck with it, and I was stuck with their change in attitude. There was a chill in the air. They weren't going to earn the millions the authors of *A Chorus Line* had. Of course they did not have the credentials the authors of that show enjoyed. They felt cheated and angry. But I make no apologies. I had fought hard for our deal and had gotten them as much as I could, probably a little more than the usual because I'd been an agent who'd made these kinds of deals in the past. So I knew what was doable and always practiced what that mighty Texan Lyndon Johnson, quoting Otto von Bismarck, called "the art of the possible."

Best of all, I was able to tie everyone, including Tommy Tune as director and myself as producer, to the movie—unheard of then at studios, which almost never ever encumber themselves with a show's talent. The creators of the show then negotiated their own deals for working on the movie, and they were all paid extremely well. I was busy congratulating myself while the creative team was busy sticking pins in my doll. It didn't matter. I loved the authors, and I loved the show. Nothing and no one could stop me from moving ahead, except Universal. They did.

CHAPTER TWENTY-NINE

Hollywood Gets Another Whorehouse

Tommy Tune started casting the movie. We placed an ad for singing cowboys to come audition at the Forty-sixth Street Theater. There was one proviso: Every guy had to have a minimum height of six feet two inches. Four thousand actors showed up on the appointed day, causing the police to shut down traffic on Forty-sixth Street between Broadway and Eighth Avenue. Tommy saw the men in massive lineups on the stage, and we remarked to each other that looking only at their heads presented a jagged skyline. Some guys were six feet five, and others no more than five feet four. And each time Tommy would ask a five-footer his height, the actor would answer, "I'm six foot two."

My first job as the film's producer was to find a location I liked where we could shoot the film. I couldn't wait to get started. Ned Tannen, whose gambling spirit had made the show possible, told me we would film it entirely in California. *What?* I cheerfully offered that I didn't think any part of California looked like Texas. Ned got a little annoyed. "Tell the audience it's Texas, and they'll think it is," he said. Given that Hawaii has been a stand-in for Vietnam, and so on, I decided to shut up and smile. To mollify me and prove he was right, he suggested I have a helicopter take me around the state. Is he really putting a helicopter at my disposal? My oh my! The chopper landed everywhere, north to south, east to west—and wherever it landed we could see mountains in the background. Worse, we could see the ocean. The open range dotted with grazing longhorns? Not there. The flatlands covered with oil rigs? Not there. Well, we could limit ourselves to two-shots and head shots. "We'll film it tight," I suggested to the pilot. We both laughed in disbelief. But when I told Ned about the ocean that existed alongside his home state, the funny thing is he didn't laugh at all. Moving on.

Universal could not be sold on Carlin Glynn and Henderson Forsythe, whose amazing performances had earned them both Tony Awards. This was hardly unusual. Many other hit shows had been remade as movies, and rarely with the actors who made them hits on Broadway. Universal demanded big marquee names, and so if we couldn't have the cast we wanted, we might as well have the biggest names in LA. Unfortunately sometimes one's wishes come true.

Although Burt Reynolds was not our first choice, he was on the studio's short list, and he wanted to do it. He wanted especially to meet Tommy Tune, and a date was set when Tommy, Pete, and I would visit him on location of *Smokey and the Bandit II* in some sleepy town deep in the South. Burt, partly undressed for the part, greeted us at his door naked to the waist and wearing high-heeled cowboy boots. His pose included a shirt rakishly draped over his shoulder. Instead of hello, he pushed a glass of white wine at me, saying: "Isn't this what you ladies drink?" "You ladies"? Is he for real? I almost rolled my eyes.

After a few minutes of chat, Burt wanted to spend some time

alone with Tommy, and they went into another room to talk privately. Pete and I sat quietly in the living trying to figure out what was going on in the other room, but we would never find out, for when Tommy returned he didn't discuss it. Our meeting was over. We politely said our good-byes and left.

Tommy was fired a few days later in the *New York Times*. Neither he nor I got the courtesy of a phone call first. His firing was public and mean-spirited, and it filled me with resentment, but left me with no cards in my hand.

Burt Reynolds turned out to be the worst thing that happened to the film. Because he was tasteless—witness his greeting at the door—he made changes to the script and the casting that turned a funny and somewhat touching show into a sadly second-rate movie. Do I sound like I'm whining? I mourned for the show for a week and then cried all the way to the bank to deposit my hefty producer's fee. Lest anyone have any doubt, big stars run big studios. In this case Burt, who was hot at the time, was the eight-hundred-pound gorilla. But I'm getting ahead of myself. Ned Tannen managed to create one last memorable moment for me before this imbroglio was over. I now started to shine up my old agent armor that was rusting in my mental closet as I prepared for a meeting with Ned to discuss director replacements.

By the time the meeting took place, we had also cast Dolly Parton, who seemed to me to be every bit as lovely as the image she projected on television. I liked her immediately. Clearly she was good casting and was also chosen because she had recently done a successful film, *Nine to Five*. It was directed by an Australian she liked, Colin Higgins, who became Tannen's first and seemingly only choice to replace TT. If it's true that in Hollywood you're only as good as your last work, then Colin's recent success with Dolly was enough for Tannen to love him. Colin Higgins, however, had never done a musical, had never been in Texas (not a requirement, but helpful), and wasn't even an American. Of course I told Ned that I would be delighted to meet him, and so a little get-together was quickly arranged.

The Colin I met was a kind man. He was sensitive and intelligent, and by the time we were introduced he seemed to know already that the film was his. So I decided to leap into creative territory. I asked him what his musical concept for the film would be. He didn't have a clue what a musical concept was. In fact he knew so little about music and Broadway musicals that I left the meeting thinking that this man couldn't find his way to a piano if it were the only piece of furniture in a well-lit gymnasium.

I was totally discouraged. I now knew that his having the job had nothing to do with any choice I had in the matter, and, worse (putting aside my ego and my lack of control), Colin's having no musical qualifications could not possibly benefit the movie we were about to make.

The next meeting in Ned's office for the purpose of discussing the creative concept was the beauty part. Even though I knew it would be useless, I told Ned straight out that I didn't think Colin, likable as he was, was the right man for the job. Picture Ned, emblematic of studio heads—dyspeptic and probably suffering from high blood pressure, upset by his day before I even set foot in his office—now listening to the exact opposite of what he wanted to hear. I might as well have just doused him with gasoline and lit the match, considering how he exploded. It was cosmic. He turned bright red, the veins popping in his neck as he screamed the following: "I don't give a fuck about what you think or a fuck about the fucking whorehouse. All I care about is seeing fucking Burt Reynolds fuck Dolly Parton's brains out for two fucking hours for the fucking fifteen-year-olds!"

"Uh-huh!" David Begelman's advice on how to answer when you don't know how to answer was coming in handy yet again. I told

Ned I'd like to go home and think about what he'd said. What now? It was clear I couldn't hold on to the movie.

It wasn't long before I got a phone call in my New York office from the business affairs department of Universal with an offer to negotiate my leaving. Two very successful television producers by the names of Tom Miller and Bob Boyett were "willing" to replace me, but I had the contractual right to be the "named" producer. If Universal, however, could deliver to these very successful chaps a major Hollywood movie with their names on the screen instead of mine, then maybe they would deliver a successful TV series to Universal. What a great bargaining chip—so Hollywood. It remains a place where everyone has an ax to grind, a place where relationships are everything. Nothing ever changes about that.

Calculating what I wanted for my departure was easy. I donned my agent's cap and prepared to negotiate. Universal turned its business affairs department loose on me. A studio insider warned me that they were getting ready to make hash of me, but I knew full well that Universal never fully understood the financial potential of a hit Broadway show back then, in spite of the fact that they were getting the box-office checks. Perhaps the lawyers and bookkeepers never conversed. I took advantage of that gap in their knowledge and traded my film salary and producer credit for additional points: 2.5 percent of gross in the Broadway and touring companies. I settled on a film credit of "executive producer," and I managed to retain part of my profit position in the film. I was delighted with the contractual result; I knew I had the better bargain. I thanked the universe for my training as an agent.

As it turned out, I never saw a penny of profits from the profitable film (hardly unusual in Hollywood, where profits are ephemeral and one's salary is usually all one ever sees), but the additional points that I bargained hard for in the show set me up financially for the rest of my life. It only takes one hit. How I would love to have another!

———

The film of *The Best Little Whorehouse in Texas* turned out about the way I thought it would. The studio was kind enough to give me a private screening, and seeing it made me want to take my name off the final credits. And I did. What bothered me was the missed potential. The hilarious truths in the Texas humor were gone, as was the sweet sadness in the original stories of the girls in the house. But there was still enough good stuff there to make it a moderately successful film—mostly based on the title and its success on Broadway—and I was delighted that Universal had had a profitable experience. It boded well for their continuing in theater.

Hollywood's lack of knowledge about Broadway has changed totally in recent years. They now understand everything. Universal has been blessed with its hit *Wicked*, and they know down to the penny exactly what it's worth. And nobody knows better than Disney that Broadway can be an enormous profit center. Little did I imagine that every studio would start taking old B movies off their shelves to remake them as Broadway musicals!

What came after *Whorehouse* for me were some stinkers of my own, four to be exact: *Wild Life*, *Open Admissions*, *Nuts*, and *The Best Little Whorehouse Goes Public*. I loved every one of them in spite of their failure. The last was a disaster that cost Universal nine million dollars. They took it on the chin. Lew Wasserman and Sid Sheinberg could not have been more understanding. They, like me, loved the musical. All of these shows had writers I loved, actors I loved, designers whose work I loved, and crews that I loved working with. They were all good experiences, and theater can be a fine, creative arena in which to play ball—or to play with your balls, as the case may be. I can think of nothing more exciting than standing hidden in a theater and watching audience members enjoy themselves as they're transported by a show that you've been a part of creating. It had been no different with Judy—always thrilling to watch what happened to the audience when she was in the spotlight, but that was all her. To be a creative intelligence on words and music that have a shot at making a little piece of theater history: That's been mine; it's been hugely rewarding.

I'm excited about producing my next musical. Tommy Tune once told me that music already on the planet, however wonderful, is not as exciting to present as new music. One takes a big financial risk to do an original musical these days, but it's well worth it in my opinion.

Judy was responsible for my falling in love with entertainment, but there was one particular film responsible for my wanting to help a show. It was seeing a black-and-white movie released in 1941, *Sullivan's Travels*, directed by one of our greatest film directors, Preston Sturges, and starring the hugely underrated Veronica Lake and Joel McCrea as Sullivan. I saw it in the late seventies; I was forty-two and just starting to produce.

In the movie Sullivan is a successful director of pointless comedies. He enjoys all the perks of the Hollywood rich: wine, women, and song. But he isn't happy. He thinks his work lacks social relevance. Sadly, he's not sure what that is. So he sets out to find it. He puts on tramp's clothing, stows a little mad money in his shoe, and sets off on the railroads. First night out, he's relieved of his shoes, and he legitimately joins the downtrodden poor. His life steadily deteriorates as the train carries him across the United States until one day he's arrested and put on a chain gang in some hellish swamp in Georgia. The prisoners are taken for a little R&R on Saturday night to a black church, where a film is shown after the sermon. (Sturges's blatant social statement here: Poor blacks are the only ones willing to give charity to those beneath them.) The movie screen is finally drawn down, and up comes a cartoon. Sullivan looks around and everyone, even he in his misery, is laughing hysterically. Sullivan now learns that his mindless comedies are a good thing. Sullivan understands that in a life where shit happens, making people laugh is a noble pursuit. Sullivan's last line is one of my all-time favorites: "Boy, there's a lot to be said for making people laugh. That's all some people have in this cockeyed caravan."

CHAPTER THIRTY

My Last Marriage

I fell deeply in love with Dave Grusin. The feelings I had for him helped me understand that I had never been in love before. I met him after *Whorehouse* was up and running. From my offices at Universal in New York City, I oversaw the daily business of the musical and the subsequent touring companies. In the process I got to know many of the execs on the West Coast. One of them gave me some material that had never gone forward as a film to evaluate as a book for a potential Broadway musical. I thought the writing was good, the story viable, and I set about finding a composer, somebody new and interesting.

I suddenly thought of this successful and immensely talented pianist, orchestrator, arranger, and composer of many celebrated film scores who had never worked on Broadway. I loved Grusin's work. He was an original and his work was amazing. I called him and he told me immediately he had no interest in doing theater. He was enjoying a lot of recognition for his superb work in recordings, personal appearances, and, of course, film, and that's where he wished to remain. He made it clear, however, that he was interested in me, and said he wanted to meet me.

David called me on his next visit to New York. I made a date with him thinking it would be my opportunity to talk him into composing this show for the studio, in spite of the fact that he had definitely rejected the idea. Either I wasn't listening, or it was again a case of refusing to take no for an answer too easily.

Once we met, I found him very appealing. He appeared to have a soft-spoken vulnerability that made you want to take care of him. There was no question that I wanted to see him again—and again—and this no longer had anything to do with Universal.

Our relationship developed quickly. Deepened even faster, and in the fall of 1979 we became inseparable. I loved climbing into bed with this man. Didn't want to get out of it. He was the most experienced lover I'd ever had. It was great. We were relishing each other's company. As I got to know his friends, I discovered there were lots of other women who found him appealing and they also wanted to take care of him. They were the wives of his friends. Happily this was all platonic. I liked his friends. They were talented and recognized. Most were big-time Hollywood players whose work I admired, and it impressed me that they admired him. He introduced me to a starry Hollywood scene, different from my own.

David courted me on both coasts, generously and charmingly, and I was enjoying him immensely. He moved into my apartment on Fifth Avenue after two months, and then, after only five months, he asked me to marry him. I was extremely flattered, but I thought it was too soon. Although I liked what I knew, I didn't yet know nearly enough. We both carried baggage. He would be my third. I would be his fourth. I hadn't yet met his family. I already knew from experience that one learned a lot from families.

I resisted his proposal; I told him that we needed more time together, but he insisted that he didn't want a long engagement. He threatened to walk if I didn't marry him right away. An amber warning light started to flash. Though I saw it, I looked away from it in spite of a voice inside me crying out, trying hard to get my attention. But I didn't want to lose him. I thought about my children, and how wonderful it would be for them to have another father figure better than their own. But had I taken the time to learn what I needed to know about his past as a father, I would have run for the hills!

I put the wedding together quickly, within a matter of weeks. We married on February 23, 1980, in Aspen, in a beautiful home on the famous ski mountain looming over the town. Aspen was a place we both enjoyed. David was born in Colorado, and as a young musician had picked up gigs playing piano in the resort when it wasn't much more than a frontier town. He'd bought some real estate back then on the residential mountain where we would build a second home together—more than merely a vacation home, although it would never replace New York.

I'd been skiing in Aspen for more than ten years at that point and I owned a little condo. By 1980 the town had grown into a world-class ski resort with lavish megahomes, not unlike the one we rented for our wedding day and night. And now, at four in the afternoon on our wedding day, the interior of the gorgeous chalet was filled with glamorous people, many of whom had flown in from both coasts and some who had skied in after a beautiful day on the slopes.

The ceremony took place in front of the big stone fireplace with the perfect log fire, and against a backdrop of gently falling, perfect snow. It was as if a set decorator had done his best work for *Town & Country* magazine. My children were there, of course, ten and eleven at the time. I recall how beautiful Jenny looked in her little red and white polka-dot gown, her hair tied up with red ribbons. They were excited and so sweet to everyone. Two of David's three children did not come, and although I found that strange, he convinced me it meant nothing and I would meet them later. I let it go in spite of knowing that his youngest lived only a few short blocks away. There was nothing to do about it in the eleventh hour.

I took the vows from the local magistrate, and I gave this man my heart.

In the first room we inhabited together as man and wife, there were two doors. One was the entrance; the other was a closet. If you know what a movie prop closet is, you know that when one opens it, suddenly all its overstuffed contents come exploding out. It's generally good for a laugh. Well, the closet in our room was stuffed to the max with skeletons, and when I cracked the door they all tumbled onto the floor, making a huge and frightening pile of horror stories. I started picking through the bones and learned things that were no laughing matter at all. I would describe my process as a due diligence that I should have done before we married. My education about my new husband began on our honeymoon.

As the first few months wore on, I discovered the problems were even more severe than I first suspected. They had accrued over many years. And I, who had always wanted a big extended family, thought that I could solve them all. That, then, was the beginning of the end of the marriage. How did my new husband react to my reaching out? Badly! I believe the guilt was too much for him to handle. I'd opened up a can of worms.

No longer my hero, he seemed embarrassed and angry by what I had unraveled, and the whole gestalt of ugly behaviors that went with his personality were manifest. He became silent and morose, a very unhappy man. Nevertheless I continued to dig in with energy and enthusiasm because I was persuaded that love and affection for his family coupled with treatment would make a difference. I will not discuss the nature of the problems because it will only cause more pain to some people about whom I once cared deeply, and a few of whom I still do. It is enough to say that what I saw broke my heart and I cried a river.

The more involved I got, the more it took a toll on me. I became clinically depressed. I couldn't function. And the more depressed I grew, the farther away my husband drew. While I was making a difference for his family, I was wrecking everything for us. As things got better outside our apartment, they fell apart within. I am totally to blame for this, I told myself. Finally, I no longer knew how to make David happy. Everything I did was wrong. Look at all the good work I'm doing, I told myself, but it had the reverse effect. I faulted myself for the wreck the marriage had become, and as I continued along that path, I lost all my confidence and self-esteem until I was nothing but a shadow of the woman I had once been. At the very bottom of my ride into despair, I became a suicidal codependent.

He didn't exactly tell me he was leaving. I found out when I went to the airport, uninvited, to pick him up and watched him come off the plane, arm in arm with his new lover.

Looking in the rearview mirror, I realize how utterly stupid I was. I managed to do the same dumb thing I'd already done too many times: taking an action without being informed. I was careless with my father when I signed over my mother's estate, and again with my second husband when I signed fraudulent tax returns. Marrying this time was no different except for the size of the consequences.

There was never any excuse in my case for not being informed. Ever. And yet I married a man without knowing nearly enough about him. How stupid is stupid? You don't need reminding, but I need to remind myself day in and day out of Einstein's definition of insanity: doing the same thing over and over again and expecting different results. The results of my earlier mistakes were grisly enough, but this last one was devastating. This dumb mistake nearly cost me my life.

CHAPTER THIRTY-ONE

The Pieces

I didn't wake up one morning and decide David was a first-class prick, but that's where I ended up. And it didn't take picking through the bones of all the skeletons in his closet to convince me. It was how I found him—an angry, disconsolate man. I think he looked in the mirror and didn't like what he saw. He was sometimes vocal about it. Or he was quiet and despairing. There was little cheer in his life. There had been little cheer in the home he came from. Doesn't everything finally go back to one's parents?

One day I heard the twisted tale of his childhood. No need to go into it, nor could I if I wanted to. I can only report what I was told by David, which is that his mother had an affair with another man while married to his father. They did not divorce; they simply moved to different floors in the house and never spoke to each other again. For as long as the boys remained at home, David and his brother, Don, carried messages between them. That's enough to make any child angry. It put both young men in the position of having to choose. From the few conversations that went down between David and me about his parents, it was clear to me whom he chose. He spoke of his father, never his mother.

One of David's favorite things to do was to go trout fishing. He loved to fish. I often thought that if he could have made a living from trout instead of from music, he would have done it. As a kid he had often fished with his father, and from time to time he would reminisce. Those were happy times. He associated no happy times with his mother. During the five years we were married, as we stood in various streams, I often thought he was there to keep that happy time in his life alive.

I also thought he had left home not liking women. This is my amateur analysis, and I told him what I thought several times over a period of three years as the marriage was disintegrating. He tried to refute it, alluding to the fact that he'd dealt with this in therapy before we even met. Well, doesn't that mean someone might have mentioned the problem before me—like one of his three former wives, or perhaps all of them? I felt as though he didn't like me from the day we married.

Not long after we wed, *TBLWIT* started to wind down. I had been making a fortune during its run. With multiple companies, thousands of dollars a week became tens of thousands a week. And then it was over. Suddenly I was earning nothing. The next show I produced was a flop. (No failures on Broadway, we call them flops.) My marriage did not respond well to my change of status. David grew silent. However, I saw an opportunity to try something I'd wanted to do for a while: I always thought I could write, and this was my chance.

It's uncanny how smart the universe is. A little voice had been nagging at me for a long time to learn more about addiction. Somehow I knew I hadn't yet learned enough about this awful disease. Indeed, what I'd gone through with Judy, with Liza, and more recently on *Whorehouse* made me want to know more. Given that I'd decided to write, I was looking around for a subject, and I thought addiction meaty material. I asked a rehab in Aspen if they would allow me to audit sessions there, and the manager of the clinic, after canvassing the patients, said I could sit in as long as I was mute. After the first two twenty-eight-day sessions, I was, however, allowed to ask questions. What an eye-opener! I totally recognized my dismal marriage in those sessions.

I'd started early in our marriage to believe that my husband was an alcoholic. It was his behavior that got me started. It wasn't that he drank so much, and it wasn't that he was ever drunk. He was functioning at a very high level. I'm talking about a man who received Grammy Awards and countless nominations for his wonderful work during the time we were married.

There was a time, he told me, when he'd smoked four to five packs of cigarettes a day. He was a workaholic. He had interchangeable addictions. When we dined out he liked to drink. Nothing unusual about that, except that I felt that he couldn't enjoy the meal without a few drinks, some wine, and a good brandy after. He asked me if I thought he was an alcoholic, and I told him that I didn't think so, that I thought he simply enjoyed drinking socially. I've since concluded that was denial on my part, plus I didn't want to offend him. I had yet to learn that alcoholism is not a matter of how much liquid fire one pours down his or her gullet; it's a matter of how much one depends on it in order to get through work, or the day, dinner, or just life in general. I believe he had dependence issues. And actually, in retrospect, I don't think that anybody asks the question "Am I?" unless they already know the answer.

As I listened to the patients in rehab week after week, they were describing conduct that seemed to define my husband. They discussed, and their counselor discussed, a whole gestalt of alcoholic behaviors that destroy: depression, impatience, anger, rage, narcissism, control, and manipulation. These patients epitomized such behavior, and I immediately concluded I was living with someone exactly like them. I was living with a man I felt I couldn't make happy no matter what I did, who couldn't be happy no matter what he did. He often came home in a quiet controlled rage. The studio was too hot or too cold; the engineer wasn't any good; the director was demanding; the producer was stupid. He didn't need an excuse to be unhappy. His face would turn into a mask of anger, and he wouldn't talk. We had silent dinners in which I became depressed, and that angered him even more. We went to bed angry, and I sensed he knew I was silently crying.

Perhaps he thought I was upset about my career, but the truth is that I was far less upset about it than he. I worried and wondered about restoring it in order to make *him* happy, but I had no solution, and in my state of mind at that moment in time, I could not have found one.

On top of this I was ministering to his children with their problems. I think it was appalling and embarrassing to him, never mind depressing the hell out of me. I was convinced he hated me for helping them and hated that they needed help. As if it was all a reflection on him. I fell apart. How could he do this to me? I blamed him, and that made me feel worse. I didn't yet know I was asking the wrong question. The right question was, How did I allow this to happen?

I couldn't seem to do anything right. And the more he seemed to hate me, the more insecure I became, until I was but a pale, needy, helpless resemblance of me. I bought his favorite foods, but that didn't matter because I couldn't cook. I made engagements with wonderful people, but he never felt comfortable with them. Whatever I took him to see in theater, he didn't like. I couldn't do anything to please him no matter how I tried. Like air from a rubber tube with a hole in it, confidence seeped out of me every day until it was gone. My self-esteem vanished. I looked in the mirror and was disgusted by the person staring back at me. If I couldn't love her, who could? Nobody, and never again! That was my answer.

This once strong, independent, tough, and intelligent person now felt gone. Sometimes I would curl up on the floor in a corner of the living room and wonder what would happen if I jumped out of the eighteenth-floor apartment window. Would I die from a coronary occlusion on the way down? Or would it take hitting the ground to kill me? I was suicidal. Tough, take-no-shit-from-anyone me!

No matter! I didn't have the courage to jump. My two beautiful children depended on me. I had to continue to function, but all I could do all day was cry. And that's what I did—spent all day crying. I didn't have time to write. I knew I was having a nervous breakdown; that I was useless to myself and that I needed help. But I was not yet ready to admit any of that out loud. I couldn't do it while he was still in the house, and oddly enough I felt I had to maintain a false front for his children, who called often from LA, Minnesota, and Aspen. I felt they depended on me emotionally.

And then he was gone. Had I been of sound mind, I would have celebrated. In my few rational moments I knew there was nothing about him to love. But now my rational moments were few and far between. Mostly I mourned, continuing to believe I had lost the one true love of my life, and everything was my fault. I was the one responsible for the affair he was having with another woman. I found it impossible to blame him for anything. Yet I knew something was wrong with my reasoning. Why? Why did I blame myself for everything? The question grew bigger as the weeks wore on. Finally I heard a little voice say, it's because you're codependent!

It was a word I'd often heard at the rehab. "Codependent." I started to think about that. I identified myself with the patients in the rehab, but most of all I identified with Judy to the extent that love and the loss of it was what mattered most to her. She was needy and dependent, and now I was also. And not only needy and dependent, I was insecure and totally lacking in enough confidence to get through the day. I thought I was offensive to everyone. I was scared to go out for fear I would do something wrong. I wanted the world to go away and take me with it. I wanted to be left alone. *And I'd gotten to this most awful place without drugs or liquor.* I had never been interested in either, and my despair did not drive me to the well-stocked liquor cabinet in the living room. However, even though I didn't pop a single pill or take a drink, I now began to realize I had become an addict. I would learn in my recovery that I had become addicted to pain. I was a rampaging codependent.

And now, finally, I understood what happened to Judy. She too was in pain—probably caused early by family matters, and then exacerbated by Louis B. Mayer, whom she absolutely hated. She drank and drugged to deaden that pain, and became addicted to doing that. Truly I believe as I write this that her addiction to pain caused her addiction to drugs and liquor. Although I didn't understand all of that when it was happening to me, I did know one thing: What happened to Judy was not going to happen to me.

The children would often come home from school and find me wearing the same bathrobe I'd been in when they'd left in the morning. How sad it was when my Jenny would come into the bedroom to tell me that smoking was bad for me. Thinking about it now is enough to bring tears to my eyes. Back then I bawled like a baby.

But I was paralyzed, and even their sweet voices urging me to come back didn't matter. I was too depressed, but too sane to want a pill. Pills for depression in the late eighties were starting to be a hip thing. Just another fad, I thought, and anything that had to do with pills was a total turnoff. Because of Judy? More than likely, but then I'd never found the drug culture anything but disgusting.

However, I needed something to ease the pain. I was so sick. I had a record player in my head, and it played and replayed the same tapes over and over and over again. What he said, what I said, what I didn't say. And none of it mattered anymore. The tapes were making me nauseous, and even if I didn't eat, I still had the dry heaves and couldn't stop them. The tapes were the worst part. I couldn't turn the fucking tapes off. I smoked, I cried, I threw up, and I lost weight.

And one day I looked at myself in the mirror, *really* looked, and I was horrified. I think more than anything else that it was my vanity that took hold. I got so scared that I got dressed and went to my first meeting at Al-Anon. What did I have to lose? I remembered from the sessions I'd audited at the Aspen rehab that Al-Anon was a place to get help, and I'd heard it was a family place, for the relatives and friends of alcoholics and drug addicts.

I knew immediately, in the very first half hour, that this was where I belonged. I listened to so many people with problems that were eerily familiar. They took my mind off my own. It helped. If one meeting was good, I reasoned five a day would be better. I ran all over the city attending meetings. Meetings became my narcotic. I was grateful to be in New York where meetings take place in different neighborhoods almost around the clock, and I never had to leave Manhattan.

Finally, after a week, I backed off and went to only one a day for a month. Every time I left a meeting I left believing I belonged there. At the end of the first month, I was feeling better enough to seek an addiction doctor, and it was she who led me little by little to the understanding that I was addicted to pain. She never said those words, although she completely understood where I was. After all, pain—mine and everyone else's—had been a constant companion in my life for a long time, and I ministered to all of it. I was pain's handmaiden. It's not a surprise to me that I started to need it.

One day, however, while in my doctor's office, and after months of repeating the same sick phrases of feeling-sorry-for-myself garbage, I finally heard, actually *heard*, what I was saying as if for the first time. With the expert help I was getting, I was compelled to listen to myself, to really hear the maudlin crap that was coming out of my mouth, and it appalled me. The words were ridiculous, and I was disgusted and embarrassed. I stopped talking. I sat silently. The shrink sat watching me. And then, all at once, I was able to find the right words myself: "I am addicted to pain. I want it." The moment I was able to say that out loud, I turned a corner. It was the most wonderful moment. I was a kid. I was so excited I jumped up and down like some kind of nut. Some kind of nut is what I had been.

It was going to be different going forward. Perhaps not overnight. But I was coming back. In that wonderful moment I knew that. It had taken me a year to get to that precious moment. During the following year, I never noticed my pain was disappearing, I felt my energy returning instead. I stayed at Al-Anon, attending a meeting a week, for five years.

Let me start here with the dictionary definition of codependency. It suited my condition so perfectly that I amuse myself by imagining it was tailored to me personally, but then I do recognize from time to time that I am not the center of the universe. Codependency is defined as "a psychological condition or a relationship in which a person is controlled or manipulated by another who is affected with a pathological condition (as an addiction to alcohol. . . .)" (I seemed to specialize in these.) "Codependency often involves placing a lower priority on one's own needs, while being excessively preoccupied with the needs of others." (That describes my concern for and care of David's children.) "Codependency can occur in any type of relationship, including family . . . and also romantic relationships. Codependency may also be characterized by denial, low self-esteem, and excessive compliance or control patterns." This definition summed me up perfectly. Narcissists (again, one of my specialties) are considered to be natural magnets for the codependent.

I can joke about this dictionary definition being written with me in mind, but trust me, it also fit everyone I met at Al-Anon. They were mothers and fathers, sisters and brothers, aunts and uncles, husbands and wives, and the grown children of all the aforementioned. I listened to all their stories and recognized me in many of their problems. I was no longer alone.

It was remarkable to me (and for a long time surprising) how I continued to find exactly the nonjudgmental help I needed. It's said that you take away from those rooms what you need and leave behind what you don't. Listening to others discuss their relationships at home, I learned a great deal about my own home, not just the one I was in, but the one I grew up in. I heard others talking about behavior like my father's, and the distress that his kind of behavior wreaks in all kinds of families. When the conversation shifted to the wives of such fathers, I thought they were talking about my mother.

Once I was able to accept that my family problems were hardly unique, I was also able to find *me*—the child who had been introduced to Judy Garland. That child was no different from so many other lonely children I heard about. I learned how to acknowledge that child, to love her, and to forgive Judy even though I might never learn to love Judy. And, having arrived in those rooms suffering a deep depression (although never as deep as Judy's, whose condition fitted the classic definition of manic-depressive), I could finally identify, at least somewhat, with how Judy felt as she valiantly tried to go forward every day.

The meetings reinforced my understanding that self-mutilation has nothing to do with love, and that Judy never needed an excuse to hurt herself. Sometimes I imagined Judy sitting next to me in those rooms. Of course that would have been impossible because of her celebrity, but I'd like to think she would have learned as much as I did.

I finally managed to say good-bye to the damage I'd allowed Liza's betrayal to cause in me. Letting go is a learned behavior, and it was hard work, but it was a great relief not to be carrying all that Liza baggage around anymore. I felt way lighter and more able to enjoy my former successes. There has always remained, however, a residue—a great sadness for Li, whose career started on a downhill slide after we parted. Liza was (and perhaps remains) every bit the codependent I was—and for good reason.

Someone in one of those rooms said, "There are two days of the week you don't have to worry about. One of them is yesterday, the other is tomorrow!" How right is that?! I've been making today count for a long time because of that lesson. Not the least of what I learned was to keep my mouth shut when someone else was talking. I'm forever grateful for the day a young man in those rooms said: "If I would only just take the cotton out of my ears and stuff it into my mouth, I'd be a whole lot better off." Oh, what a gift! An agent hardly ever shuts up. I finally discovered how much more I could find out if I kept my mouth closed. My last husband actually told me everything I had needed to know before I married him. He didn't use words like "controlling," "manipulative," and "narcissistic," but the messages were all clearly there. I didn't hear them because I wasn't really listening.

Sharing my own experiences in those rooms started me on the road to recovery. Finally, by the late eighties, after taking a good look at the totality of my married experiences, I was able to let all the anger and depression go, and I was then ready to go to court, which is where the legal hassling ultimately led David and me. It was nasty stuff, and the details are boring, but the finale was better than any eleventh-hour finish on Broadway.

To start with, I looked at my soon-to-be-ex-husband sitting there, and I felt nothing. I wondered how I had allowed myself to make such a poor judgment. My first instinct, which was to get to know this man better before we married, had been the right one.

And now I would pay for my mistake in court. I was disgusted with myself.

The prim little (and I mean tiny) judge, who revved up his machismo by arriving clad in black leather on a huge Harley Hog, sat as tall as he was able to as he listened to my husband's lawyers tell him that it would be a shame to give me anything in the divorce. "Take it all away from her," my husband's lawyer boomed out in a stentorian tone. "Don't let her suck on the hind tit of wealth. You will be destroying her. Take it all away," he said. "Then, like cream rising to the top, she will do what she has to in order to succeed once again." I couldn't believe my ears.

The judge, however, found this argument very compelling, and that's just what he did. He gave all the investments, bought with a great amount of my earnings, to David. My attorneys hardly spoke at all. I didn't understand it, and at that point there was nothing I could do about it. I might have done something later, but I was anxious to be done with it and to move on. That the judge gave the home we'd built in Aspen to David was only right because he'd owned the land before, and he'd invested the lion's share of the construction costs.

I was awarded a lousy cash settlement, which didn't come anywhere close to the money I'd invested in our different real estate ventures in Colorado. It was a sick joke. Like cream, I curdled just listening to the judge. But it was finally over, and here's the bottom line: When I came out of this dark tunnel, I was so much stronger. I don't think I know many as strong as I.

I am deeply grateful to all the people who inhabited those rooms. I share a silent bond with them that will never be broken because I live the lessons I learned in those rooms every day of the week. I can no longer be tested without my thoughts immediately flying back to some meeting that informed me how to react with understanding and with grace.

CHAPTER THIRTY-TWO

TGIF (Thank God It's Finished)!

I still find it interesting, in retrospect, to look at how my career functioned in my marriages. It was the third person in bed. In both my success and my failure!

In my first marriage I used my ambition like a steamroller to mow my husband down. I was young and stupid, thoughtless and unkind. And when I achieved a certain level of success, I dumped him. He deserved far better. I'm grateful to myself for apologizing to him.

In my second marriage my success made it difficult for my husband to stand on his own two feet once he'd lost his business. But that was his own doing, so who cares that he was never again able to measure up!

My last husband (and I love being able to say that) married a success. He was good with that. During our marriage it was my career this time that went south. The huge earnings and all the attendant glitter disappeared. He was not so okay with that. One of my opening-night flops that my husband and a friend drank their way through stands out as a particularly low moment for me—but just one of many.

So my career brought about behavior both good and bad from me and those closest to me. Had our relationships been solid enough, had the men I married had a stronger sense of self, had I been more confident and tolerant, perhaps my career would have mattered less. For sure, my career wasn't the only factor that determined the success or failure of those unions. It would be a gross oversimplification for me to lay the demise of each marriage at the feet of my profession.

However, having made all the above disclaimers, as a dedicated career woman who defines herself by her career, I need to repeat my feeling that *having it all is not possible.* Had I made good choices for myself instead of bad ones, I think I still would have had to make many more compromises than I was willing to make because I know what a career demands. I would have had to let go of a Hallmark-card version of life, a picture-perfect existence, and instead let things happen as they do in life without sweating it. I couldn't. I always wanted it to be perfect. It was far from. Some aspect of my life or someone I loved always drew the short straw. Sometimes it was one of my beautiful children, or both of them: at other times it was my husband, and very often it was me. And I dealt with it badly.

Since my last divorce, I've enjoyed affairs and relationships, but I'm no longer interested in finding the same slippers under my bed two weeks in a row, nor do I want to babysit anyone's enlarged prostate. I want to be neither a nurse nor a purse. (I love that expression.)

There is one life lesson I've adopted that is the most important of all. It counts with me more than listening, and more than being present, more than living in the moment. It is that I never need to be 100 percent right ever again. Just recently I was reminiscing with my daughter about a silly event that took place one morning many years ago. She remembered the incident one way, I another. My memory was so vivid; apparently so was hers, and our recollections were totally different. It was a setup for an argument. (As it proves there's no such thing as objective reality!) That long-ago morning was a seminal moment for me, because I realized exactly then that my third marriage was over. David had been out the night before with the woman who would become wife number four. We had visited friends in Santa Fe, and now we were leaving; and I was leaving my marriage behind although I would stubbornly cling in needy fashion a bit longer.

Those few awful hours are as crystal clear to me as if it were yesterday. I was fine with Jenny's memory of the moment. I didn't need to convince her that I was right, nor do I ever need to do it with anyone else. Being right is simply a way to perpetuate an argument. I can allow everyone else in my life—those I know, and strangers who are just passing through—to be right. It doesn't mean I'm wrong; it means we don't argue. I don't lose arguments anymore; I simply don't have them. I love that.

CHAPTER THIRTY-THREE

Climbing the Mountain

Fast-forward. I am on safari in Africa, at Tarangire National Park in Tanzania to be exact. Paul Oliver, one of the greatest safari guides in East Africa, says, "Let's do something daring. I've never tried this with a client." Okay! "Let's take some bedrolls and leave camp. We'll sleep out in the wild tonight." I had already walked twenty miles across the savanna with Paul, who carried a rifle he wouldn't use, and Osidai, a Masai whose machete was a simple extension of his arm going back to the time he was a child. I'd wanted to get a real feel for the country, and I could think of no better way than to walk. We were sometimes in elephant grass over our heads, inhabited by poisonous snakes and every other dangerous tiny creature. In this new adventure we'd be outside the park in the dark with the elephants crashing around, and with whatever lions were prowling the night. Sleeping out sounded fully scary enough to be interesting.

We stretched out our bedrolls on a high rock because, as I had learned in Paul's camp—where elephants cruised constantly—that if you had to run from an elephant, running up a rock could save your life. Elephants don't climb rocks. Our rock that night was twenty feet high. Next to us was a rock that was at least five or six stories high. That's where the baboons went to get away from the lions that fed at night. They climbed their rock at precisely 6:00 p.m. every single night of the year, at the exact moment in equatorial Africa when the sun goes down. Paul knew that he could treat me to this amazing sight: hundreds of baboons, some with babies on their stomachs or on their backs, scaling this tower at breakneck speed to their nests above.

That night's episode was nothing short of fabulous. We brought a good bottle of wine and a battery-operated disc player so that we could listen to Beethoven and Mozart as we watched forest fires burning in different places on the wall of the Great Rift Valley. Paul, a little more worried about the lions than he was willing to admit, didn't get much sleep, but I had no trouble, and when I awoke in the morning, I put the Barbra Streisand concert album on the CD player. I loved that album, and so did the big baboons! At 6:00 a.m. on the dot, the sun came up, and the baboons came down. Just as we were preparing to leave, at least a hundred of them (those with good taste) sat at complete attention in a long line stretched out in front of us, their paws in their laps, until the last song was played. Not one so much as coughed. We stared at them, and they stared back, and it was clear they loved Barbra as much as I. I thought long and hard about calling her to say, "I've seen big baboons line up to hear you sing." I feared she might not understand. (I am a big fan of hers; I think she is a great lady.)

I fell so in love with Africa on the first trip, I decided I wanted to celebrate my sixtieth birthday by climbing Mt. Kilimanjaro. There was nothing to keep me from doing it, and no reason why I shouldn't treat myself. I already enjoyed hiking in Aspen, where I still owned a condo, and I thought I was as strong at sixty as I had been at thirty. (Not true.) I devoted the summer just prior to my birthday to getting in better shape. I did this in and around Aspen, where just about every week my friend Barbara Eisberg and I climbed a fourteen-thousand-foot peak. (Colorado boasts fifty-four of the monsters.) We also hiked to twelve and thirteen thousand feet the other days, and I regularly took my copy of the *New York Times* to the top of Independence Pass (12,095 feet) so that I could improve my lung capacity at the same time as I improved my mind.

Finally, on a bright, sunny September 6, 1996, I flew back to New York to drop off unnecessary luggage, quickly go through the mail, pick up my passport, and go for it. The plan was to be in Nairobi on the seventh, Arusha on the eighth, and be climbing on the ninth, lest Barbara and I lose even an iota of the valuable acclimatization gained on the roof of Colorado.

The night before the climb started we stayed at a modest hotel not far from the access route. Our chief guide, Capanya, visited us to introduce himself, go over details, tell us what not to pack, what we could expect, and what he expected from us. Our excitement was tempered by trepidation, and neither of us slept.

The next morning we joined the men who would take us up. They were all Masai: two guides, Capanya and Sekeyan (who both turned out to be incredibly capable), a cook, Manasee (who climbed carrying four large egg cartons in his hands so that we could have sauces), and ten fabulous porters. It looked like a small tribe supporting us: That's what we wanted and thought we needed, and that's what we paid for—first class.

The climb would take seven days: five going up, two coming down. We were starting out at ninety degrees Fahrenheit and ending at twenty below zero the night before summiting. This meant carrying a lot of food and clothing. Beyond fourteen thousand feet, there would be no firewood; therefore it was mandatory for the outfitter to supply stoves and fuel. There were two two-man sleeping tents: one for us and one for our guides, a dining tent, a lavatory enclosure, and a cook tent that would also serve as a dormitory for the porters. Some outfitters allow their porters to fend for themselves in the elements, but not our classy outfitter. Going first cabin meant that the guys who carried eighty pounds each for us all day would at least enjoy warmth and shelter all night. God knows they deserved it.

The two guides spoke excellent English, the cook could make himself understood, and the rest knew about five words each. Those words were "Bruce Willis," "Arnold Schwarzenegger," and "Nike." This, however, did nothing to stop us from communicating. I would take my face creams and lotions into their tent each night and talk about everything from face-lifts to American politics—all of which they loved hearing about—and then, invariably, they would question me about their biggest concern: AIDS. They wanted—needed, really—to know how they could have a relationship with a woman—a woman they might one day marry—and not get sick. I told them how, and they never had any trouble understanding me. But I'm getting ahead of myself.

When they first caught sight of Barbara and me, I could see slight smiles on their faces, not smiles of greeting but smiles of gratitude. They were looking at two old ladies who were going to give them the weekend off with full pay. They figured—and this was confirmed to me later—that we would have a nice stroll for three days through the unique vegetation of the Shira Plateau, and when we got to "the rock" it would be all over, as in "Down we go."

On the third night we made camp at the foot of "the rock," the last enormous, very steep side we would have to climb to reach the top. Capanya gave us a pep talk at our first-class dinner, and got up from the table to demonstrate how he wanted us to walk the next morning. "Step, breath, step, breath," he said, emphasizing the rest after each footfall. We had breakfast at 5:00 a.m., packed our gear, and hit the rock walking. And I mean just that. We were putting one foot in front of the other without a breath in between. (God bless Colorado!) I heard Capanya issue new orders at the lunch break that resulted in changed expressions and a great deal of chatter. Swahili is a language in which many syllables are repeated, (*tutu a nana* = "See you again"), and at top speed it sounds like the language a child might invent, whimsical and lyrical. "What did you say to them?" I asked Capanya, although I thought I knew exactly what he'd said. Still, I wanted to hear him say it.

"I told them, 'Pack everything tight. We're going to the top!'"

Yes! Yes! Yes! It was the moment of greatest victory for me, even greater than being at Uhuru Peak, the roof of Africa—not that there was anything wrong with that. "We're going to the top!" That's what it's always been about for me: taking risks, stepping off a cliff, attempting to get to the top, and having fun doing it. And I figured if I could climb Kili at sixty, there was nothing I couldn't do. I am happy. I am healthy. I have a beautiful family, and I do it all!

I remember closing my eyes and resting my head on the plane cushion as the 737 left Nairobi on the way to Frankfurt and then on to New York. I thought about the frightened girl who stood in the middle of a room in the Plaza Hotel and put out a small fire all those years ago. I also thought about the young woman who stood in the middle of Judy's life for a while and put out grass fires all over the place. The experience changed her. She was braver; she risked more. The grown woman now had the courage to fight fires wherever she found them, and putting them out allowed her to see the world around her more clearly, though she sometimes got burned.

The old woman's own raging fires have now cooled, and she no longer bears any ill will toward anyone. She owes Judy something for the changes. Gratitude? I'm not sure that's the right word. Whatever it is, it would have been a much lesser life without her.